# ACKNOWLEDGEMENTS

The authors and publisher would like to thank the following individuals, institutions and companies for permission to reproduce photographs and illustrative material in this book:

The Association of British Travel Agents 195; Advisory, Conciliation and Arbitration Service 166; Advertising Standards Authority 195; ©The Board of Trustees of the Armouries 30; Bob Battersby/Tografox.com 25, 87, 106, 108, 222; Courtesy BSM 35; British Standards Institution 196; Café Direct 22; Courtesy Companies House 14; Corbis 95/Nathan Benn 58, Yann Arthus-Bertrand 37, Gary Braasch 38, Jacques M. Chenet 32, David Cummings, Eye Ubiquitous 2, Dex Images, Inc. 190, Lowell Georgia 4, Charles Gupton 264, Edward Holub 149, Lester Lefkowitz 60, Ghislain & Marie David de Lossy 268, Michael Mirecki 119, Kevin R. Morris 137, 187, David Muench 42, SABA/James Leynse 135, Paul A. Souders 73, Michael St. Maur Sheil 146, LWA/Dann Tardif 11, Bill Varie 90, John Zoiner 126; Derbyshire County Council 26; Equal Opportunities Commission 161; Forest Stewardship Council (*FSC Trademark* ©1996 Forest Stewardship Council A.C.) 129; Getty Images/Luis Castenada Inc. 74, Ron Chapple 179, Chris Close 70 (Newcastle), Color Day Production 171, Jerry Driendl 70 (Sydney), Romilly Lockyer 89, Stephen Munday 19, Chris Ryan 79, V.C.L. 7; Hello! 115; Investors in People UK 182; Journey Latin America (www.journeylatinamerica.co.uk) 111; Life File/Ken McLaren 2; Meridian Broadcasting Limited 33; Courtesy ©Microsoft 116; PA Photos/European Press Agency 243, Phil Noble 57; Popperfoto/Reuters 17; Remploy 95; Rex Features Ltd. 26, 51/Andy Drysdale 47, Gunther Heidrun 84, Steve Lyne 276, Sipa Press 106, Ray Tang 134; Ronseal (*Ronseal, Ronseal does exactly what it says on the tin* are registered trademarks of The Sherwin-Williams Company) 110; J Sainsbury plc 62; Science and Society Picture Library/Science Museum 156; Science Photo Library/Simon Fraser 128, Ed Young 96; Still Pictures/David Drain 141, Mark Edwards 76, Andre Maslennikov 139; Tesco.com 100; Topham Picturepoint 123; Trades Union Congress 61; WHSmith 62, 82.

Crown copyright material (82, 121) is reproduced with the permission of the Controller of HMSO and the Queen's Printer for Scotland.

Every effort has been made to trace and acknowledge copyright. The publishers will be happy to make suitable arrangements with any copyright holder whom it has not been possible to contact.

# CONTENTS

# ----→-→ INTRODUCTION

The Applied GCSE is designed to let students develop knowledge and understanding of business through the practical investigation of a range of business organisations. It is designed to help prepare students for further study, or for the world of work.

**The Applied GCSE in Business is a Double Award. Candidates will be awarded grades from A*A* to GG and it is strongly recommended that schools and colleges allocate double curriculum time to reflect the importance of this.**

This book is designed to be used by students following any of the main examination board specifications for Applied Business Studies at GCSE. There is an accompanying teachers book which provides further help, advice, assessment materials and examples as well as answers to exercises in this book (where appropriate). The book is designed to be accessible to all levels at GCSE but, at the same time, to contain all the knowledge, and underpinning understanding and explanation, necessary for the successful completion of the course.

The specification consists of three parts:

**Unit 1: Investigating Business**

**Unit 2: People and Business**

**Unit 3: Business Finance**

Assessment is through two portfolios (one each for Unit 1 and Unit 2) and an externally set and marked examination (for Unit 3). Each Unit carries equal weighting, i.e. one third of the marks available.

Unit 1 requires students to undertake an investigation of two contrasting businesses (different sizes, locations, markets, structures, ownership etc.). Unit 2 requires students to undertake a detailed study of a single medium to large sized business, and Unit 3 to understand and be able to apply the elements of business finance. The structure (and assessment) is very similar to Part 1 GNVQ Business, which this specification will replace.

Unlike the traditional GCSE, there is a large element of coursework (66.6%) which is internally marked and assessed and a smaller element of examination.

# HOW TO USE THIS BOOK

This book is divided into the three Units in the same way as the specification. Although some details of each examination board specification are different – i.e. there may be different emphasis on particular sections of the content – they are all based on the same QCA Criteria. Where such differences are significant, these have been pointed out, especially in the advice to students on carrying out oral presentations, tackling the examination, or putting together a portfolio.

## Units 1 and 2

Each Chapter in the portfolio units (Unit 1 and Unit 2) shares common features. Different features are appropriate for the Finance Unit, as test practice will be required.

### KEY SKILLS
**Information Technology 2.x**

Here you will find exercises linked to the main Key Skills of Communication, Application of Number and Information technology.

### FACT FILE

*Here you will find extra information that is useful, relevant, or just provides an extra dimension to the knowledge and understanding in the Chapter.*

### CITIZENSHIP

*This is a new National Curriculum subject so you should take the opportunity to study it through your other subjects. This provides information and suggestions for investigations and discussions that will help you to fulfil the Citizenship programme of study.*

### TRUE OR FALSE?

*This box contains some statements that many people often get wrong.*

*(see foot of page for answer)*

### Classwork activity

An exercise, discussion or activity that should be carried out in class. Often this involves some sort of group work.

### ACTIVITY

These will help you to understand and apply the knowledge that you have learned. They are graded through the use of bullet points.

✦ is a thought starter: an easy activity that everyone should be capable of completing;

✦✦ is a slightly harder task, although it should still be possible for most of you to complete it

✦✦✦ is a task that requires more thought or greater explanation. In these tasks you may be asked to analyse, evaluate or explain.

### For your portfolio

This contains pointers towards the sort of work or investigations you could be planning, or carrying out, towards your portfolio.

### True or False answer

True. You will find the answers, and a brief explanation, at the foot of the page.

## KEY *TERMS*

Some terms in the main text are highlighted; these are key terms, concepts or methods. A lot of words are used in a specialist way in Business and it is vital that you understand the importance of using the correct terms.

### What you need to do:

This shows what you need to achieve to succeed at each level of the portfolio. The examination boards have expressed the assessment in three levels.

- To achieve Level ❶   is usually a basic description
- To achieve Level ❷   is usually a further explanation or analysis
- To achieve Level ❸   is usually a detailed explanation and analysis, often requiring you to give advice to managers on improvements that could be made

**HOMEWORK ACTIVITY**

This could be a fairly simple task, or advice or directions on carrying out an investigation.

## EXTENSION EXERCISE

This sort of exercise may feed directly into your portfolio work, with suggestions for investigations, discussions or further work to extend your understanding.

### Unit 3

The chapters in the Finance Unit do not use some of these features, but instead have features that are important for an examination. These are:

**FOR YOUR EXAMINATION**

✓ ✗ Tips and hints on how to do well in an examination situation.

**LEARNING ACTIVITY 1** ——— *Key Skills:*

This includes a reference to the particular Key Skill that will also be practised. Learning Activities are often numbered so that you can tackle them in sequence in order to fully cover a particular financial concept or exercise.

## EXAMINATION PREPARATION EXERCISE

A detailed exercise to check your knowledge and understanding. You should try to do them 'unseen' and can also use them to revise for your examination.

### What have I learned?

Because Finance is examined, you will need to revise. This will help you to test your knowledge and to prepare for examination.

# SECTION 1

# BUSINESS
## Investigating Business

# CHAPTER 1

# Business aims and objectives

People start businesses for many reasons. Most people think that this reason is to do with making a lot of money, or a lot of profit, but it is not always the case. Entrepreneurs – the people who take the risk of starting a business – have many different aims and objectives. Often, the main aim is to provide an income for themselves, for which the business may indeed need to make a profit. Sometimes, however, people will have other, quite modest, aims – perhaps to provide a local service where none existed beforehand; to use a particular skill or qualification; or perhaps because they have certain knowledge or expertise. They may even be in business just because they enjoy doing something or because they want to work for themselves: to be independent, rather than have to work for a boss.

**Figure 1.1** *A National Park – but what are its objectives? The people walking in it may have achieved the objective of independence*

## TRUE OR FALSE?

*The process of performance monitoring and review (checking how well you are doing), target setting and evaluation is only applicable to businesses.*

*(see foot of page for answer)*

## Commercial aims

A larger business is likely to have written aims that form part of its overall policy or strategy. These may be included in the business's mission statement, vision statement or other corporate publication:

- A mission statement outlines the general long-term goals of the business.
- A vision statement usually has more to do with the image that a business wants to project.

Some aims are called commercial aims – those that have a direct bearing on the commercial efficiency or profitability of the business. The most common of these is profit, but others include increasing market share, increasing competitiveness and producing a better or bigger range of products. Examples include Kodak, the leading photographic business, which has a Corporate Vision Statement, which says 'Our heritage has been and our future is to be the world leader in imaging'. Their mission statement outlines their main aim of 'Total Customer Satisfaction and our consequent goals of Increased Global Market Share and Superior Financial Performance'.

## Social aims

Some aims are 'social' rather than commercial. For example, Sky TV aims 'to inspire people by exposing them to a world of opportunities', while the Body Shop wishes 'to dedicate our business to the pursuit

True or False answer

**False.** The process can and should be applied to your own work. You should set yourself SMART targets, monitor your progress and plan further targets when those are reached.

of social and environmental change'. The aim of a business is usually a statement of what it wants to achieve in the long run. Coca Cola, for example, wants to become the 'beverage of choice' (replacing even tea and coffee); Heinz aims for its tomato sauce to be 'the world's favourite ketchup, on every table'.

Aims can therefore be seen as not only long term, but in some cases, almost impossible to reach. They may be stated in a way that makes them unachievable (*every* table; *total* customer satisfaction), but this does not stop the organisation from trying to reach the aim, and from always working towards it. Look at the business aims given above and think how any of the businesses mentioned would know if their aim had actually been reached!

## Stating aims

A large business may state its official aims in a statement that is part of the business's policy. The *mission* statement of First Direct, the telephone banking arm of HSBC, is to 'create harmony between the services it provides and the way people live their lives with simple, straightforward products'. BUPA, the private health care and insurance company, has a *vision* statement of 'Taking care of the lives in our hands'.

A smaller business will also have aims, but these may be expressed in a much more informal way or not publicly stated at all. These are likely to include aims such as:

• surviving as a business or expanding
• providing goods and services to the wider community
• competing effectively with rival businesses – making sure that they match them in terms of price, quality and range of products
• being innovative – a business may want to be seen to be at the 'cutting edge', the first with new technology, products or processes.

## Profit as an aim

Some businesses have aims that are openly about increasing profit. Cadbury Schweppes aims to 'maximise shareholder value', for which profit will be needed. Few businesses, however, state their aim as 'maximising profit'. It could be argued that all business aims are profit-related, that without achieving a profit, a business would be unable to improve its service, compete or expand. Aims that might also lead to increased profits include maximising sales, improving product quality, increasing market share, and being more efficient.

## Service as an aim

Organisations such as local authorities and councils responsible for services, may have broad goals of efficient service delivery, which

**Classwork activity**

You have been asked to explain what is meant by 'business objectives' to a Year 7 class.
• Write a paragraph, in simple language, to explain what a target is, and an objective.
• Write down five of the most common objectives and define them.
• Create a wordsquare or crossword that the Year 7 class could answer using the above information.

**True or False answer**

*Figure 1.2* Mountain Rescue: the aim is to provide an efficient service

may be expressed in statements about efficiency and effectiveness to the local community. There are also public bodies that have been set up and funded by government, are accountable to government, which have a public duty to provide a particular service. Examples include the National Parks Authority, the National Rivers Authority and The Countryside Commission. Other organisations are more concerned with efficiency and providing a service rather than in making a profit. These may include charities that aim to provide funds in support of a cause or to help people with problems, and voluntary groups such as Mountain Rescue organisations, providing a voluntary service in mountainous areas of the country.

Many business organisations also have aims that are not linked to profit, such as being environmentally friendly, or providing educational services (eg providing speakers to schools and colleges). Even in these cases, it could be argued that the good reputation or image which the business earns will lead to more custom, more sales and more profit.

## SMART objectives

While aims show what the business is generally trying to achieve, objectives are specific, measurable targets that can be used as stepping-stones towards those aims. The objectives of a business will need to be measurable – indeed, many objectives are deliberately set as SMART objectives or SMART targets.
SMART stands for:

- **Specific** – you should know when an objective has been reached by making it as definite as possible
- **Measurable** – you should, where possible, be able to measure whether the objective has been reached, or see how close you are to it
- **Attainable** – a target that it is not possible to achieve is not a valid objective

- **Relevant** – it should form a sensible part of the organisation's overall planning
- **Time-related** – organisations should be trying to achieve the objective in a specified time period.

For example, Cadbury Schweppes, the chocolate and soft drinks giant, has an overall aim to increase the value of the business for shareholders. To achieve this aim, it has set itself specific objectives, including financial objectives such as increasing earnings per share by 10% each year, doubling the value of shareholders' investment every four years and generating £150 m of cash every year that can be used for projects (this cash is the amount left after dividends have been paid and new plant and equipment bought). Each objective follows the SMART principle.

Objectives are often chosen so that they will not be easy to reach; they therefore set a challenge to the business. Can the business, for example, produce new, more or better products or services than in the previous time period?

## Cycle of objectives

The cycle of objectives is a constant one – the reaching of one target is really just a signal that a new target should be set. Reviewing targets means that a business constantly looks at how close it is to achieving targets, what steps need to be taken in order to achieve targets and what new targets may be set. Such reviews help a business which is failing to hit targets, to see what needs to be changed to ensure success.

The cycle of setting and reviewing objectives goes through the following stages:

- set objective
- plan how to reach objective (strategy)
- communicate strategy to team members
- organise resources
- coordinate and control
- monitor and review progress
- re-plan as necessary
- achieve objective
- set new objective.

It is a true cycle, with the last point beginning the whole process again.

**CITIZENSHIP**

*Imagine a business in your local area which employs many local people, and causes major pollution. As one of its objectives, it has decided that it wants to become more environmentally friendly. Unfortunately this means closing down a major part of the plant and no longer employing two-thirds of the current workforce.*

*Discuss what you, or your local community, might think of this. Write a letter to a local councillor to give your views.*

**KEY SKILLS**

Communications: read the company reports of two different companies; extract the mission statement or vision statement and comment on how effective or realistic it is.

**ACTIVITY**

Identify a small local business and a large multinational one, then:

✦ list the sort of objectives which the small business might have

✦ list the sort of objectives which the multinational has

✦✦ point out which objectives they are likely to share, and why

✦✦✦ decide which objectives will ONLY the small business or ONLY the multinational have.

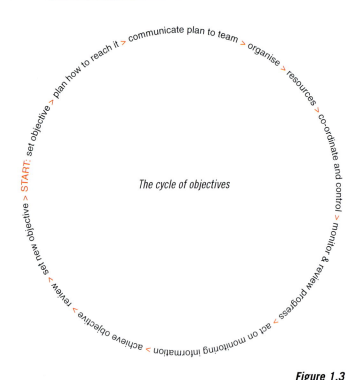

The cycle of objectives

**Figure 1.3**

## Qualitative objectives

Some objectives cannot be easily measured. These are what are called **qualitative** objectives, because they refer to quality rather than quantity. A business may review these by being able to state how much closer they are to their target than when the targets were last reviewed. Such objectives include:

- Customer satisfaction – a satisfied customer will return to make repeat purchases rather than taking business elsewhere. Some businesses try to measure customer satisfaction by looking at numbers of complaints, monitoring repeat purchases or setting measurable targets (eg complaints reduced by 20% in six months).
- Being socially aware. Many businesses aim to be socially or environmentally aware – either in their treatment of workers, suppliers or customers; eg, ensuring that they pay a fair price for produce coming from poorer countries, or making sure that they do not exploit labour. Many businesses now use 'social marketing',

## KEY TERMS

- Commercial aims – those directly linked to profitability
- Cycle of objectives – the process by which objectives are set, reviewed and achieved
- Entrepreneur – the person who takes the risk in setting up a business
- Mission statement – outlines the general long-term goals of the business
- Objectives – shorter-term targets to be reached on the way to achieving the aims
- Qualitative objectives – targets linked to quality that it is difficult or impossible to measure
- SMART objectives – objectives that are specific, measurable, attainable, relevant and time-related
- Social aims – those that are linked to service or the community
- Vision statement – outlines the image that a business wants to project

# EXTENSION EXERCISE

Wall's hold a major share of the ice cream market for 'impulse bought' ice creams (brands like Magnum and Cornetto that people buy to eat immediately), with nearly three-quarters of the market. Nestlé/Lyons Maid has nearly 10% of the market, and Mars 9%. Suggest possible objectives for each business, and possible targets on the way to achieving the objectives.

linking a product to an environmental or social issue (eg Sky TV developed a social objective to 'help young people see what they could be' through its Reach for the Sky project).

- Developing a good reputation – many businesses rely on attracting trade by building up a good reputation. This is often true of small businesses providing a personal service, which rely on word-of-mouth recommendation rather than on advertising or promotion. It is also true of large businesses who want to build up a good corporate image.

## Conflicting objectives

Although the groups within a business may all agree with the general aims of the business, they may disagree about the ways of achieving these aims. For example, greater efficiency may be an aim, and it may be achievable by investing in new technology or training labour (or even by buying new technology and sacking labour). There is therefore likely to be conflict between those who want the technology and those who don't. Often these conflicts can run very deep.

Airlines have hit two big problems in recent years: a global downturn in air travel since the terrorist attacks on America in 2001, and an increase in public awareness of DVT (deep vein thrombosis). DVT is also known as 'economy class syndrome', in which people can die due to the cramped conditions in aircraft on long distance flights. In response to the first problem, the airlines have to increase security, to make travellers feel safe. This, of course, adds to traveller inconvenience and slows down the process of boarding an aircraft. The conflict is between providing the fast, efficient service which customers want, and the levels of security which customers also want. In response to the second problem, airlines could create more leg-room by taking seats out, but this would reduce the number of passengers they were able to carry – a conflict between safety and efficiency. In both cases (increased security in one, the provision of special cushions, exercises and advice in the other), airlines are eating into profits in order to keep market share.

**Figure 1.4** Airlines have to try to balance a number of conflicting objectives such as passenger convenience vs. security

- To achieve Level ❶ you must be able to give a basic description of the activities, type of ownership and aims of each business you study.
- To achieve Level ❷ you must show a clear understanding of the objectives of the business and how they may be monitored. You need to show how the ownership of the business is suited to its size, ownership responsibilities and profit distribution.
- To achieve Level ❸ you must be able to judge how businesses might need to change their aims or objectives in the light of changed circumstances.

CHAPTER 2

# Sole traders and partnerships

There are many different ways in which a business may be legally owned and organised. Two of the most common forms of ownership are the **sole trader** and the **partnership**. Both are very easy to set up and this is one of the reasons why they are so popular.

**Figure 2.1** *Sole traders include the keepers of small shops, tradesmen and women and many other small businesses*

## TRUE OR FALSE?

*A sole trader is the only person working in a business.*

*(see foot of page for answer)*

## One-person business

A sole trader is a business that is both owned and controlled by one person. The sole trader takes all the responsibility for the business and is responsible for all the decisions.

### Starting up

The sole trader is the easiest form of business to start up. You can start trading as a sole trader without any formal process of setting up at all. All you actually need to do is start trading.

For certain businesses there will be legal requirements before you can trade (like licences to sell alcohol) but these only apply to some businesses. Most businesses need no legal requirements at all.

True or False answer

**False. There is nothing to stop a sole trader employing as many people as s/he wants to.**

### Why set up?

For many sole traders it is likely to be one or more of the following reasons:

- to make enough income to live
- to make a profit
- to be their own boss
- to be independent
- to use their own special skills
- to provide a service.

## How is the business financed?

Because the amount of money needed by a sole trader is generally small, it is usually the owner's personal funds which are used to finance the business. These may be in the form of:

- personal sources – money saved up from previous employment or received for a pension; sometimes insurance or redundancy payments
- other family sources – or borrowing from friends
- personal loans from a bank – this could also be permission to borrow in the form of an overdraft
- grants – organisations like the Prince's Youth Business Trust (which helps young business people under 30) might put money forward to help a good idea.

## Liability

Liability means the responsibility for the debts of a business. In the case of the sole trader, the owner is personally and completely responsible for all of the debts – an unlimited responsibility. If they cannot pay the debts out of current income, they can be made to pay by having their possessions sold. This is called **unlimited liability**.

This is a very important idea in business: when a person sets themselves up in business, they are actually risking all that they possess if that business should fail with unpaid debts. Many businesses rely on being able to obtain goods on credit before selling them, and could easily be left with unsold stock which they will still have to pay for.

## Bankruptcy

This means that the businessperson does not have enough assets to pay the debts of the business. The people who are owed money (creditors) can take the businessperson to court to try to get their money back. The court can make the person bankrupt and order possessions to be sold to pay off debt. Only when all the debt is cleared can the person ask the court to discharge them from being

### Classwork activity

Imagine that you were setting yourself up in business. Decide on a business idea and then write down what you think you would have to do. Compare your list with a partner's. Which do you think is more accurate? You could ask someone in business if s/he went through the same stages.

### HOMEWORK ACTIVITY

Write a list of the main sources of finance for a sole trader.

Use the internet to find out what organisations might give a grant to a business (try searching under 'grants for new businesses').

List three of the organisations, and say why you think each is important.

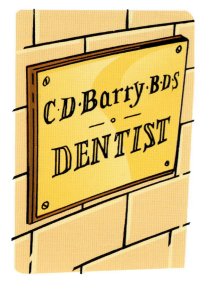

**Figure 2.2** *A sole trader, like this dentist, has unlimited liability*

bankrupt. Until this time they are not allowed to borrow money, operate a credit card or have a bank account.

## Profits

Set against the disadvantage of unlimited liability is the advantage that the sole trader does not have to share profits with anyone (except the government, in the form of taxation).

## Paperwork

There is no paperwork to complete before setting up the business, but there have to be some simple accounts so that the government can calculate the tax. This means that both a Profit and Loss account and a Balance sheet have to be provided for tax purposes. The sole trader is also responsible for his/her own National Insurance contributions – the deduction that is paid by workers to provide such things as unemployment benefit and the National Health Service. These are paid at a lower rate than if the sole trader was an employee.

## Advantages

Apart from those advantages already outlined, sole traders:
- are flexible – they benefit from being able to make decisions quickly in response to any changes
- usually need little capital in order to start up
- are able to manage staff at a personal level
- can keep their financial situation to themselves. Only the tax authorities need to be supplied with any detail about the business, and then only enough so that they can accurately assess taxation.

## Disadvantages

There are also disadvantages apart from unlimited liability. A sole trader may:
- find it hard to expand due to the lack of capital and the risks associated with borrowing
- not be able to receive the advantages that big firms can from buying in bulk, or from using specialised staff
- not pass on or sell the business. There is what is called a 'lack of continuity'. Because the business does not have a separate legal existence from its owner, when the owner dies or ceases trading, so must the business.

## Partnerships

Partnerships share many features with sole traders. The main difference between a partnership and a sole trader is that, in the partnership, there is more than one person. This means more than one person:

- taking the decisions
- sharing the responsibility
- sharing liability
- sharing profits.

A sole trader may take on a partner for any or all of the above reasons but is unlikely to take a partner just to help with workload. After all, the sole trader can easily employ someone to do that.

## Starting up

A partnership is just as easy to start as a sole trader. Two people just have to agree to share the decisions, or start to work together as joint owners of a business. If this happens, they are automatically partners and share both responsibility and profit. The minimum number of partners is two; the maximum (except in some special cases) is 20.

## Advantages of a partnership

Partners have the same advantages of independence, flexibility and privacy in financial affairs as sole traders. In addition a partner may bring:

- extra expertise – specialists such as bankers, lawyers, builders, accountants and medical practitioners will form partnerships so that they can provide a complete service; eg a carpenter, a plasterer and a bricklayer may be able to cope with most building jobs; a law firm might have different specialists in family, criminal and company law.
- extra money into the business – the sources of finance are the same as the sole trader, but there are more of them!
- extra help with the workload of the business
- help with the decision-making of the business and a share of the liability for debt; this means that responsibility is shared.

**Figure 2.3** *Partnerships gain from extra expertise in the business*

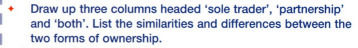

## ACTIVITY

+ Draw up three columns headed 'sole trader', 'partnership' and 'both'. List the similarities and differences between the two forms of ownership.

++ State and explain one good reason for taking a partner.

++ State and explain one good reason for not taking a partner.

## FACT FILE

The Partnership Act 1890 is the main Act of Parliament which governs the way in which partnerships are set up, run and dissolved. If a partnership is formed without any formal or written agreement, this Act covers the conduct of the business. It lays down that all profits and responsibilities are shared equally unless a Deed of Partnership has been drawn up to vary these conditions. The Deed cannot vary the liability of partners, which must be shared equally unless a partner is a 'sleeping partner'. (This is where a partner contributes finance to the partnership and shares in its profits but has no part in the actual running of it.)

## Liability

There are no real benefits to a partnership in terms of liability. The partnership still has unlimited liability and now each partner is responsible for the debts of the firm up to the limit of their personal wealth, whether or not they had anything to do with creating the debt. This last point is important; partners are said to be 'jointly and severally liable', meaning that they share joint responsibility but, if any one partner cannot pay his or her share of the debt, the others are still responsible for it.

## Disadvantages

The biggest disadvantage is the shared unlimited liability. Not only is each partner now responsible for their own debts, they are also responsible for the debts incurred by any member of the partnership. Other disadvantages include:

- possible disagreements that may happen now that decision-making is shared
- partners making decisions on their own (these are still binding on the partnership)
- lack of continuity – the same problem as the sole trader in that it does not have a separate legal existence to its owners. Should a partner decide to leave the partnership, or to retire, or become bankrupt, or dies, then the partnership ceases to exist and will need to be re-formed.

## KEY *TERMS*

- Sole trader – a one person business. The term is used interchangeably with sole proprietor and sole owner
- Liability – the responsibility for the debts of a firm
- Unlimited liability – responsibility for the debts of the business is only limited by a person's personal wealth
- Bankrupt – declared by a court as being unable to pay debts; a person remains an undischarged bankrupt until debts are paid and they are discharged by the court
- Partnership – wherever two or more people are operating a business as joint owners (a formal agreement is not needed)
- 1890 Partnership Act – this lays down that everything in a partnership is shared equally by the partners
- Deed of Partnership – the agreement which can vary the terms of the Partnership Act

# EXTENSION EXERCISE

For your portfolio work, you will need to compare either a sole trader or a partnership business with a business that has a different type of ownership. This will be easier if you fully understand the nature and problems of sole traders and partnerships. Discuss the answers to the following questions:
- Why do you think that the sole trader is the most common form of business ownership in the UK?
- Which sector or sectors of the economy do you think that most sole traders and partnerships will be found in and why?
- Why do sole traders and partnerships carry unlimited liability, even though they could limit it by becoming a limited company?

Not every sole trader or partnership is intent on growing larger. Many are happy to stay small, or the nature of their business keeps them small. This may be because the business:

- is local
- provides a personal service
- provides a specialist service
- needs the flexibility to respond quickly to changes in demand
- has only a small or niche market for what it is producing.

## What you need to do:

- **To achieve Level ❶**    you need, for each organisation, a description of the type of ownership and the type of liability that the owners have.
- **To achieve Level ❷**    you need a clear and coherent explanation of the type of ownership and liabilities.
- **To achieve Level ❸**    you need a detailed explanation of why the particular type of ownership is appropriate to your targeted businesses and how this might affect the owners' liabilities.

CHAPTER 3
# Limited liability companies

Sole traders and partnerships both have unlimited liability – the owner or owners have responsibility for all the debts of the business – and may have to sell personal possessions in order to pay those debts. There is therefore a risk to the owners that they could lose money. Owners may be willing to take this risk if it means that they all control of the business and receive the rewards. In many cases, however, owners do not necessarily want to control the business, and do not want to have to carry this level of risk. Business owners can limit their risk through creating a limited liability company.

**Figure 3.1** *Companies House, in Cardiff, records essential details of limited companies*

## Three parts: limited liability company

The three parts to the term – **limited**, **liability** and **company** give clear clues of what it is all about.

- **Liability** is the responsibility of the business for its debts.
- **Limited** means that this has now been restricted. All that the owner can actually be asked to lose (to give up in order to cover the debts of the business) is the amount of money that they originally invested. They cannot lose any more than this. 'Limited liability' therefore means that the business has limited the responsibility of its owners for its debts. In effect, the business now has the responsibility, not the owners, so no call can be made on their personal assets or wealth.
- **Company** shows that the business now has a separate legal existence from its owners. It has been created as something completely separate from its owners (with a sole trader or partnership, the owners *are* the business). As a company, it can be bought and sold and passed from one owner to another as if it was a product.

## Aims

The aims of a limited liability company will vary with the size of the business. Small private limited companies may have similar aims to sole traders and partnerships – survival, security and a reasonable income. By becoming a limited company owners are reducing their own financial risk. In the case of larger businesses, they could be looking to raise money for expansion – this is usually the case when a business becomes a public limited company. The business may also be trying to make sure that its shareholders receive the best possible return for their investment.

# Setting up

Setting up a limited company is a much more complicated process than setting up a sole trader or a partnership. There are legal formalities, and much of the information about the business is made available to the general public. This is the reason why many businesses remain as sole traders or partnerships.

To set up as a company, a business needs to follow these steps:

1 The owners must decide on a company name. This must then be registered so that no two companies are using the same name. This also protects companies from anyone trying to trade under their name.
2 They must register the business with the Registrar of Companies at Companies House in Cardiff. You can look at www.companieshouse.gov.uk/ and see the sort of information that is needed. Companies House also produce information booklets and lists of frequently asked questions (FAQs). People intending to set up a company can check trade names, internet site names and patents from this site. Information is also available on which people are barred from being company directors and why.
3 The owners must draw up two main documents: the Memorandum of Association and the Articles of Association.

## Memorandum of Association

This document outlines the information about the company that must be available to the public. It must include the name of the person making the application, and the name and address of at least one director (this must be their home address – Post Office boxes are not allowed). It must also include the registered address of the company, the purpose of the company and what capital it hopes to raise, along with the name of the Company Secretary. It must also say whether or not shares are to be offered to the public and if so, how many. Finally, there has to be a statement of limited liability.

## Articles of Association

These are the internal rules of the company, its owners and its organisation. The Articles must

• list the directors' names
• say who has what voting rights
• outline the rights of shareholders
• say when and how shareholders and directors are to meet
• say how profits are to be divided.

Shareholders can later change these articles, as long as the changes do not disagree with the Memorandum.

**TRUE OR FALSE?**

*It is easy to set up as a public limited company.*

*(see foot of page for answer)*

**HOMEWORK ACTIVITY**

Copy out the following passage and put the correct words in where the blanks are:

Limited liability means that the business's _____ for debt _____ is _____ to the amount put in by shareholders. It must use _____ after its name if it is a public limited company, or _____ if it is a private limited company, in order to _____ people of its status.

True or False answer

**False.** Setting up as a plc is a complicated and expensive process. The business must provide a lot of information and accounts, and must be trying to raise a large amount of capital. There are also special rules which it must follow.

## Certificate of Incorporation

The company only comes into existence and can start trading once it has its Certificate of Incorporation from the Companies Registrar.

Once the company is set up, it must warn everyone who deals with it that it has limited liability. It does this by including the word 'Limited' or abbreviation 'Ltd' after its name if it is a private limited company (Jones the Builders Ltd), or the abbreviation 'plc' after its name if it is a public limited company (Jones the Builders plc).

# Advantages and disadvantages

Limited liability companies have the disadvantage of having their affairs (directors, accounts and financial affairs) being made public and of being more complicated and more expensive to set up than sole traders or partnerships. Companies are also liable for different types of taxation.

The benefits of having limited liability are so great, however, that many businesses decide that the advantages outweigh the disadvantages. In the UK, there are over half a million private limited companies and many hundreds of public limited companies.

A **private** limited company is different from a **public** limited company:

- private limited companies do not sell shares to the general public, whereas a public limited company does
- a plc produces an annual report and set of accounts which are made available to anyone who asks for them, whereas only the basic accounts of private limited companies are available, for a fee, from Companies House
- setting up as a public limited company (called 'floating' a company) is a very expensive and complex process, but one which allows a company to raise a lot more capital. There are also drawbacks – because anyone can buy shares in a company, it is possible for an owner to lose control of his/her own business. If someone is able to buy a large enough block of shares, then they can take control of the company and carry out changes or policies against the wishes of the original owner.

# How is the business financed?

Companies will raise finance through the use of

- owners' funds – the owner's own money
- banks and other financial institutions – borrowing money
- credit – obtaining goods, machinery etc on a promise to pay in the future
- shareholders' funds – the money raised from the sale of shares in the company
- share issues – public limited companies can raise finance by further share issues.

**Figure 3.2** Bill Gates, CEO of Microsoft, addresses the company AGM

## Control

In a company that has shares, each share has an equal amount of control – one vote at the Annual General Meeting of the company. This means that the more shares a person has, the more control s/he has. Anyone owning a large enough block of shares can elect him/herself as a director and make decisions. If a person has enough shares to have absolute control of a company (ie more than 50% of the shares), then they can make all of the decisions on their own. This is called having a 'controlling interest' in the company. Sometimes one shareholder has a 'majority shareholding'. This means that s/he has a large enough block of shares to outvote any other single shareholder. Look at the diagrams to see what a controlling interest and a majority shareholder mean.

## Who takes the profits?

Profits may be put back into the business ('ploughed back') to buy more stock or machinery, or to help with expansion. These are called

A controlling interest. This slice of shares is more than half.

A majority interest. This slice of shares is bigger than any other single slice.

**Figure 3.3**

retained profits. Alternatively, profits may be shared out amongst the shareholders of the business. In this case, each share receives an equal share of the profit – called a dividend. Therefore the more shares you have, the more of the profit you receive. If the dividend were 10p per share, then a person with 10 shares would receive £1; one with 100 shares £10 (100 × 10p), and so on.

## Winding up

A company may decide that it can no longer be profitable, or its creditors (the people to whom the company owes money) may decide that they want to be paid. In either case, the company may be forced to 'wind up'. This means that it will stop trading and sell off its assets (stock, machinery, buildings, order books etc) in order to raise as much money as possible. This is called liquidation – turning the assets into money. Sometimes this is voluntary; the business's owners deciding that the business is no longer a 'going concern'. Sometimes the creditors may apply to the court for the company to be compulsorily wound up. In some cases, an outside agency (called a receiver) may be brought in to wind up the company.

## Limited liability partnership

Recently, the Government has introduced a new form of business ownership, which combines some of the benefits of a partnership with some of the benefits of a limited liability company. It is called a limited liability partnership. The main difference between a limited liability partnership and a limited company is that a limited liability partnership is taxed as a partnership and has fewer restrictions on how it can be organised. Limited liability partnerships are not available for all types of business – eg a non-profit making enterprise could not be a limited liability partnership.

Two or more people operating as a partnership can set up as a limited partnership by filling in an incorporation form (to establish the company) and paying a fee to Companies House. The form asks for:

## KEY *TERMS*

Articles of Association – the internal rules of the company

Companies House – where companies and their details must be registered

Company – the separate legal body created when a business is incorporated

Company Secretary – the person appointed to look after the legal affairs of a company (not an ordinary secretary)

Controlling interest – having more than 50% of the shares in a company

Dividend – a part of the profits given to each share

Liability – the responsibility of the business for its debts

Limited liability – limiting this responsibility to the amount the owner has risked

Majority shareholding – having a large enough block of shares to outvote any other shareholder

Memorandum of Association – the document that outlines the information about the company and must be available to the public

Retained profits – profits not given to shareholders but put back into the business

## EXTENSION EXERCISE

Write to three public limited companies for a copy of their annual report and accounts. What does

- the speed of their response
- the quality of the documents
- the content of the documents

tell you about the company?

- the name of the limited liability partnership
- the address of the registered office
- the name, full address and date of birth of each member.

In most respects, limited liability partnerships are very similar to limited liability companies.

## What you need to do:

- To achieve Level ❶   you need, for each organisation, a description of the type of ownership and the type of liability that the owners have.
- To achieve Level ❷   you need a clear and coherent explanation of the type of ownership and liabilities.
- To achieve Level ❸   you need a detailed explanation of why the particular type of ownership is appropriate to your targeted businesses and how this might affect the owners' liabilities.

CHAPTER 4

# Co-operatives, charities and mutuals

Businesses exist to produce something – a product or service. This is usually managed through an input–process–output model. What this means is that a collection of inputs (raw materials, skills, machinery, etc) is brought together and through a process (such as manufacturing or delivery of a service), an output is produced.

- In the case of co-operatives, some or all of the process is carried out by a group of people working together for their mutual benefit – in other words, so that each one of them benefits from the

***Figure 4.1*** *Charities often use events like the London Marathon as fund-raisers*

enterprise, with no one person gaining more than another. A mutual society maximises benefits to its members.
- In the case of charities, the difference is in the aims of the organisation. A charity should aim to maximise the benefits to the people that it is targeting; this could be the poor, the homeless, or 'good causes' identified by an organisation such as the National Lottery in the UK.

## Classwork activity

Why do you think producer co-operatives are often found in the agricultural industry?

Draw up a poster with at least five bullet points, which could be displayed at an agricultural venue like a market or agricultural show. It should be bold, bright – and persuasive!

## Aims

The aims of a co-operative will be to produce the maximum benefit for their members. This may not mean maximising profit; but instead aiming for something else, such as a fair price for labour or goods. A charity will also be aiming to maximise benefits, but this time for the people or cause that it is targeting. This could be anything from wild animals to underprivileged children. A mutual society is similar to a co-operative, in that its members have set it up. It is owned by, and run for the benefit of, its members.

## Co-operatives

There are four main types of co-operative:
- a group of producers who have joined together to sell their produce – a **producer** co-operative
- a group of workers sharing labour and the profits from their labour – a **worker** co-operative
- a group of consumers who have joined together to bring about lower prices – a **consumer** co-operative
- a group of people who have joined together to provide financial benefits – a **mutual** organisation.

A co-operative is therefore a group of people who have joined together to:
- share resources
- produce goods or services
- work
- buy or sell goods or services
- secure financial security or benefits

The aim is to gain shared or mutual benefit of the members of the group.

## HOMEWORK ACTIVITY

There is another type of mutual not mentioned here, called a credit union. Find out about credit unions – what are they, who would use them, and why.

## Mutual societies

Some types of co-operative organisations are called mutual societies. The two main groups of mutual societies are insurance companies and building societies: people traditionally either saved to protect themselves from a risk (such as fire) or to be able to build a house. Other societies were formed for more modest aims, such as to be able to afford a decent burial. Later, mutuals provided ways for people with money to invest it, in order to maintain an income. Often the only people who could save money were those in the professions, or those who had been married to someone in the professions. This explains why some insurance companies have odd names like Legal and General, Clerical and Medical, and Scottish Widows.

**Figure 4.2** *The Woolwich – a mutual building society*

Insurance companies work on the principle that everyone pays a fee (a **premium**) into a central fund, and anyone who suffers a misfortune is compensated from this fund. As not everyone will suffer a loss, the society should be able to cover the losses that are made. In some cases, funds were set up to cover things that were going to happen, such as death, funeral expenses, retirement.

Building societies were originally set up so that people could cooperate in the building of houses and, when every member in a group had a house, the society would be closed. Mutual societies put their members first. It is the members who own the society, therefore the society does not have to please shareholders or other owners.

## Demutualisation

The market for financial services such as bank accounts and loans used to be restricted to banks. The Government deregulated the market so that other businesses could also compete. This has led to a number of mutual societies seeking to 'demutualise', so that they

**CITIZENSHIP**

*Much medical research and care is funded through charities such as Cancer Research, Leukaemia Research, the British Heart Foundation, the Multiple Sclerosis Society and Macmillan Nurses. Discuss whether you think it is right for funding to be raised in this way, or should government provide the funding for these services, and pay for it through higher taxation?*

**ACTIVITY**

A number of successful worker co-operatives have been formed by workers taking over a business which the previous owners thought could no longer be a success.

✦ Suggest five reasons why the new owners have a greater chance of success than the previous owners.

✦ Compare your answers with a partner to make a longer list.

✦✦ Put the reasons in order of importance.

✦✦✦Which do you and your partner agree are the most important? Why?

**Figure 4.3** *The traditional way to collect for charity*

**Figure 4.4** *Café Direct and Fairtrade products are produced by co-operatives*

can provide services in the new markets that are now open to them. For example, building societies are allowed to operate current accounts and issue credit and debit cards, and banks are allowed to issue mortgages (loans for house purchase). Some societies, such as Scottish Widows and the Halifax Building Society (now the Halifax Bank), have demutualised, with cash or shares being given to members to compensate them for their loss of ownership and control. Others (such as the Yorkshire Building Society) have remained as mutuals, saying that this is in the best interests of their members.

## Charities

Charities are organisations that have been established to provide help to those in need of it (such as the poor and the sick), or to support 'good' causes (such as protecting wildlife or the environment). Many of them (particularly large charities such as Oxfam or Cancer Research) have directors and managers who are paid a salary, and may even be incorporated (see Chapter 3), but no one shares in the 'profits' of the organisation except the good cause itself. Even the examination board that sets this course is a charity!

A charity may collect its inputs – in the form of donations of materials, money or labour – without having to pay for them. It may use these inputs to produce a service, or the service it produces may be the redistribution of the materials it collects. Some charities may actually produce goods or may just use business techniques to market themselves or to raise funds. They can be considered as businesses because they produce a service.

## Producer co-operatives

Producers who join together to share resources, expertise, and marketing form these co-operatives. Often such co-operatives are based around agriculture. Co-operatives are especially important for agricultural producers who may only use a piece of specialised machinery once or twice a year – perhaps at harvest or planting time. It is much more economical for them to share the expense of such machinery. Agricultural producers can also co-operate to sell their production. In rural areas of the UK, for example, there are farmers' markets, where farmers can sell direct to the public. The cost of holding and advertising such markets will be shared amongst the farmers.

### Fairtrade and Sunkist

In South America, smaller producers of coffee (and most farms are small) have joined together to co-operate in the branding and marketing of their own produce. They have been helped in this by charities whose aim is to ensure that small producers are not being exploited. Many operate under the Fairtrade label, which tells consumers that the money they pay for goods is being fairly distributed – in the case of coffee, that it is going to small coffee growers rather than big corporations. Café Direct is one such label, representing a co-operative of small coffee producers. Their combined crop shares facilities, marketing, packaging and distribution, where this would not be economical for any one of the farms on its own.

Small farmers in richer parts of the world also use such organisations – growers of oranges, lemons and limes in California have joined together to market under the co-operative 'Sunkist' label.

# Worker co-operatives

At one political extreme, the state or government owns everything (communism); at the other extreme, everything is owned privately (capitalism). In Scandinavia, co-operative ownership is very common and is known as the 'third way' between communism and capitalism. The workers own and benefit from the co-operative and often receive state support.

Worker co-operatives are where a group of workers decide to share the work, decision-making and profits of an enterprise between them. The major features of worker co-operatives are shared:

- ownership
- work
- decision-making
- risk
- profit.

The workers own the factory, plant, machinery etc themselves. In the UK, some co-operatives have been created as workers bought out businesses that were threatened with closure. They share the work as equally as possible between the members, taking into account each member's particular skills or expertise. Decision-making may be possible through a meeting of all the workers in a small business, or the workers may appoint some of the members to take decisions. Some co-operatives will even employ specialist managers who are not members of the co-operative.

With shared risk and shared profit, each worker puts in an equal amount of money, has an equal say in the decisions and takes an equal share of the profit. The Industrial Common Ownership Society will give help and advice to worker co-operatives.

## Advantages and disadvantages

Worker co-operatives suffer fewer industrial relations problems. They produce better motivation in workers who are working for themselves.

**FACT FILE**

There is a difference between a profit-making business, a not-for-profit business and a non-profit making business. Most businesses will try to make a profit – and co-operatives are no exception to this even though they may have other aims as well. A not-for-profit business, like a charity, may make profits from some of its activities (such as the sales of clothes in charity shops) but this is not its main aim.

Non-profit making organisations are different. Perhaps the best example is that of an amateur sports team or club, where members pay subscriptions that contribute to a clubhouse or other facilities. Such organisations often have no paid staff, relying on volunteers to carry out the necessary duties such as treasurer or club secretary.

# KEY TERMS

Charities – organisations established to provide help to those in need of it or to support 'good' causes

Co-operative – a group of people working together for common benefits

Demutualisation – the process of turning a mutual society into a company with shares

Liability – responsibility of the owners for the debts of the business

Mutual society – similar to a co-operative

# EXTENSION EXERCISE

Find out exactly what is meant by a company 'limited by guarantee'.

Find three companies that are limited by guarantee and outline exactly what their activities are.

What else do they have in common?

They also tend to be more aware of their responsibilities to the local community, because this is where the workers live.

Disadvantages include difficulty in raising investment capital and difficulties in expansion. There can also be difficulties with decision-making, if each member feels that they must have their say. This is not always very efficient.

## Consumer co-operatives

The modern consumer co-operative movement in the UK was started by a group of people now known as the Rochdale Pioneers. In Victorian times, factory and mill owners often did not pay workers in cash, but in tokens that could only be used at the owner's shop, or in goods. Often the goods sold in these shops were poor or overpriced.

In 1844 a group of workers in Rochdale, Lancashire, fed up with such practices, formed a consumer co-operative called the Rochdale Society of Equitable Pioneers and opened their own grocery shop. Each member gave just £1 to set up the business. The business sold basic goods at fair prices and did not intend to make a profit. Any surplus was divided up between the members so that everyone benefited.

### It's all at the Co-op

Nowadays the Co-op is big business. The co-operative retail society (CRS) has a turnover in excess of £8,000 m and 5,000 retail outlets nationwide. The CRS has adopted the principles that were laid down by the Rochdale Pioneers:

- Each member has only one vote, regardless of how many shares in the society s/he owns.
- Anyone may buy a share and become a member of the society, regardless of race, colour, creed or religion.
- Goods and services are sold at reasonable prices.
- After usual business expenses have been paid, the profit or surplus is returned to the members.

Profit is divided between members according to how much money they have spent with the society. This is called a dividend.

**Figure 4.5** *A co-operative retail outlet*

## How is the business financed?

Mutuals and co-operatives are financed through the contributions of members. Producer co-operatives will put in equal amounts in order to buy plant or machinery; worker co-operatives will each contribute the same amount; consumer co-operatives will put in equal amounts to establish the business by buying stock, premises or equipment. They may also be helped, in the UK, by the Co-operative Union.

In 1869, 25 years after the founding of the original Rochdale co-operative, the Co-operative Union was formed. This is a body that helps and advises on the formation of new co-operatives. It now forms an umbrella body under which are the CRS, the Co-operative Wholesale Society (CWS) and other co-operative enterprises such as Co-operative Funeral Service, Co-operative Insurance Society, Co-operative Press, Co-operative Bank and Co-operative Travel.

Charities are financed by the donations of people who want to support the good cause. Some charities have grown into multi-million pound businesses, but they are still funded by voluntary donations – of money, goods, time and labour.

## Liability

Co-operatives usually operate as companies – with, therefore, limited liability. Smaller co-operatives may operate almost as partnership organisations, with unlimited liability and shared decision-making.

Charities may have a lot of assets, and may also need to borrow money or obtain credit from supplier. They therefore have liabilities. Many charities have liability 'limited by guarantee'; this means that a few people have taken on the role of members and agree to guarantee the debts. The 'guarantees' are, however, in name only and are usually no more than £10 a head. 'Limited by guarantee' is really a warning that debts are unlikely to be paid should the charity fail. Companies limited by guarantee are nearly always charities and are never seeking to make a profit.

## What you need to do:

- To achieve Level ❶    you need, for each organisation, a description of the type of ownership and the type of liability that the owners have.
- To achieve Level ❷    you need a clear and coherent explanation of the type of ownership and liabilities.
- To achieve Level ❸    you need a detailed explanation of why the particular type of ownership is appropriate to your targeted businesses and how this might affect the owners' liabilities.

CHAPTER 5
# The public sector

All of the businesses that you have read about so far have been owned privately. That is to say, individuals own them. Sole traders are owned by one individual, partnerships by two or more, limited companies by shareholding individuals, co-operatives by a group of people. Some businesses, however, are owned and run by the government. This could be local government, national government, or even international government bodies like the European Union. The government, on behalf of the public, holds these businesses and organisations. Businesses of this type are therefore called the **public sector**.

**Figure 5.1** *The armed forces are controlled by central government and used on state occasions as well as in conflict; in this case, the funeral of the Queen Mother*

## Public sector size

At its largest, the public sector consisted of much of the country's primary industry – coal mining, shipbuilding, the iron and steel industry, the railways, electricity, gas and water. It also included The Post Office, the BBC, telephone and telecommunications systems (part of the post office at the time), British Aerospace, British Airways, British Petroleum (BP), the National Bus Company and London Transport (buses and the underground), plus many smaller undertakings such as airports, a road transport fleet and air traffic control.

The public sector is now quite small. Privatisations include: BP, Cable & Wireless, gas, electricity, water, coal, steel, British Airways, the National Bus Company and British Rail. Currently under the possibility of being privatised are Air Traffic Control and The Post Office. The government has, however, kept a share in some of the new technology industries.

## Reasons for the public sector

Why would government want to hold a business organisation? There are a number of reasons:

1. The government may not trust certain services to private ownership, eg the Royal Navy, the Royal Air Force and the Army.
2. Some things might be considered too dangerous for individuals to own, eg nuclear power.
3. Some services are so essential that it could be dangerous to put them in private hands who might only let people who could afford the service have it.
4. It is not possible to make a profit from certain services, so no private business would be interested. How, for example, could a private business charge for street lighting, or road maintenance?
5. Some services are considered an essential right to everyone and are therefore provided by the government. These include health services and education.
6. Private individuals or private industry may not be able to afford the investment necessary, eg building a new railway.
7. Private businesses would not provide amenities (like parks, gardens and swimming baths) as they would not be profitable – yet government thinks that people have a right to these things.
8. The government itself needs to be administered by officials who are more interested in efficiency than profit – the civil service.

Some of these goods and services are provided at a local level, some at a national level, and others by special bodies set up by government to provide them.

## Local government services

Elected locally, your local council is responsible, by law, for providing certain services. This is usually because they are services that must be available to everyone. In other cases it is because private businesses could not make a profit out of such services. Legally, the council must provide and pay for:

• the education service
• refuse collection
• the fire service
• the police.

Most councils also provide other services such as:

• housing
• public parks and open spaces
• public buildings like libraries, museums and art galleries
• leisure and recreation facilities like swimming baths
• objects for public enjoyment, like statues and fountains.

### TRUE OR FALSE?

*The public sector does not include public limited companies.*

*(see foot of page for answer)*

### FACT FILE

*Many of the private companies created by privatisation had the chance to operate against the public interest in order to make more profits. Because of this, each industry has been appointed a 'watchdog'. This is a person who observes the privatised businesses to make sure that they are not acting against the public interest. Examples include Oftel (to regulate telecommunications), Ofgas (for the gas industry), and Ofwat (for privatised water suppliers).*

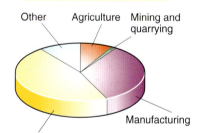

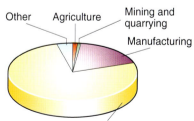

**Figure 5.2** *How the structure of UK industry has changed over the last 20 years*

## Classwork activity

Draw up a table to show whether the following businesses are in the public sector, the private sector, or could be in both:

- National Health Service
- Parcel Post
- Co-operative Bank
- Bank of England
- The BBC
- Yorkshire Television
- BSkyB
- Hospitals
- The armed forces
- Emptying household bins

Add five more examples of your own and then ask a partner to say whether they are in the public sector, private sector or could be in both.

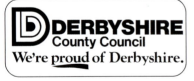

Figure 5.3

Councils may also provide support for music, the arts, transport, or other areas where they feel that support is needed.

### Local government income

The council's income comes from three sources:

1. the uniform business rate (UBR) charged on all businesses
2. the council tax charged on all households
3. the revenue support grant – extra support from central government.

## Regional government

In Scotland, Wales and Northern Ireland, there are now regional assemblies or, in the case of Scotland, a Parliament. These bodies have been given some of the powers that the national Parliament in London used to have, in a process known as **devolution**. This means that these bodies can take certain decisions to benefit their own people. For example, in Scotland, there is a different system of funding students and paying student fees.

## National government

The national UK government (which sits at the Westminster Parliament in London) is responsible for central essential services, such as the navy, army and the printing and distribution of banknotes.

Government departments also provide some services which the government wishes to keep control over – such as The Stationery Office (which prints and publishes all the proceedings of the Houses of Parliament and all proposals for Acts of Parliament, as well as the actual Acts). Traditionally, such government bodies were recognisable by being part of the monarch's government and therefore with the heading 'Her Majesty's' (as in Her Majesty's Inspectors of Schools'), but in many cases this has now been dropped in order to give a more modern image.

### Public corporations

Also under national government are business organisations that were set up by government in order to carry out a particular service. Public corporations are created either by being directly set up by government (such as the BBC) or by an industry being nationalised (ie taken into public ownership). These bodies rely on the government for funding and can be controlled by government. Examples of these public corporations include the BBC and the Post Office.

### The Post Office

The Post Office has a duty to be as efficient as possible. It provides a national postal service – even in areas where this is not profitable such as remote villages or Scottish islands. It costs approximately £13 to send a letter from Land's End to John O'Groats (ie the length of the UK), but because it is a national service, this journey costs the consumer the same as sending a letter next door – ie one stamp. A business seeking to make a profit would be unlikely to continue with non-profit making services like this. Some governments have thought that some parts of the postal service could be run more efficiently by private businesses, and have threatened to allow private businesses to compete with the Post Office. This is already the case with some business mail services and parcels.

### The BBC

The BBC is not a commercial television station, and carries no commercial advertising. The BBC is intended to provide a national broadcasting service including educational and religious programmes, which people are entitled to watch by paying the licence fee. Because it is a public corporation, however, it is often accused of being biased towards whichever political party is in power.

## QUANGOs

These are semi-independent bodies set up by central government, usually with a Board or Council to run them. There are hundreds of bodies carrying out various different functions and providing different services, ranging from The Sports Council and National Park Planning Boards to the Environment Agency, the British Waterways Board (in charge of canals) to the British Tourist Board, the National Rivers Authority (in charge of keeping rivers clean) and Learning and Skills Councils. Because appointments to the boards of such bodies are made by government, there is much criticism of the way in which QUANGOs are put together. Equally, because they have to answer to nobody, there is criticism of how they operate.

## From public to private – why?

There are a number of reasons why a government might want to move public sector businesses into the private sector. These include:

- **Cost** – taxpayers' money is used to run the public sector; some governments have felt that this was not the best way to spend taxes
- **Efficiency** – some governments believed that private industry, looking for a profit, would be more efficient than a public body that did not have to make a profit
- **Security** – some public ownership was for reasons of security (such as British Petroleum, to ensure that Britain always had oil supplies)
- **Monopolies** – some public ownership was originally regarded as the best way to control natural monopolies (where a single business operator is likely to be more efficient than competing operators)

**HOMEWORK ACTIVITY**

Find out which companies supply gas, electricity, water and telephone service to your home. Find out which companies have provided each 25 years ago.

Have the companies changed? Explain in what ways, and why.

**For your portfolio**

Look at how your chosen businesses are affected by the public sector. What dealings do they have with public sector businesses? Are they happy with the service that they receive? Interview a manager or owner to see if they agree with privatisation, and why.

like water, electricity and the railways. Government has now decided that it can introduce some competition in some areas
- **Politics** – a change in political views can mean that public sector industry is no longer seen as a good thing.

## From public to private – how?

There are a number of ways in which public sector businesses are transferred to the private sector:

- PFI – the Private Finance Initiative. This brings private money into public projects. An example is the Royal Armouries in Leeds, where the builders paid for the project, but in return can charge entry fees
- PPP – the Public Private Partnership. This is where some public money is matched by private industry money. This is the proposed method of financing the changes to the London Underground

**Figure 5.4** *The Royal Armouries in Leeds – a PFI project*

## ACTIVITY

✦ Outline five ways in which public sector businesses can be transferred to the private sector.

✦ Give five reasons why public sector businesses might be transferred to the private sector.

✦✦ Explain which of these reasons you agree or disagree with, and why.

✦✦✦ Suggest three industries that you think the current government should either
- take into public ownership or
- privatise

and give reasons for your answer.

- Privatisation – selling public corporations into the private sector by offering shares to the public (the opposite to nationalisation, where private businesses are taken under state control)
- Deregulation – allowing and encouraging competition in areas where monopolies or licensing had existed before (eg on the railways, the buses, financial services)
- Introducing charges – such as for dental work and eye tests
- Internal markets – this is where departments within corporations and councils have to compete with each other to provide the best service at the lowest rate. For example, a school meals service will set itself up as a private concern and bid to provide school meals; a private contractor will bid to collect bins.

## Owner's liabilities

In a business in the public sector, liability is not really an issue. The debts of the business are the responsibility of the owner; the owner is government, and the government can always raise more taxes or borrow more money should it need to pay the debt. In fact, one of

## KEY TERMS

- Deregulation – opening up certain markets to competition
- Devolution – passing some of central governments powers to regional or local government
- Internal market – introducing competition within operations in order to gain the benefits of competition
- Local government – your local council
- National government – the government elected at a general election
- Nationalisation – taking businesses into public ownership
- PFI – private finance initiative: a way of persuading private industry to invest in the public sector
- PPP – public private partnership: another way of persuading private industry to invest in the public sector
- Privatisation – returning businesses to the private sector
- Public corporations – bodies set up by government to run certain organisations in the public sector
- Public sector – those concerns owned/controlled by government
- QUANGO – quasi-autonomous non governmental organisation
- Regional government – bodies set up in parts of the UK to carry out some of the functions of government
- UBR – uniform business rate, charged on all businesses

## EXTENSION EXERCISE

Find a project local to your school or college that has been the subject of a PFI or PPP initiative (it could be a museum, a road, a hospital, an educational project, a public transport project, or a public amenity). Find out as many facts about the project as you can. State your opinion on the scheme. Would it have been better paid for from taxation? Why? Or why not?

the problems with businesses in the public sector was that no one was really worried about the debt. Publicly-owned businesses did not have to be efficient, or profitable, as the government would always bail them out. Sometimes this cost many millions of pounds, and it is one of the reasons why governments have decided to return industries to the private sector.

## What you need to do:

- **To achieve Level ❶**    you need, for each organisation, a description of the type of ownership and the type of liability that the owners have.
- **To achieve Level ❷**    you need a clear and coherent explanation of the type of ownership and liabilities.
- **To achieve Level ❸**    you need a detailed explanation of why the particular type of ownership is appropriate to your targeted businesses and how this might affect the owners' liabilities.

## CHAPTER 6
# Franchises

Franchises often appear under the heading of 'type of business ownership' when, more accurately, they are a type of business organisation. Franchises really consist of two halves – a franchiser, who provides the franchise, and a franchisee, who buys the franchise. A franchise may be owned by a sole trader, by a partnership, by a limited company or by a co-operative. The profits, responsibilities and control will all be shared according to the type of business ownership chosen. Liability will be limited or unlimited according to the type of ownership. Most franchisers will be large businesses and are therefore likely to be public limited companies. Most franchisees will be small businesses and are therefore more likely to be sole traders or partnerships.

**Figure 6.1** *The Body Shop – a well known franchise operation*

## How does a franchise work?

For a franchiser, a franchise is a way for its successful business to expand and share its success. For the franchisee, it is a low-risk way for a person or group of people to start in business.

The people with the successful business decide that they would like their product (remember, a product includes both goods and services) to be sold or distributed more widely. However, they do not want all the costs and risks of setting up, for example, new branches or outlets. They do, however, want to keep the image, which they have created (their 'corporate image') and trade on its success. They therefore expand by letting someone else sell the product in return for a fee or payment. The person with the successful product is called the **franchiser** (in some books this may still be spelt in the old way of 'franchisor'). The person buying the right to sell the product is called the **franchisee**.

Examples of successful franchise operations include Burger King, Prontaprint, SnappySnaps, Wimpy, KFC, the British School of Motoring, McDonald's, The Sock Shop, Tie Rack, Avis car rentals and The Body Shop. McDonald's, for example, is the largest fast food group in the world and has franchises in over 150 countries. It has never operated more than a handful of outlets itself since it was founded in 1948, preferring to use franchising to achieve expansion.

## Different franchises

Sometimes a franchise involves the provision of a service, using the existing equipment of the franchiser. This is the case with the railway network in the UK and with commercial television stations. In the case of commercial television, the franchiser is the Independent Broadcasting Authority. In the case of the railways, the franchiser was Railtrack – the public limited company which used to own the rails, signalling equipment and so on that train operators need.

In both cases, businesses bid to buy a franchise to provide a particular service. GNER, for example, has the East Coast Main Line and associated routes and stations. Virgin has the West Coast Main Line, Scotrail provides rail services in Scotland and Connex provides commuter services in the South East. Your own television region (eg Yorkshire, Meridian, Anglia, Grampian, Border, Carlton) has bought the right (the franchise) to broadcast programmes in your area and to pay for this through advertising revenue.

## Aims

- The franchiser is likely to have profit maximisation or taking a larger share of the market as its main aims and it uses the franchise route as a means to expand and to compete.
- The aims of the franchisee are likely to be the same as those for any other small trader, or business start-up. Initially the franchisee will be looking to survive, to provide a reasonable income for themselves and to break even. Franchisees may eventually decide that they want to expand, but this is unlikely.

## Why set up as a franchiser?

Franchising is a reasonably cheap and low-risk way of trying to achieve the aim stated above, as a means to expand the business. The franchiser gets money in two ways:

**Figure 6.2** *Holders of a broadcasting franchise*

True or False answer

False. Franchises are a type of business operation – they can be owned in many different ways.

## TRUE OR FALSE?

*Franchises are mostly in fast food businesses.*

*(see foot of page for answer)*

# CITIZENSHIP

*McDonald's is a global business, operating in over 150 countries. Most of its outlets are franchises, run by local traders or businesses. Investigate how McDonald's succeeds (or fails) in being global but having consideration for local problems and issues.*

## KEY SKILLS

The two documents that you create for the classwork exercise – a description of a business which includes a logo and an application form for a franchisee – will help you to reach Communications Key Skill C2.3. To reach it completely, your business description should be as detailed as possible.

1 The fee charged for the franchise. This may be several hundred or even several thousand pounds. In the case of franchise holders such as the railway companies or independent television stations, it may be a promise to invest or to provide a certain quality of service that is required. The franchiser may not even sell the franchise, they may just rent it to the franchisee.

2 The franchiser usually collects an amount based on the franchisee's sales. This will be a percentage of sales turnover (price $\times$ quantity sold), and is called a royalty. This means that the more successful the franchisee is, the more the franchiser will gain from them. It is therefore in the interest of the franchiser to make sure that

- they provide the best possible service to their franchisees
- they chose their franchisees very carefully.

## Advantages and disadvantages

There are few disadvantages to the franchiser – the company keeps control of the operation, expands at a much reduced cost and ensures that it receives an income through fees and royalties. The major disadvantage is the damage that can be done to the reputation of a company by the failure of even one of its franchisees. Imagine the damage that would be done to KFC, for example, if a branch was found to be selling out-of-date and infected chicken. In this case, the damage of bad publicity to the parent company, the franchiser, would be much greater than that to the individual franchisee.

### Classwork activity

Work with a partner. Each of you should draw up details of a franchise operation as if you were the successful business choosing to sell the franchise. You should include details of the type of business, its corporate image and why it wants to expand in this way.

Create a logo for your business to help represent its corporate image.

Write down how someone wanting to buy a franchise from you would have to apply and create an application form for them to fill in.

Apply for a franchise in your partner's business.

Would you accept the application? Why? or why not?

True or False answer

**False.** While there are many franchises associated with fast food, there are many others in businesses such as printing, insurance, high street shops, photography, entertainment and transport – as well as television broadcasting and the railways.

34

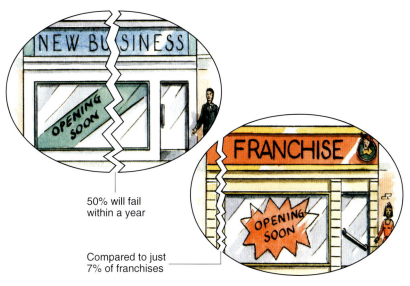

50% will fail
within a year

Compared to just
7% of franchises

**Figure 6.3** *New start-ups compared to franchises*

## Why be a franchisee?

The main reason for buying a franchise is the low risk attached to this way of starting a business. Because the product is already established and successful, the franchisee is much more likely to succeed. In fact, less than 7% of franchises fail in any one year (compared with a figure of over 50% for other forms of small business), and over 90% make a profit.

### Advantages and disadvantages

Franchisers may also provide many benefits to the franchisee apart from those they get from being able to use the corporate image of the franchiser. For example, the franchiser may provide national advertising and promotion, uniforms and staff training and other essentials such as suppliers. All McDonald's franchises use the same ingredients, the same suppliers and the same menus. In many cases the franchiser will also guarantee an exclusive area for the franchisee so that they are not competing with other 'branches' of the same business.

**ACTIVITY**

✦ What is a franchise? Describe the difference between a franchiser and a franchisee.

✦✦ Explain the advantages and disadvantages of a franchise operation to
• the franchiser
• the franchisee.

✦✦✦ Explain why a business would consider using franchising to expand rather than any other route.

**For your portfolio**

You should have a section in your portfolio called 'My businesses – type of ownership'. If one of your businesses is involved in franchising, you need to explain how – is it a franchiser or a franchisee? Why has it chosen this particular way of operating? How successful is it? If it is not

involved in franchising, you should consider why not. You could consider:

• is there too much competition in the area that the business operates in?
• has the business found a better way of expanding?
• is the business not interested in expanding – does it have other aims?

**Figure 6.4** *The British School of Motoring (BSM) operates franchises*

In other cases, the franchiser may provide the point of contact so that franchisees can meet customers. For example, the British School of Motoring offers franchises to driving instructors to run a business under the BSM brand name. Driving instructors will have already passed the Driving Standards Agency exams themselves or may have taken a New Driving Instructor course from BSM to train and qualify for their Approved Driving Instructor registration. All instructors receive a training car in BSM livery, marketing support, business training, administrative back-up and, most importantly, the services of staff at more than a hundred BSM centres throughout the country to receive, meet and greet their customers.

The major disadvantage lies in the amount of control which the franchiser has over the franchisee. In some cases the restrictions placed on the franchisee may make them feel more like managers than independent owners. A franchisee at a McDonald's franchise outlet would not be allowed, for example, to introduce his/her own uniforms or add different dishes to the menu, and may even have to follow certain rules about when to open and close, and how often or thoroughly to clean.

## Selling a franchise

The commercial franchiser will advertise the sale of the franchise in a specialist directory such as The UK Franchise Directory or Franchise World Directory, and invite people to apply for the franchise. A person wanting to buy a franchise will have to prove to the franchiser not only that they can afford to buy the franchise, but that they have the right qualities to run a business and are not likely to fail and spoil the franchiser's image. This means that the process

## KEY *TERMS*

- Corporate image – the way that a business projects how it wants to be regarded by other people
- Fee – the initial payment to buy the franchise
- Franchise – the right to trade under an already established name
- Franchisee – the person or organisation which buys the right
- Franchiser – the person or organisation which sells the right
- Royalty – a payment made to the franchiser from the franchisee, set as a percentage of the franchisee's turnover
- Turnover – a figure worked out by multiplying the quantity of product sold by its price

## EXTENSION EXERCISE

Look at the two businesses that you have chosen and consider the different ways in which, within the same business area:

- a small business might decide to start up
- a larger business might decide to expand.

For each way, suggest the best form of business ownership and why it would be the most suitable.

of applying for a franchise is usually a very complex one, involving the preparation of business plans, interviews and other means of selection. In the case of a successful franchiser business, there will be no shortage of applicants for the franchises being offered; this is because franchising offers such a safe and established route into business. The Body Shop, for example, receives over 10,000 applications each year for the few opportunities that are available.

## What you need to do:

- To achieve Level ❶    you must be able to give a basic description of the activities, type of ownership and aims of each business you study.
- To achieve Level ❷    you must show a clear understanding of the objectives of the business and how they may be monitored. You need to show how the ownership of the business is suited to its size, ownership responsibilities and profit distribution.
- To achieve Level ❸    you must be able to judge how the number of other businesses involved in the same activity as your chosen businesses might affect their aims or objectives.

CHAPTER 7

# Business location

One of the most important decisions a business has to take is where to locate. Whether it is manufacturing a product or providing a service, and whether small, medium or large, a business must consider a number of factors. Ideally, the location will keep costs to a minimum while helping to generate maximum revenue, while the overall aim is to be successful. Some factors affecting location decisions will be under the business's control, while others will be quite outside its power. Sometimes, decisions about location will be influenced by outside bodies such as the government, the European Union, development agencies and local councils.

**Figure 7.1** *Road systems are part of the infrastructure of an area or region, and important factors in location*

## Factors to consider

There are a wide variety of factors that ought to be considered. For some businesses, only a few factors will be really important. Other businesses may have to consider and balance a complex mixture of location factors. Possible location factors are listed below with the sorts of questions that a business might ask.

## TRUE OR FALSE?

*Businesses can locate where it is most convenient for them.*

*(see foot of page for answer)*

**Figure 7.2** *Sometimes location is obvious and a business, like fishing, has no choice*

## Classwork activity

1. List the three most important factors in locating these businesses:
   - a coal mine
   - a textiles manufacturer
   - a chemicals company
   - a supermarket
   - a garden centre.
2. Add three other businesses to your list and list the important factors for them.
3. Decide, for each case, which factor is the most important.
4. Share your answers with a partner. Do you agree?

## Supply of a suitable labour force

- Is there an adequate supply of workers?
- Do those potential workers have the right skills?
- Are there training facilities nearby if needed?
- Will the business be able to pay sufficient wages to attract enough workers? Businesses may find they can pay lower wage rates in areas of high unemployment.
- Do the local people have a positive attitude towards the development of the business?

## Cost of the site and buildings

A business will need to consider such things as:

- How long will the site/building be needed, and so should it be rented or purchased?
- Will the site need to be drained and levelled?
- Is it a disused green field site, or on a well developed industrial park?
- What are the level of rates payable to the local council?
- If there are extra risks with the site/building, will this raise the insurance premiums?
- Is there room for expansion?

## Advice and financial help

Throughout the twentieth century and in the twenty-first, there have been some regions in the UK with higher rates of unemployment than others. Within these regions, there have often been small areas with very high rates of unemployment. It was not until after 1945 that governments began to use techniques to help reduce unemployment in the problem regions. Most of these aimed to persuade businesses to locate in the regions of high unemployment. Such regions were called 'assisted areas' because financial assistance was available to many businesses, either expanding in or relocating to those areas. Over the last 50 years, the types, amount and sources of assistance have changed and so have the regions identified as having unemployment problems.

## Assistance

The major forms of assistance include advice and information from:

- County Councils' Business Development Units. This provides funding advice and practical assistance in assembling business plans, for businesses proposing to create or protect jobs.
- District Councils, who have economic development officers to give advice on local development issues and opportunities.

## True or False answer

**False.** Although they would like this to be the case, there are many restrictions over where they can be: eg a business producing dangerous chemicals should not be located near where people live.

- Learning and Skills Councils. These look after smaller organisations which give information and counselling support to all types of business.
- The Rural Development Commission (RDC). This supports businesses with between five and 50 employees in manufacturing, service, tourism and some retailing. Support includes training courses on both rural skills and business skills.

## Financial assistance

This is available from:

- British Coal Enterprises Ltd, which provides loans or investment capital for job-creating projects in former coalfield districts. The support is limited to 25% of the total funding package or £5,000 per job created over three years.
- the Department of Trade and Industry, which can provide various forms of financial help for businesses in the assisted areas. Regional Selective Assistance for manufacturing and some service businesses of any size is available for investment projects. The level of grant is the minimum for the project to proceed and is linked to the number of jobs created or safeguarded. Regional Enterprise Grants may also be available in some parts of the assisted areas, for small businesses undertaking investment projects or innovation projects. There is special support for businesses with up to 250 employees developing new products.
- the newly-created Learning and Skills Councils, which can provide a mixture of grants and interest free loans to new businesses.
- the RDC, which can offer top-up loans at fixed interest rates for projects in rural communities.

### Other organisations

There are a number of other organisations both in the private and public sectors who offer loans and grants. These include:

- the commercial banks such as Barclays, Lloyds and HSBC
- Northern Enterprise Ltd
- Northern Venture Managers Ltd
- The Prince's Youth Trust
- The Royal British Legion
- some of the District Councils.

## Premises

Business Development Units at County Councils keep a register of all advance factories and industrial sites in their county. There is a wide variety of units available for purchase or on lease. These are provided by organisations in both the public and private sector, including the County Council, the District Councils, English Partnerships and the RDC.

**TRUE OR FALSE?**

Locating on a greenfield site means locating in a field.

(see foot of page for answer)

**HOMEWORK ACTIVITY**

Research into the kind of help and assistance available to businesses in your locality.

Explain how this help and assistance might influence business's location decisions, using examples of real businesses.

*For your portfolio*

Whichever businesses you choose to investigate and report on for your portfolio, you need to:

- identify which of the above factors might have
- influenced the location of the particular businesses
- discover whether any of the reasons for the chosen location are changing, and how this might affect the businesses.

**True or False answer**

**False.** Greenfield sites are actually sites where there has been no industry before – they do not have to have been agricultural. Brownfield sites are those where industry used to be located.

## Business Training

This form of help is often forgotten about and yet is very important. Again there are a number of organisations providing a wide range of training. Providers include the regional LSCs, University Business Schools and specialist training organisations like Entrust.

## Help from the European Union

Parts of the country are able to receive financial assistance from the EU through its Regional Policy and Regional Fund.

## Other forms of help

The Government tries to influence the location of industry through the creation of Enterprise Zones. These are quite small areas which often have pockets of particularly high unemployment. The area may have suffered from the decline of a major industry, and it may have a number of derelict business properties or industrial estates. The idea is to make them like 'mini-Hong Kongs': ie, to encourage a lot of new enterprise so that as the area becomes more prosperous the benefits spread out to surrounding neighbourhoods. Over 24 such zones have been created over many years. The major bonuses are:

## CITIZENSHIP

*The effects of industry can be seen in many places, even though the industry may be long gone. These include canals. Find out where your nearest local canal or waterway is and arrange to go, with a group, to clean up a section of it.*

## KEY SKILLS

Application of number: Choose three possible sites near where you live for a new supermarket that will employ 300 people. Find out from your local council (and any other sources) what grants or financial help would be available for each site. You should also estimate the cost. Put all the financial information together in a report recommending the most suitable site.

## ACTIVITY

Nissan Motor Manufacturing (UK) Ltd started to build its production plant at the old Sunderland Airfield in 1984. The geography of the site itself was very important as it offered a large expanse of flat land, making new building and expansion easy. The site offered excellent infrastructure, with both the A19 and A1 close to the site, plus nearby deep-water ports.

The area was well known for its engineering background and the excellence of its training colleges. Nissan's research also suggested that there was a very positive attitude among the local people towards the development. The company also had the support of trades unions. As the site was part of an enterprise zone, there were grants worth £100 million available. However, this was not such an important factor for Nissan since the company planned to invest over £900 m.

♦ Read the passage and identify all the factors the company considered when choosing Sunderland.

♦♦ Make a two column table with the columns headed 'location factor' and 'description'. Put the location factors you have identified in order of importance, and describe each.

♦♦ Explain how you decided the order of importance.

♦♦♦ Suggest which of these location factors might change, and explain how the changes might affect Nissan's location at Sunderland.

- free rates for up to 10 years
- tax advantages
- easier planning controls on new premises, so it should be quicker to build and get operating
- other financial help, but this depends where the zone is located.

## Transport links for supplies and distribution

Transport can have a major influence on your decision:

- Are there adequate transport systems for the site? – road, rail, air, river/canal, ports
- How far are the transport links from the site?
- Are there adequate communication systems, especially telephone facilities?
- Are there ancillary businesses to help production take place? For example, are there businesses to deal with waste disposal, to repair machinery, to transport the finished product and to supply computer services?

FACT FILE

*Canals are still used for some commercial and industrial traffic. They are particularly useful for transporting pottery, as there is no jolting. Their only disadvantage is that they are slow, but this does not matter if the time taken for delivery is planned into a schedule.*

## Suppliers and raw materials

If the product loses bulk or weight as it goes through the production process, then a business will achieve the lowest transport costs by locating as near the supply of raw materials as possible. If these materials or parts are imported, then a business will wish to locate near deep-water ports. The assembly of the product may require a large number of small parts and components. In this case, the business will need to locate near to other businesses supplying these items; and you can see from the Map of Nissan's site that it has several suppliers very close to its main factory.

### Geographical factors

Other more geographical factors to consider include:

- Water supplies – will there be adequate supplies of clean water? This is very important for businesses using large quantities of water like paper manufacture, pharmaceuticals and electricity generation.
- Prevailing wind – which direction does the wind usually blow? For some businesses that create smell, smoke or dust during the production process, it might be important for the usual wind direction to take these pollutants away from areas of population.
- Waste Disposal – are there adequate facilities for dealing with the waste created during the production process? Some businesses create a good deal of waste during production. Various laws strictly control how this should be disposed of safely.

## KEY TERMS

Assisted areas – areas that the government gives extra help to because of high unemployment or industrial decline in the area

Enterprise zones – a smaller area, targeted by government for extra help

Infrastructure – the transport and communication networks available

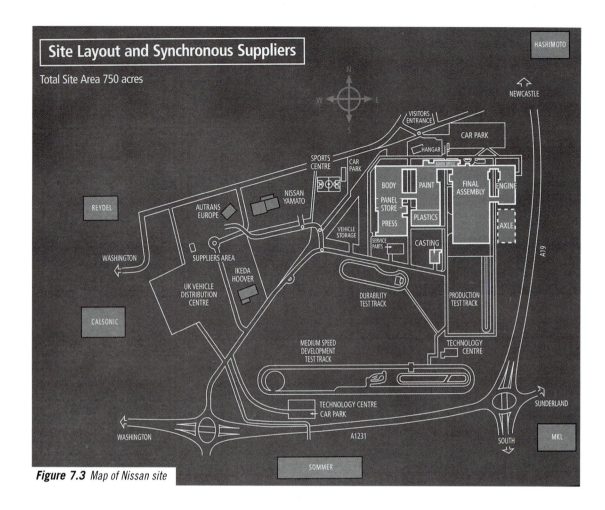

**Site Layout and Synchronous Suppliers**

Total Site Area 750 acres

**Figure 7.3** *Map of Nissan site*

• Safety – are there any specific safety issues to consider when considering location? Some businesses make products that are dangerous or use production processes which are dangerous to the public. These businesses will need a site far away from people's homes. Typical examples include fireworks factories, nuclear plants, chemical processors and petrol refineries.

# EXTENSION EXERCISE

Compare the location factors of your two chosen businesses with two similar businesses. In each case:

• Identify the location factors of the extra businesses.
• Are there any different factors affecting the businesses' locations?
• Are the same factors of differing importance?
• How might your two chosen businesses improve their locations?

## Competitors

Many businesses are attracted to site their operations close to their main competitors. In some instances, this might be because the labour supply in that area has the necessary skills. In other cases it might be because that is where the market is located. Sometimes, businesses may wish to share knowledge or even research projects, leading to the need to be in close proximity. Generally, as an industry develops, businesses often find that all the necessary extra facilities and experience grow with it. These might be ancillary businesses such as machine repairers or transport businesses; or perhaps the expertise of local banks and advertising agencies to deal with the needs of that type of industry.

## Customers

If a product gains bulk or weight during the production process, transport costs may be kept down by locating near to the large centres of population who are going to buy the products in largest quantities.

Even where this is not the case, businesses that depend on large sales to mass markets will wish to locate near the largest centres of population. The spread of the car and better roads has made this a little less important, and hence the development of the out-of-town shopping centre.

## History and traditions

In the past, sources of power supplies were a very important consideration when locating a business. The early woollen mills located next to rivers so that water power could drive the early looms. Steam power generated by coal soon took over, thus leading to many industries locating in the coalfield areas of the country. The creation of electricity and North Sea gas industries, together with a national grid system for distribution, has helped most businesses become more footloose when considering power supplies.

For some industries, the original reasons for location have disappeared. For example, the centre of the pottery industry is in the Midlands, but the reserves of China clay were exhausted long ago. The area now has other benefits that outweigh the extra costs of transporting in china clay. New businesses will be attracted by the skilled labour force, by the businesses experienced in dealing with the needs of the industry, and by the tradition of the area.

Sometimes a business locates at a particular site by chance. For example, many of our oldest businesses became established in an area because the original owner happened to live there.

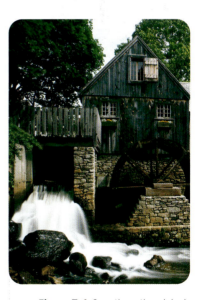

*Figure 7.4* *Sometimes the original reasons for location are obvious*

## What you need to do:

- To achieve Level ❶    you will need to describe the location of your two chosen businesses.
- To achieve Level ❷    you will need to compare the locations of your two chosen businesses and give the main reasons for the choice of location.
- To achieve Level ❸    you will suggest and justify changes that could be made to the locations of your two businesses that could make them more effective and assess the impact of location choice on overall organizational performance.

# CHAPTER 8
# Types of business activity

While some businesses will carry out one single activity, there are many that carry out two or more activities. In your investigation you will need to decide what the main activities of your chosen businesses are. A key decision will be in identifying whether the business is involved with goods, services, or both. There are many ways of grouping business activities and so it may be useful to start your exploration by making sure you know about the common system of grouping activities by industrial sector.

**Figure 8.1** *Three different businesses, each carrying out a different business activity – but all essential to the economy*

## TRUE OR FALSE?

*The utilities of gas, electricity and water are part of the primary sector.*

*(see foot of page for answer)*

## Industrial Sectors and the Chain of Production

As a product is made, it passes through several stages along a chain of production. At each stage, the producing business will try to add value until the product is sold to its final consumer.

One well known example is the production of Kellogg's breakfast cereals. It begins with the planting, ripening and harvesting of maize. This is imported into the UK where it arrives at Seaforth. After storage it is then milled to remove the parts that would harm freshness and taste. The milled 'grits' are taken by road to Manchester where it is flavoured, cooked and dried. At each stage it is checked for quality. The next stage is to roll the maize into flakes, which are then toasted at high temperatures. At last, the cereal can be put into inner liners and then packed into cartons. The cartons are collected into cases for storage in the warehouse, before being transported by road to the country's supermarkets and then onto consumers' breakfast tables.

Just like the example of Kellogg's cereals, every product has a chain of production with each stage linked to the next. There might be a different number of stages but these may be grouped under three main headings or industrial sectors.

### Primary sector

Virtually every product will start in the **primary sector**, where the raw material is extracted. Industries involved in the extraction of raw materials are quite varied. The most obvious examples are the mining of coal and the extraction from quarries of such things as iron ore, granite and limestone. Other industries that are particularly important for the UK are the extraction of oil and natural gas.

Forestry in all its forms is also part of the primary sector. This includes the felling and logging of trees but, in Asia, could also include rubber plantations where rubber trees are tapped and rubber resin is collected in pots from each tree. Agriculture covers the most obvious western world farming activities of animal rearing and arable production; but world-wide, a huge number of crops is grown, from tea to cotton, and from coffee to rice. A final industry to recall in this sector is fishing.

## Secondary sector

Once the raw material has been 'harvested', it will enter the **secondary sector** where it is processed or manufactured into a finished product. In this sector there may be a very large number of production stages before the final product is ready for sale. The more complex the product, the more stages it is likely to go through. This sector also covers a large number of different industries and activities.

Some products will need to be processed such as that described for cornflakes. This might also apply to both oil and beer where the product has to be refined from the original raw materials. Some products will have to be 'simply' assembled from pre-produced items, and in the modern-day car plant, this is the general rule. Many of those car parts have to be manufactured at some point and this secondary stage of production is often referred to as the manufacturing stage. A final industry to include in the secondary stage is construction, the building of houses, factories and shops.

## Tertiary sector

Finally, the product will enter the **tertiary sector**, where the product will be distributed to organisations prepared to sell it on to the final consumer. Tertiary production includes all types of services, such as the commercial services of banking and advertising, and the direct, personal services of doctors and hairdressers.

These stages of production are said to be part of a chain because they are linked together as illustrated below. You should remember, of course, that various services will also be needed at each stage to help production take place. For example, the services of a bank will be needed by virtually every business involved in the chain, as will transport.

**HOMEWORK ACTIVITY**

Write down three advantages and three disadvantages for an business which operates solely on the internet.

## For your portfolio

1. Consider the different forms of business activity in your local area. Establish some categories of business activities and identify one example of a business for each of the activities you have identified.
2. Give a description of the size of each business activity you have identified, suggest reasons for their locations and how these reasons might have changed over time.
3. Describe the processes used by each of your businesses to provide the product or service.
4. Describe the main competitors for each of your chosen businesses and suggest any external factors and trends that might be affecting the businesses.

| | | |
|---|---|---|
| **Primary** | Extractive industries eg quarrying, farming, fishing, mining, forestry | *Trees extracted from forest* |
| **Secondary** | Manufacturing, processing and construction industries | *Trees are stripped of bark, planks cut to size, parts are joined together to complete an item of wood furniture* |
| **Tertiary** | Distribution, Direct and Commercial services | *Pine furniture shop* |
| **Consumer** | | *Consumer* |

***Figure 8.2*** *The chain of production for wood furniture*

## Classifying Business Activity

There are many ways of grouping or classifying business activity. The following five are the most common:

- sale of goods
- client services
- manufacturing
- producing raw goods
- other services

## CITIZENSHIP

*Discuss whether the government should support declining industries in order to maintain employment, or whether it is better to let them decline and let the people employed in them look for new jobs.*

### Sale of goods (eg retail, wholesale, mail order, internet)

In simple terms, this involves the selling of a good or service to a consumer, usually at a shop or some other outlet. The range of retailing outlets is quite extensive, and the range of goods and services being offered is almost beyond belief. There are still one-off traders with a single outlet offering personal service, or a small range of items such as hairdressers and small newsagents.

**Variety chain shops**

A common sight on today's high street is the variety chain or multiple, offering several different types of goods and operating from a large number of branches located throughout the region or nation. Marks and Spencer, Woolworths and Littlewoods could all be placed in this category, although all three have had their problems over the years and have had to re-launch themselves or their products. While Woolworths is an ever-present sight in most high streets, Littlewoods has sold off several of its shops and developed clearer links with its

**Figure 8.3** *Many stores now locate together in large retail parks such as Bluewater in Kent*

home catalogue business, by extending its Index catalogue sales at its high street shops. Marks and Spencer has suffered from the success of many new competitors and has had to develop at out-of-town shopping centres as well as in the major high streets.

**Supermarkets**

Most supermarkets have moved into becoming superstores, selling much wider product ranges from ever bigger outlets and with ever bigger car parks alongside. The development of discount retailers and hypermarkets has been more uneven, with businesses such as electrical retailers Comet maintaining steady sales patterns while furniture businesses such as MFI seem to peak and fall. The DIY business is very buoyant, but the structure of the industry is undergoing much change, as mergers and sell-offs have created new opportunities for some well known names such as B&Q and Homebase.

## ACTIVITY

Data from Barclays Bank informs us that 98% of businesses employ less than 250 people, and those 98% account for 60% of the employed UK workforce. 99% of UK businesses employ less than 100 people.

✦ List all the local businesses which you think employ no one (you could use Yellow Pages to help you).

✦ List all the local businesses which you think employ less than 100 people.

✦ List all the local businesses which you think employ less than 250 people.

✦ List all the local businesses which you think employ more than 250 people.

✦✦ Next to each business write the nature of its activity.

✦✦✦ What conclusions can you draw from the information collected?

## 🔲 KEY *SKILLS*

Application of number. Using the table of employment by industry, present a chart of 12 line graphs, showing each category of industry over the nine year period. Each line needs to be labelled and should be in a different colour. Choose a suitable scale for the employment figures to show the changes to best effect.

### FACT FILE

*Every day, consumers purchase millions of goods and services from supplying businesses in the UK. In most cases these transactions have required a face-to-face interaction, or perhaps a voice-to-voice interaction when the deal has been done over the telephone. This may end sooner than we expect if sales through the internet continue to expand at present rates. Predictions for transactions via the internet in the UK during 1999 were just under £1 bn. By 2005 this is predicted to rise to a staggering £18 bn. Direct sales avoiding our traditional outlets will mean the death of the salesman. Every business in the country will have to start planning for a new way to organise their business activity, and new tactics are being launched with the AA giving 10% discounts for customers buying insurance online, while the Prudential's Egg finance provider will now only accept new customers through the internet.*

### Specialist retailers

Most high streets have a wide range of specialist retailers, with many being part of a multiple organisation. Restaurants, opticians, bakers, travel agents, estate agents, banks and building societies probably make up the biggest proportion of retailers on your high street, but even here change seems to be speeding up. For example, many banks are closing smaller branches as tele- and internet-banking services seem to grow in popularity.

### Internet sales

Many traditional high street retailers have set up sales links through their own websites on the internet. Computers may be ordered direct from Time, clothes may be viewed and ordered on the Marks and Spencer web site, and you can even do your supermarket shopping at Tesco or Asda from your arm chair. In addition, there are several companies selling goods and services only through the internet.

### Mail order

Mail order businesses are the ones most likely to suffer from the rise in use of the internet for purchasing goods and services, although there is no obvious downward trend yet. Home catalogue business has suffered some decline, but newspapers, magazines and 'junk' mail still offer a multitude of opportunities for the public to send off or phone in orders.

### Cash and carry

At one time, cash and carry wholesalers seemed to be a growth area for the sale of goods. These large warehouse organisations still exist and help to supply small retailers, but the growth in size of most types of retail business has limited their progress. Businesss such as Macro and Costco continue to operate by breaking down bulk purchases from the manufacturers into smaller quantities for sale both to retailers and directly to consumers.

## Client services

These are services provided to individual clients such as financial, health care, leisure and sport and internet.

### Health care

Health care services include the more obvious elements of personal service such as general practitioners (doctors), hospitals, dentists, physiotherapists, and opticians. An obvious trend at one end of this personal care industry is the direct marketing to the public of some parts of health care. BUPA advertises its private medical schemes including its own hospitals, while both opticians and dentists are a far more noticeable part of high street outlets. With clinics offering tattoo removal or various forms of plastic surgery, and even general practitioners setting mission statements, the whole health care industry is undergoing rapid change in its activities.

### Leisure and sport

Leisure and sport activities are a growth area with definite increases in specialist leisure providers such as gyms and dance studios, in leisure clubs linked to hotels, in the creation of golf clubs and finally in team sports. The growth of Premier League football clubs and their spin-off commercial enterprises is also reflected in other team sports, most notably the move to professional rugby union.

**Financial services**

Financial services have become very competitive as banks, building societies and insurance companies all target consumers with financial products and services. Consumers are faced with a barrage of advice, both on the best way to save and invest their money and on ways to borrow money for that new three-piece suite, the car of your dreams or that larger house. These same organisations are also competing with each other to attract business customers.

## Manufacturing (eg consumer and capital goods)

This type of business activity covers a multitude of businesses producing a multitude of products, but even so, some broad types may be picked out. In terms of goods made for direct sale to consumers, clothing manufacture is one industry involving particular production techniques and skills, while the food industry covers two areas – processed and frozen food production. One large section includes the manufacture and assembly of consumer durables, ranging from cars to fridges, and from televisions to microwave ovens. Other industries include the refining and distilling of diverse products such as oil, beer and alcoholic spirits.

The capital goods industry is important: in this, machinery and equipment is manufactured for the purpose of making other goods and services.

## Producing raw goods (eg agriculture, fishing for food, forestry and mining)

This includes agriculture, fishing, quarrying, forestry and mining. These have been described earlier in this chapter as part of the primary sector. In the UK these primary sector industries employ small numbers of people, with under 500,000 now employed in total.

**Figure 8.4** *Financial services – a very competitive sector*

##  KEY TERMS

Primary production – a first stage of production where raw materials are extracted

Secondary production – at this stage, raw materials are manufactured and processed into the final good

Tertiary production – this is the provision of services of all kinds both to business and to the general public.

## EXTENSION EXERCISE

Carry out research into the latest trends in consumer expenditure and write a report detailing your findings. Start by looking at the data available from the ONS on the internet – www.statistics.gov.uk

## Other services (eg transport and communications)

The trends in these industries are difficult to plot with real certainty. In general there is an increase in demand in both industries. In transport, rail travel has suffered after various fatal accidents, while bus travel has also declined as more people own cars. In communications, the demand for products such as mobile phones may have peaked and yet the demand for internet-related communications is beginning to increase. Other services that could be included here are the utilities of gas, electricity and water.

## Number of people employed in different activities

Earlier in the chapter you were introduced to the three main industrial or production sectors – primary, secondary and tertiary. These sectors are rather too broad to use effectively when we want to examine and explore the range of business activities. In particular, by breaking the sectors down into more parts we can see in more detail the employment changes taking place. The table below based on data from the Monthly Digest of Statistics shows this.

There is no information included in this data on the trends in full- and part-time working. It is expected that the increases in part-time working mainly come from retailing, distribution and catering where part-time working is already very strong. There is also expected to be an increase in part-time work in the more professional activities of consultancy, computing and financial services. In other words, such people may be expected to combine a number of part-time posts or activities to create the equivalent of a full-time position. Some estimates suggest that by 2010 there will be nearly 8.75 million part-time jobs, which compares with 6.84 million in 1998 and just 4.8 million in 1980.

| Industry | 1990 | 1991 | 1992 | 1993 | 1994 | 1995 | 1996 | 1997 | 1998 |
|---|---|---|---|---|---|---|---|---|---|
| Agriculture, forestry, fishing | 294 | 287 | 290 | 307 | 280 | 253 | 261 | 275 | 282 |
| Mining and utilities | 396 | 370 | 333 | 289 | 255 | 231 | 222 | 221 | 211 |
| Manufacturing | 4605 | 4196 | 3983 | 3808 | 3823 | 3918 | 4002 | 4055 | 4033 |
| Construction | 1114 | 1025 | 925 | 840 | 840 | 814 | 859 | 940 | 1066 |
| Wholesale & retail trade | 3574 | 3512 | 3503 | 3483 | 3570 | 3619 | 3728 | 3840 | 3928 |
| Hotels and restaurants | 1242 | 1215 | 1200 | 1162 | 1173 | 1235 | 1245 | 1270 | 1276 |
| Transport & communications | 1371 | 1352 | 1334 | 1297 | 1293 | 1285 | 1302 | 1322 | 1376 |
| Financial services | 1045 | 1024 | 992 | 961 | 966 | 984 | 959 | 982 | 1014 |
| Real estate, Renting, Computer | 2395 | 2355 | 2363 | 2442 | 2455 | 2604 | 2945 | 3137 | 3262 |
| Public admin & defence | 1385 | 1404 | 1406 | 1400 | 1382 | 1345 | 1346 | 1299 | 1272 |
| Education/health services | 4062 | 4103 | 4146 | 4139 | 4172 | 4221 | 4237 | 4268 | 4280 |
| Other services | 900 | 885 | 913 | 939 | 932 | 943 | 1024 | 1047 | 1081 |
| TOTAL | 22383 | 21728 | 21387 | 21066 | 21141 | 21452 | 22128 | 22657 | 23080 |

*The number of people employed in different industries (Monthly Digest of Statistics)*

NB All figures are in '000s, are for the whole of Great Britain and are recorded in June of each year.

The Office for National Statistics (ONS) collects a huge amount of data on our spending habits. The Stationery Office publishes this data in books such as *Social Trends* and on its website. This example shows data taken from *Social Trends No 31*.

| | |
|---|---|
| Household goods | 143.0 |
| Rent, water and sewerage charges | 77.9 |
| Food | 54.9 |
| Transport and communications | 54.4 |
| Clothing and footwear | 33.5 |
| Alcohol | 32.6 |
| Recreational and cultural activities | 28.1 |
| Financial services | 25.9 |
| Fuel and power | 13.6 |
| Tobacco | 12.0 |
| Other services | 84.4 |
| All household expenditure | 560.3 |

*Household expenditure in the UK by UK citizens in £ billions for 1999*

## What you need to do:

- To achieve Level ❶    you must be able to describe the activity of your two chosen businesses.
- To achieve Level ❷    you must be able to compare the activity of your two chosen businesses and identify the main differences between them.
- To achieve Level ❸    having fully explored the activity of your two chosen businesses, you need to be able to suggest and justify changes to their activity that might enable them to be more effective.

CHAPTER 9

# Introduction to functional areas

Each business has to carry out certain tasks in order to operate, regardless of its size, its type of ownership and the business sector in which it exists. These tasks are usually referred to as the **functions** of the business. In a large business, specialised departments may carry out the functions. In a smaller business, it is likely that one person will carry out a number of different functions. Certainly, in the case of a sole trader, it is the owner who will carry out all of the functions in the business.

**Figure 9.1** *James Dyson has the organisational skills required to be a successful entrepreneur. His Dyson vacuum cleaner is now a world leader. The business grew from a strong emphasis on the Research and Development function. However, the work of the other functional areas (eg Sales and Marketing, Production) also contributes to his success*

## The functions

A business exists to produce a good or service. To do this it takes certain inputs – like raw materials and labour – and passes them through some sort of process to create an output – the good or service that the business produces. (This is called the product, which can be either a good or a service.) The tasks or functions, which a business must carry out, are

- to raise enough finance to be able to afford to carry out the business
- to find out if there is a market for the product
- to bring all of the factors together in order to produce the product
- to ensure that labour, as a factor, is available, trained and capable of doing the jobs required
- to carry out the manufacturing, processing or other procedure
- to deliver the product to the identified market
- to let people know that the product is available
- to persuade people to buy the product
- to cost and price the produce
- to keep all the financial (and other) records
- to make sure that customers are happy with their purchase, and with the service
- to communicate decisions within the business and to people outside the business.

Each of these functions may have a separate department; in some cases they may be important enough to be split into several departments. Most commonly, the functions are carried out as shown in the table below:

| Function | Functional area |
|---|---|
| To raise enough finance to be able to afford to carry out the business<br>To cost and price the produce | Finance |
| To find out if there is a market for the product<br>To let people know that the product is available<br>To persuade people to buy the product | Marketing and Sales |
| To ensure that labour, as a factor, is available, trained and capable of doing the jobs required | Human resources management (HRM) |
| To carry out the manufacturing, processing or other procedure | Operations |
| To deliver the product to the identified market<br>Making sure that customers are happy with their purchase, and with the service | Customer services |
| To keep all the financial (and other) records<br>To communicate decisions within the business and to people outside the business | Administration |

*The functions of each business department*

### True or False answer

In a really large business, there will be other subdivisions. For example, a distribution department could handle getting the product to the customer. Making sure that transport and deliveries (both of raw materials and of finished stock) are efficiently organised could be handled by a Logistics sector. Operations could be serviced by a separate Research and Development area, which is looking into new and better products, and a separate Production area, which is manufacturing the products. Marketing could be further divided into sales, advertising, promotion and public relations.

## Interaction

The interaction between the different functional areas is also important. Any part of a business's operations is likely to involve more than one functional area. Therefore the areas have to communicate with each other and work together closely. Think about how a business's functions would have to interact in the following circumstances:

1 A new product idea is developed, but will the customer like it?
2 A new machine is invented which is more efficient at carrying out production.
3 A number of complaints have been received about late delivery of goods.

**A new product idea is developed, but will the customer like it?** As a minimum this will involve

* Research and Development in developing and testing the product
* Finance in costing the materials needed and the production process
* HRM in hiring the right workers
* Marketing in conducting market research to see if customers will buy the product – and at what price
* Finance in seeing if the business can afford to charge that price
* Marketing in advertising the product
* Distribution in making sure that the product is delivered to outlets.

**A new machine is invented which is more efficient at carrying out production.** As a minimum this will involve

* research into the efficiency of the new machine
* costings by Finance to see if the machine is affordable
* HRM retraining the existing workers (or hiring new ones and having to make the existing ones redundant).

**A number of complaints have been received about late delivery of goods.** As a minimum this will involve

* Administration in recording the complaints
* Customer Service in dealing with the complaints
* Logistics in finding out the cause of the problem
* HRM in solving the problem through hiring, firing or training workers.

**Figure 9.2** *Even the smallest business has to carry out the different functions*

True or False answer

## For your portfolio

Draw up a table to show how the functions are carried out. First list the functions that are carried out in your chosen businesses. Then list the functional area that deals with each function (if your business has functional areas). Add a column to show the name and job title of the person who carries out each function.

## CITIZENSHIP

*Find one law that protects workers. Make a poster to explain what it does.*

Functional areas need to be efficient in themselves, and also to communicate efficiently and effectively with the other functional areas. Any breakdown in communications will cause the business to be less efficient than it could be. In any given situation, two or more functional areas will be involved. Even if there are only one or two workers or owners in the business, the same functions still have to be carried out – the difference is that they are not carried out by a specialist.

## Managers

An owner may decide to employ a professional manager to help with the organisation of his or her business. A large enough business may even decide that it wants a professional manager for each functional area – a departmental structure with departmental managers to manage them. Managers are employed to

- set targets and make decisions
- share their knowledge and expertise in a particular area
- provide many of the necessary links in an organisation. They can link horizontally (ie across the organisation) with managers at the same level, to keep the business running efficiently. They can also link vertically (ie up and down the business) with more senior managers and owners, and also more junior managers and staff

One of the main reasons for dividing a business up into functional areas is to take advantage of specialisation in those areas. A specialist manager, in a specialist department, will find it easier to solve problems, to take informed decisions, and to help to achieve the aims and objectives of the business. One of the disadvantages of small businesses is that they are not able to take advantage of this specialist knowledge.

## Organisation

A business needs to be organised so that it can carry out its functions. Organisation structures are covered in detail in Chapter 25, but it is worth mentioning something about them here. Imagine that you are just starting up in business. You will need to carry out several functions yourself:

1 You will have to gather funds that you need to buy the raw materials and other inputs for your business. You will be risking these funds in your business venture.

2 You will need to organise the inputs, the process and the sales of the outputs.

As a risk-taker, you are called an **entrepreneur**. An entrepreneur is the person who has 'enterprise' – this can mean an idea or the organisational skills to put an idea into practice. Entrepreneurs take the risk so that they will benefit from the rewards. They are hoping to benefit from the future profits of the business. The entrepreneur is therefore the person who actually puts the structure together and tells the functional areas what they need to do.

## IT and flexibility

In the middle of the last century it was common to find businesses where the functional areas were kept separate. If a manager wanted to send a letter, he would dictate it to a secretary (part of the Administration functional area), who would type it up and bring it back for signature. It would then be taken by a clerk to be posted. Information Technology has made much of this unnecessary. Managers in many businesses would now be expected to use a computer effectively. This could mean, for example, typing letters, dealing with email and keeping letters. Most workers in efficient businesses in the twenty-first century would be expected to have at least some IT skills that can help their own area – and therefore the business – run more smoothly.

## Efficiency

The success of the business depends on the efficiency of the functional areas in carrying out their duties. This efficiency can be

*Figure 9.3*

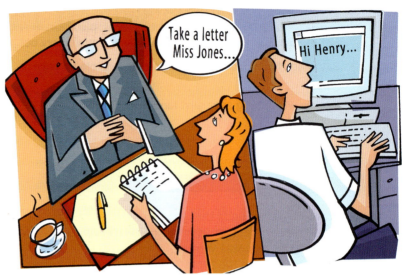

**Figure 9.4** *Methods of communication have rapidly changed*

measured by how much each functional area helps the business to achieve its aims and objectives. Each functional area or department will contribute towards the success of the business by carrying out its own specialised task or tasks. It must also interact efficiently with the other functional areas of the business.

This means that areas must communicate clearly with each other and work closely together. The efficiency of the functional areas is therefore bound up with the efficiency of the communications channels in the business. If even one functional area is not pulling its weight, or if communications are poor between just one functional area and another, the business will not be running efficiently. The effectiveness of each functional area therefore depends on the effectiveness of all the other functional areas and on their ability to work together.

# EXTENSION EXERCISE

Find out which economist first thought of the idea of specialisation, and how it was first applied.

## What you need to do:

- **To achieve Level ❶**    you will need a description of some of the purposes and activities of each of your chosen organisation's functional areas. For some specifications this excludes HRM and Customer Resources, as they are included elsewhere.
- **To achieve Level ❷**    you will need a detailed explanation of the purposes and activities of your chosen organisations' functional areas; you will need to explain how the functional areas relate to the aims of the business and how they support each other.
- **To achieve Level ❸**    you will need a thorough account of the purposes and activities of your chosen organisations' functional areas; you must analyse how effectively functional areas work together.

# CHAPTER 10
# Human Resources Management

The human resources of an organisation refers to the people who work there, their knowledge and expertise, and their efficiency. The human resources functional area looks after all aspects of an employee's welfare in an attempt to coax the best out of the employee. This means that it is responsible for recruiting staff, training and appraising staff and motivating staff to succeed. In a small organisation, the owner may carry out the function, or an agency may be hired for the job. In a larger organisation, there will be a separate human resources department.

**Figure 10.1** *Retention: when a player in a team is performing well, s/he may be offered incentives such as a better contract or rate of pay, in order to keep him/her*

## The role of a human resources department

A look at some of the job roles that may have to be carried out in a large human resources department will give an idea of the sort of areas covered.

- recruiting – seeing what jobs are needed in the organisation, putting advertisements in the correct places and dealing with applications
- interviewing – finding out who are the best candidates for a job by asking questions or setting tasks and tests
- training – making sure that staff are fully capable of doing a particular job efficiently
- negotiating – carrying out discussions so that employees and employers can agree on wage and salary levels, and conditions of work
- appraising – checking on the efficiency and effectiveness of staff and pointing out ways in which they might become more effective.

## Recruitment and selection

Recruitment and selection is the process of finding and choosing, from the widest possible selection of applicants, the best people to meet the needs of the organisation. This means that the human resources department must:

- define exactly what job needs doing and provide good information about the vacancy

**TRUE OR FALSE?**

*In most large organisations, Human Resources has replaced Personnel.*

*(see foot of page for answer)*

True or False answer

**True.** Human Resources is seen as covering much more than the old Personnel departments, in looking after all elements of an employee's welfare, training etc.

## TRUE OR FALSE?

*There are extra payments in some industries called 'noise money', 'dirt money' and 'danger money'.*

*(see foot of page for answer)*

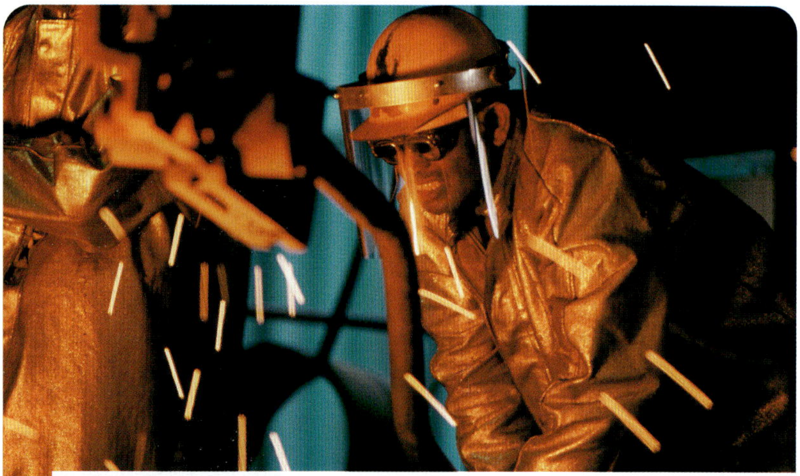

***Figure 10.2*** *Some people have to work in dangerous or uncomfortable conditions and earn extra money for doing so*

## Classwork activity

Draw a timeline to show the stages that an employee would pass through:
- in getting a job
- during the employment
- in finishing the employment.

- advertise for staff in the right places and at the right time
- ask for the right information from jobseekers
- be professional and efficient in dealing with applicants
- be able to choose candidates through an interview or other appropriate process.

Jobs are defined by the employer who analyses what is required and then writes a job description, which can be sent out to applicants.

Advertising must be in the correct place, otherwise jobseekers will not see the advertisement. This depends on the nature of the organisation and the type of employee that they are seeking. A small trader might only need a card in a newsagents window; other outlets include 'situations vacant' in local papers and, for better qualified or experienced staff, national job advertising. This could be through the trade press for a particular industry or through national newspapers. Many newspapers have particular days for particular types of job. Job centres are provided by the Department of Employment and aim to reduce unemployment by providing a free site for employers to advertise.

## HOMEWORK ACTIVITY

Find an article in a newspaper which describes how someone (such as a sportsperson, a businessman or a show-business personality) has been offered more money or incentives to persuade them to stay in a job. Bring it in to make a display on retention.

## Retention

Retention means keeping the staff that the organisation wants to keep. If an organisation has gone to the trouble (and expense) of hiring the best possible staff for a job, the last thing that it wants is for that person to want to leave. This means that the business may have to use some sort of incentive in order to keep certain members of staff. In some businesses, this consists of small rewards for length of service ('stars' or badges may be awarded, as in McDonald's). Other businesses offer regular pay rises, possibilities of promotion, pension arrangements or shares in the business. Many of the offers –

True or False answer

True. These may not be the official names, but such extra payments are made for working in extreme conditions.

and amounts – can be linked to length of service in an attempt to keep staff.

In some industries, retaining staff is a big problem. For example, in teaching, recruitment to the profession runs at a high rate due to the many incentives offered by government to persuade people to teach. Retention, however, is poor, with many new teachers leaving the profession within a couple of years of starting.

In other cases, key workers may be retained through special share or salary deals. This could apply equally to a key director in a business, or to a top footballer; each will be in a position to negotiate favourable terms if s/he is still doing a vital job in the organisation.

## Dismissal

Sometimes a business does not want to retain a member of staff, but actually wants to do the opposite – to get rid of them. Workers can be dismissed from a job if they are not carrying it out properly or abusing their position. Minor offences will be dealt with by a disciplinary procedure. For example, if a worker was often late, they would receive:

- first an informal verbal warning
- if the offence persists, a formal verbal warning
- next, a written warning of dismissal if the offence continues
- finally, a notice of dismissal.

Workers can be sacked on the spot (a summary dismissal) for serious offences such as stealing, fighting or being drunk.

Workers also leave because of retirement and redundancy, and it is the job of human resources to deal with these. Human Resources will deal with pension rights and arrangements for people who reach retirement age. Human resources will deal with redundancy rights and payments; this occurs when a job is no longer needed, often because of new technology (eg much engineering and design drawing that was done by hand can now be better carried out by computer packages).

## Training, development and promotion

Businesses will be more efficient if employees are properly trained, so it is in the interests of employers to make sure that they provide

**For your portfolio**

Look at the aims and objectives of your chosen businesses. Explain how the operation of Human Resources in those businesses helps to meet those aims.

**CITIZENSHIP**

*What are the rights and responsibilities of both employers and employees under Health and Safety legislation? Do you think this is fair to both?*

**ACTIVITY**

- ✦ Draw up a job advertisement (you could use IT for this) and display it on the wall.
- ✦✦ Draw up a job description to go with it
- ✦✦✦ Choose one of the jobs displayed (not your own) and apply for it.

**Figure 10.3** *Off the job training often takes place in educational institutions*

training. It is also in the interests of employees – if they are trained, it makes them more valuable to their employer. Almost all businesses, even the smallest, will have some form of induction training – this is the training which a new employee gets when s/he first joins the organisation, and can be as simple as letting him/her know when breaks are and what to do in case of emergency.

Other training may take place during work ('on the job') or away from work ('off the job'). Training on the job is usually practical; training off the job can be practical, but can also cover theory at a college or other educational institution. Larger businesses may have a staff training or staff development programme, which Human Resources either run themselves or arrange for outside trainers to run. In smaller organisations, training may be more often 'out of house'.

An appraisal (by which an employee's work is studied) can lead to the identification of training needs, and is often used in this way. All groups, by law, have equal opportunities to work, train and be promoted. This is included in equal opportunities and anti-discrimination legislation.

## Working conditions

Once the employer formally offers the job and the candidate accepts it, a Contract of Employment is drawn up. This is the legal agreement between the employer and the employee, and is designed to protect both.

Included in it, among other things, are details of the conditions of employment – the normal hours of work, entitlement to holidays and holiday pay and sickness benefits. Trades unions have worked hard over the years to make conditions safe, fair and as comfortable as possible, and to give workers rights to extra pay, for example, for overtime, or having to work in dirty, noisy or dangerous conditions.

> **KEY SKILLS**
>
> IT. Create a CV for yourself. Make sure that you update it whenever there is something worth adding on!

> **KEY TERMS**
>
> Appraisal – checking on the efficiency and effectiveness of staff and pointing out ways in which they might become more effective
> CBI (Confederation of British Industry) – the national organisation that represents employers
> Contract of Employment – the agreement between the employer and employee that outlines their roles, rights and responsibilities
> Equal opportunities – giving people the same chances
> Human Resources – includes both the people in the organisation and their ideas and welfare
> Induction – initial training into the operation of a business
> Job description – the tasks and responsibilities of a job
> Negotiating – carrying out discussions so that employees and employers can agree on wage and salary levels and conditions of work
> Recruitment – advertising for new staff
> Redundancy – when a job role is no longer required
> Retention – the ways in which a business keeps its staff
> TUC (Trades Union Congress) – the national organisation that represents trades unions

## Employer organisations and trades unions

Employers join together and form organisations to provide help and support for each other. These may be trade associations (eg The Society of Motor Manufacturers), local organisations such as Chambers of Commerce and Chambers of Trade, or national organisations. The most prominent national organisation for employers is the Confederation for British Industry, usually known just by its initials as the CBI. It also holds an annual conference and represents the views of employers to the government.

Employees have the right to join a trades union at their place of work. Trades unions have always worked to improve conditions of work, health and safety and pay and conditions of employment. Most trades unions are members of the national body – the TUC. Sometimes the employees will negotiate directly with the employer; sometimes a negotiator may be brought in. Large Human Resources departments will employ staff trained in negotiating skills.

**Figure 10.4** *The TUC – Trades Union Congress – has a membership of trades unions*

## Health and Safety

Both employers and employees have a duty to work in as safe and healthy a way as possible. Part of this is the responsibility of the employer, part is the responsibility of the employee:

- employers have a responsibility to make sure that working conditions are safe and that rules are laid down for safe practices
- employees have a duty to work in as safe a way as possible and to follow safety rules where they are laid down.

### HASAW

The main piece of legislation is the Health and Safety at Work Act 1974. The major requirements of this Act are to ensure that both employers and employees act in as safe a way as possible in the workplace. The working environment must be safe and employers must provide all necessary safety clothing and equipment. All businesses with five or more employees must display a written safety policy, and inspectors appointed by trades unions have the right to check that employers are following the rules. Many of the other regulations are based on this legislation or amendments to it. It is itself based on earlier legislation, in particular the Factories Act 1961 which covered general health and safety issues such as proper washroom and toilet facilities, adequate ventilation, fire exits, heating and lighting and the fitting of guards on to machinery.

The Act set up the Health and Safety Executive (HSE), with inspectors who can check that premises are safe. The HSE also investigates accidents.

**FACT FILE**

One of the problems of training is that it can make staff more attractive to another business. If a business pays to train a person, that person can then apply for a better job, meaning that the business that has paid out, loses out. Someone who is so well-trained and experienced that they are at the top of their profession might even be 'head-hunted' – ie offered more money to work for a rival business. Businesses have to balance carefully the training needs (and the costs of training) with the likely benefits.

## EXTENSION EXERCISE

Work in a group of three or four to look in a different national newspaper on each day of the week, to see what types of jobs are on offer. Draw up a table to show which newspapers run which types of job advertisements and when.

## What you need to do:

- To achieve Level ❶    you will need a description of some of the purposes and activities of each of your chosen organisation's functional areas. (For some specifications this excludes HRM and Customer Resources, as they are included elsewhere.)
- To achieve Level ❷    you will need a detailed explanation of the purposes and activities of your chosen organisations' functional areas; you will need to explain how the functional areas relate to the aims of the business and how they support each other.
- To achieve Level ❸    you will need a thorough account of the purposes and activities of your chosen organisations' functional areas; you must analyse how effectively functional areas work together.
- A detailed study of Human Resources is required for Unit 2.

CHAPTER 11

# Finance

The Finance function in an organisation may be carried out by a separate department, just one person, or by an external agency. If an organisation is large enough, it may have its own financial or accounting department. A small organisation may have someone appointed to carry out the finance function – eg the treasurer of a club. Some organisations will hire an accountant to carry out most of the financial accounting and record-keeping that they need.

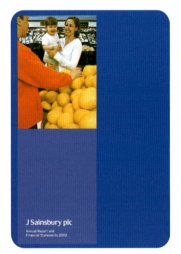 

**Figure 11.1** *Company reports are produced annually*

## Overview

In many businesses – particularly the sole trader – many of the functions of the Finance 'department' are actually carried out by the owner. However, it is one area where, because of the complexity of the area, and the expertise needed, even the smallest business would be well advised to employ a specialist (an accountant) for at least some of its financial needs.

However it is organised, the Finance function manages the flows of money coming into and out of a business.

- it is responsible for keeping records and accounts, and for understanding and interpreting those records and accounts
- the advice of the finance area will be crucial to planning in the organisation

- it will also be responsible for paying wages and salaries (and making sure that there is enough money to pay them)
- it will be involved right at the start of the existence of the business – in raising the initial or 'start-up' capital – and in the day to day running of the business
- it will advise the business on whether or not it can afford to keep trading or should close down.

A large Finance department (or specialist organisation like a firm of accountants) will have many specialist job roles to deal with particular aspects of accounts. However, the main job in the finance functional area will be that of the accountant. The chief accountant in a larger organisation will have to maintain an overview of how each part of the business is performing. S/he will have to decide which parts of the business are doing well, which need support, and where that support can come from. S/he will advise management on appropriate courses of action – and in many businesses will be a part of the management structure.

## At the start . . .

The Finance function will be involved right at the start of the business's existence. Before the business can even start trading, it will be responsible for obtaining the capital with which to buy the necessary resources. The initial finance is likely to come from the owners' own resources (called owner's funds, or owner's capital), ie the personal wealth of the people setting up the business. For sole traders, partners and co-operatives, this is their money which gives them some control over the business, and a share in the profits.

A company might raise money by selling shares (shareholder's funds). For shareholders in limited companies, the money may bring a part in decision-making but, in many cases, it will not. It will, however, always bring a share in the business's profits (providing it makes any!). In all cases, the money is 'sunk' into the business. It is not a loan, but is permanently invested in the business. It is part of the Finance function to keep up-to-date records of where money has come from, and where it has gone to.

There could also be grants available from government or other bodies. It will be the job of the finance function to apply for such grants.

Many businesses will also start by borrowing some of the money that they need. Again, this will be organised as part of the Finance function. This is called 'debt finance' and could be in the form of loans, overdrafts or credit. The Finance function will have to organise the payment of interest on any borrowed funds, and the payments for goods or services obtained on credit.

### TRUE OR FALSE?

*Businesses have to produce accounts so that members of the public can see how well they are doing.*

*(see foot of page for answer)*

### Classwork activity

Write an information leaflet aimed at younger students, to explain exactly the tasks which a Finance function in a business carries out. You should also explain why this function is important.

### HOMEWORK ACTIVITY

Write to a company (any company that is listed on the Stock Exchange) for a copy of its report and accounts. You can then use this to show the different ways in which the financial dealings of companies are reported.

True or False answer

**False.** Not all businesses have to reveal financial information. Sole traders, partnerships and co-operatives that are not companies do not have to reveal accounts. This is one reason why many small business owners do not wish to become a limited company.

## ... and at the end

When a business ceases trading, it is the Finance functional area that has to sort out who is owed what, and how the business might be able to pay some or all of the debt. It could arrange for the sale of assets, for example, or for the business to be declared bankrupt. The Finance area will have a major say in any decision as to whether the business can afford to keep trading or not.

## Financial Accounting

The Finance area will be responsible for two distinct types of accounting, financial accounting and management accounting. Financial accounting looks at the flows of money into and out of the business that have already happened. It gives a historical picture of how well the business has been doing. In the case of small organisations like sole traders and partnerships, the information can stay private. Companies, however, have to make certain information available to the public. The main financial accounting documents prepared by the Finance area for financial accounting are the cashflow statement, the profit and loss account and the balance sheet.

- The cashflow statement shows the cash coming into and going out of the business at a particular moment. It is often called a 'snapshot' of the business's finances.
- The profit and loss account is, again, a historical document, showing the profits and losses made over a period of time.
- The balance sheet shows the main things which the business owes (its liabilities) against the main things which it owns (its assets).

Limited companies must produce a profit and loss account and a balance sheet, by law. Public limited companies must also produce the cashflow statement.

**Figure 11.2** *Financial accounting is about taking a 'snapshot' of the business's current financial situation*

## Management Accounting

Management accounting involves the internal financial information of the business. It is not information that has to be made available to anybody else but the organisation's management. It is concerned with looking at costs and revenues, and with setting budgets. Management accounting looks at the decision-making that takes place, using predictions and forecasts. The main documents prepared by the Finance area are the cashflow forecast and the break-even forecast.

- The cashflow forecast shows the amounts of money which the business predicts it will spend and receive on a month-by-month basis. This allows it to plan.
- The break-even forecast shows the amount of sales which the

**True or False answer**

**False. The money is not lent to the business, but 'sunk' into it. Shareholders can try to get their money back by selling shares to other people, not from the business itself.**

64

business thinks it will have to make in order to break even – ie in order to raise enough sales revenue to cover its costs.

Whether the business is small and employs an outside accountancy firm or whether the business is large and operates its own department, yearly accounts must be created. For sole proprietors, partnerships and shareholders in private limited companies, these are mainly for the owners to analyse their personal financial interests and for the tax authorities to calculate the amount of tax owed. Public limited companies have to publish their annual accounts formally and these may be looked at by the general public, other businesses, shareholders and the tax authorities.

## Auditing

The importance of the financial transactions of a business – and of the accuracy of the various accounts and documents that have to be produced – is such that there is a special role of checking that everything is correct. An auditor (either an accountant or a firm of accountants) will be brought in to check the figures and calculations of the Finance area, and to make sure that everything is accurate. This only applies to the financial accounting documents of a business and, in particular, to those documents that must be produced by law or for taxation purposes (or both).

The auditor checks that figures being used are correct, that they have been entered correctly, and that all calculations are correct. In the case of a limited company it is expected that the accounts will carry the auditor's signature to say that these represent a 'true and fair account'. In many situations where the person handling the accounts is doing so on behalf of someone else (eg the treasurer of a society), an auditor will be used.

*Figure 11.3* Management accounting is about looking into the future and planning

### For your portfolio

Look at the way that financial records and accounts are kept in your chosen business. Is it the owner who keeps the accounts? Is it an externally hired agency or person – an accountant? Does the

organisation have a separate finance department? Write out the details.

---

**REPORT OF THE AUDITORS TO THE MEMBERS OF THE ROBERTS FISHRODS PRIVATE CO LTD**

We have audited the financial statements of the company on the following pages in accordance with auditing standards.

In our opinion, the financial statements have given a true and fair view of the state of the company's affairs at 31 July 2002 and of its results and cash flow statement for the year ended. These have been properly prepared in accordance with the Companies Act, 1985.

Davies & Lawder
Chartered Accountants

25 September 2002

*Figure 11.4* An audit statement

Write out the following passage and fill in the blanks:

✦ The finance area is responsible for both _____ accounting and _____ accounting. _____ accounting looks at the _____ of money into and out of a business that have already happened. It gives a ____ picture of how well the business has been doing. The main _____ accounting documents are the cashflow statement, the profit and loss account and the balance sheet. The _____ shows the cash coming into and going out of the business at a particular moment. It is often called a _____ of the business's finances. The _____ shows the profits and losses made over a period of time. The _____ shows the main things which the business owes (its ____) against the main things which it owns (its _____).

✦✦ Describe which accounts must, by law, be produced by limited companies

✦✦✦ Explain the difference between the two types of accounting.

## KEY SKILLS

IT and Application of number: take the accounts from either one of your chosen businesses, or a company report, and make them easier to understand by creating graphs and charts. You could use IT for this.

## FACT FILE

Cashflow. Many businesses fail, not because their business idea isn't good, or because they don't have customers, but because they have failed to manage the flows of cash into and out of the business.

There will be a flow of money both into and out of any business. The important thing is to manage the flow so that there is neither too little nor too much cash. Think of it as water flowing into and out of a bath. As long as the flows are even, the level of bathwater will remain the same. Even if sometimes the water flows out very quickly, and sometimes flows in very quickly, the bath can generally cope with it and settle down to its old level again. Money may flow quickly out of the business – on payday, or when a bill comes due to be paid. It may flow quickly in, when the business is paid for work completed. The trouble is when the flows happen unexpectedly and on a large enough scale to cause a problem. If too much water flows out of the bath, the level can fall to nothing. This will be even worse if water stops flowing in. In business, flows of money are not regular: large sums of money can flow out, while the flow in can dry up.

The important thing for a business to be able to do is to predict when this will happen, and make arrangements. If the business can see that it is about to run out of money, it can borrow some (like using a bucket to top up the bath). Banks are usually happy to lend to businesses that have enough financial sense to be able to predict when there will be a problem. It can also happen that a business actually has too much cash when inflows are much higher than outflows. The solution in this case, is to take some of the cash and put it elsewhere, like in an interest earning bank account (like baling water out of the bath).

## KEY *TERMS*

Assets – what the business owns
Auditing – the job done by an auditor, which is to check the accounts for accuracy
Debt finance – start-up capital that has been borrowed
Financial accounting – looking at the past performance of a business
Liabilities – what the business owes
Management accounting – using financial tools to make predictions for the future
Owner's funds – start-up capital from the owner's own money
Start-up capital – the money initially raised so that the business could start trading

## The central role of Finance

The Finance functional area will always play a central role in a business organisation. Without its ability to raise the initial capital for the business to begin trading, none of the other functional areas could operate. Without capital, materials cannot be bought, goods will not be produced and therefore revenue will not be earned because there will be nothing to sell. The finance area also has the job of watching over the expenditure of other areas to make sure that they don't overspend (or plan to overspend). In this way it can make sure that each area is working together and working efficiently. It helps to set the aims and objectives of the business and, in particular, will be heavily involved in financial aims, such as maximising profit or revenue.

## EXTENSION EXERCISE

Explain exactly what finance was likely to have been needed to start up each of your chosen businesses. What were the major sources of this finance in each case?

## What you need to do:

- To achieve Level ❶   you will need a description of some of the purposes and activities of each of your chosen organisation's functional areas.
- To achieve Level ❷   you will need a detailed explanation of the purposes and activities of your chosen organisations' functional areas; you will need to explain how the functional areas relate to the aims of the business and how they support each other.
- To achieve Level ❸   you will need a thorough account of the purposes and activities of your chosen organisations' functional areas; you must analyse how effectively functional areas work together.

CHAPTER 12

# Administration and IT support

The Administration function in an organisation may be thought of as the 'scaffolding' or 'skeleton' that holds the organisation together. It deals with all the time-consuming but essential tasks that have to be carried out to keep the business running smoothly. Traditionally, it would have been mostly involved in writing letters, answering telephone calls and dealing with other paperwork such as filing and record-keeping. Nowadays, the Administration function covers a much wider area, owing to the fact that many of these tasks are now more easily carried out by computer applications. The Administration department will usually provide the support to allow people to make the best use of information technology.

**Figure 12.1** *All parts of a business's administration – security, communication, maintenance, record-keeping*

## The size of Administration

As with many of the other functional areas, the size of the organisation will be a significant factor in deciding who actually carries out the administrative tasks. If the business is a small one, such as a sole trader, then the owner is quite likely to carry out many of the administrative tasks him/herself. However, as a business grows, one of the first areas where it is necessary to employ an expert is often that of administration. If the business owner has the good sense to see that filing, accurate record-keeping and organisation are essential to efficiency, and that employing someone with keyboard and organisational skills will help to meet efficiency targets, then s/he will take on an administrator.

## Traditional areas

The traditional areas in which the Administration function operates include clerical work such as typing records or letters, the collection and distribution of mail, the keeping and filing of records, the organisation of meetings and responding to customer enquiries.

## Typing

This has been replaced in organisations with the term 'keyboarding', as almost all traditional typing now takes place via a computer keyboard. Letters, memos, reports and other documents all need to be typed up. Many managers now do at least some of the actual typing themselves, as, for example, when a meeting record is kept on a word-processing file. This means that the administrator does not have to re-type the document but can use the electronic copy instead.

## Record-keeping

Records are now usually kept electronically, on a database. However, many organisations still keep paper records, and it is the job of the Administration function to make sure that these are filed properly. The main purpose of filing documents in a systematic way is so that they can easily be found again should the business need them for any purpose. For example, a business may need to know which of its employees is qualified to do a particular job, and could find out by referring to application forms. In many businesses, a multi-skilled worker carries out these jobs, with records being kept both on computers and on paper, and with new technology being introduced to speed up as many of the old time-consuming tasks as possible.

## Mail

In a large organisation, incoming mail needs to be sorted and sent via the internal post to various departments. At the same time, outgoing mail needs to be collected. It also needs to be stamped or franked, and a record made of where it is going. Even in a small organisation, it will save the time of a manager or owner if an administrator deals with the mail. S/he will be able to filter out the letters (such as circulars and other junk mail) that do not need to be dealt with; will be able to answer some of the less important queries him/herself, and can pass on the letters requiring the owner's or manager's personal attention.

In terms of efficiency, a specialist manager or worker is better employed at his or her own job than in opening mail. The administrator is the specialist for carrying out that particular function.

## Meetings

The Administration function is responsible for the organisation of meetings. This is a much more complex process than may at first be thought. It involves finding a suitable venue, inviting participants, checking availability (of venue and participants), organising any facilities that are needed (such as overhead projectors and screens), and organising catering, parking etc. It also involves keeping a record of the meeting and circulating this in the appropriate format to the meeting members.

### Classwork activity

Look at the fire extinguishers and electrical equipment in and near to where you are working. You could also look at the ones in your chosen business or businesses and answer the following questions:

- What information is contained on the green slip attached to electrical equipment?
- What information is contained on the fire extinguisher labels.
- How often do you think each has to be checked?
- Why?
- Who is responsible for arranging the checking?

### True or False answer

**False.** Sometimes it will be more efficient for a number of people to actually meet – perhaps signatures are needed, or the quality of an item needs to be seen or felt.

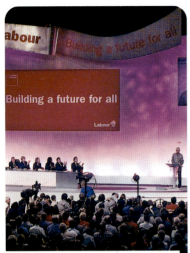

**Figure 12.2** *Large meetings and conferences take a lot of organising*

Meetings may be anything from a one-to-one meeting (perhaps between a manager and a staff member, or a sales manager and a client) to presentations to hundreds of delegates.

## Function rooms

Many hotels now provide function rooms and facilities for meetings that are held outside the premises of a business (perhaps between different branches of a business, or to show a presentation to a group that is too large for the business to cope with). The Administration function will liaise with the specialist members of staff at the hotel and, in this way, the work of organising the meeting is shared. The hotel will usually sort out seating, presentation materials, catering and parking, leaving the administrator to cope with the rest.

## Video-conferencing

Even in the area of meetings, technology is beginning to take over. While face-to-face meetings are important, they can be achieved via a video link.

Video-conferencing has some disadvantages. These include:

- not being able to read a person's body language (important in a meeting)
- not being able to 'network' (Networking involves the information and decision-making that can be made as a consequence of meeting people. It takes place in the 'social' breaks to a meeting, such as on arrival, at coffee, or at mealtimes.)

However, the advantages are that the business does not have to pay for travel (or travelling time) so that video-conferencing is much cheaper than actual meetings. Imagine the cost of a three-way meeting between managers situated in Australia, America and the UK. Video-conferencing will cost only a fraction of this.

**HOMEWORK ACTIVITY**

Find out, from the regulations, what are the minimum and maximum temperatures for your school or college. Find out what you are supposed to do if you think that the temperature is too high or too low.

**For your portfolio**

Look at the aims and objectives of your chosen businesses. Explain how the operation of the administrative function in those businesses helps to meet those aims.

**Figure 12.3** *Much easier and cheaper to video-conference than to travel between Sydney and Newcastle!*

## Responding to enquiries

The Administrative function may respond to enquiries on paper, by telephone or made electronically. These could be internal – from other departments or areas within the business – or external, from customers or suppliers for example. Reception and the telephone switchboard may be part of Customer Services or Administration. They will deal with all visitors to the business and will give the first impressions of the firm both to visitors and to callers. It is the importance of this first impression that makes their work so vital.

## Health and safety

There are legal requirements which must be met in shops, offices, workshops and factory premises. They involve the comfort and safety of the workers; eg there is a minimum and maximum temperature at which people are expected to work. The Administration function monitors and checks to make sure that conditions are being met.

For example, in the area of safety, both electrical equipment and fire extinguishers and alarms have to be regularly checked by a professional and certified as being in safe working order. It is the Administrative function that will make sure not only that these checks are carried out, but that they are carried out in the right time period and by the right, qualified, people.

## IT Support

The Administration function is responsible for providing support for software applications such as word-processing, payroll, accounts, databases, e-communications and other e-transactions. This will range from technology-based communications systems such as fax machines and video-conferencing, through to the filing and recording systems used by the various departments.

In a large organisation there could be a separate Information Technology department to deal with these areas. This would still be considered a part of the Administrative function. An Information

### ACTIVITY

✦ Administrative tasks are often carried out according to systems. Write a system for each of the following:

- answering the phone
- sorting the post
- filing customer accounts

Each should have as many points as necessary to make sure that the job is done efficiently, and records are kept.

✦✦ Exchange your systems with a partner and see if you can find anywhere where the system could be improved.

✦✦✦ Explain why it is important for administration to have systems.

71

## KEY *TERMS*

Networking – informal meetings that can be more powerful than formal ones
Video-conferencing – 'meeting' via a video link up

## EXTENSION EXERCISE

Three business people based in different parts of the world need to discuss a multi-million pound take-over deal. Explain what the advantages and disadvantages of video-conferencing or face-to-face meeting would be. What would you recommend and why?

Technology section would be likely to provide hardware support – ie trouble-shooting problems with machinery and its operation. Administrative IT support is likely to be focused on software support – training people how to use software and ensuring that it is both used properly and to its full capability. It will also manage e-mail systems, allocate storage space on central servers to individuals and departments, and manage and monitor internet access.

In a small business, these functions may be carried out by the owner, or could be managed by bringing in an outside, specialist, agency.

## Cleaning, security and premises maintenance

There are other tasks which have to take place in an organisation to keep it running smoothly, but which are not usually noticed by either the customers or the workers. In fact, it is only when such tasks are not properly carried out that anyone will notice!

Workers expect a clean and tidy environment, with machinery and equipment that function properly; customers and visitors expect the same. It is part of the Administrative function to provide cleaning and maintenance services, at the least possible inconvenience to the efficient running of the business. Many cleaning and maintenance operations are therefore carried out outside of normal office hours.

Security may be part of the premises management teams role, or, in many cases, may involve the hiring of an outside agency. Security is equally vital in both small and large businesses, and could range from simple systems of padlocks and passwords in a small business to security cameras, electronic alarms and security guards in a large business.

## Engine oil

It is important that the Administration function interacts smoothly with all other departments. It is vital to the efficient functioning of the business. You could compare its role to that of oil in a car engine. it keeps everything running smoothly and efficiently.

CHAPTER 13

# Operations

Remember the business model? Certain inputs are processed in order to produce an output – the product. Every business needs a set of inputs. It is the job of the functional area that covers **operations** to make sure that there are enough of the inputs, and that they are of sufficient quality. The Operations area obtains, organises and uses a variety of resources including people, premises and equipment. Part of the Operations function will also be to organise and oversee the actual production process.

**Figure 13.1** *Production may mean that a process is taking place, as with making steel from iron ore*

## Inputs

Operations produces products (goods and services) by making best use of the various inputs that are needed. These are:

- **Land**. This includes land that is worked (such as agricultural land, mines and quarries) and the land that is needed for buildings to stand on. The sorts of buildings that are needed for businesses are often called business premises. These include all kinds of places of work such as offices, shops, factories, railway premises etc. Land (a location for the business) is still needed even when it is a service that is being produced. Even a mobile hairdresser or an internet-based business needs somewhere to work from.
- **Equipment**. This includes any vehicles needed by the business, machinery, plant (a term usually used to refer to large machines or fixtures used in industrial processes), tools, equipment and computers.

## Classwork activity

Choose three items that you are carrying, wearing, or are in your classroom.

Write out the inputs, processes and outputs for each one.

Explain which is the most expensive and why.

- **People**. A business may need general labour, or specialist staff. The people needed may include operators, managers, support staff and other specialists, some of which work directly for the business, some of which are brought in from outside.
- **Materials**. Manufacturing and similar businesses need the raw materials that are going to be used in manufacturing products. Many businesses do not deal in raw materials, but do deal in selling finished products. This means that the materials they need are the products for selling.

## Separate departments

Operations covers such a wide area that, in many businesses, it is divided into different specialist departments. For example:

- specialist buyers of materials working for a purchasing department
- a special area where production is organised
- a department devoted to quality and the hiring, training
- other details to do with people may be handled by the Human Resources department.

Remember, a business will still need the various functions to take place, even if they are not in separate departments. Operations may not be in a single functional area but be spread across the business, with each area being responsible for its own purchase and management of the specialist inputs it requires, and of its own processes.

## Production

Some businesses are actively involved in making products. Such businesses are likely to have a production department as part of their

***Figure 13.2*** *Production in many businesses is automated and can be carried out by robots*

operations set-up. Once a product has been designed, its manufacture or assembly has to be carefully planned. It is the production area that will have to make these decisions which may include:

- what types of raw materials will be needed
- where they will be sourced and transported from
- what quantities of raw materials will be needed
- how the materials will be delivered and stored
- what machinery, equipment and tools will be needed
- how many workers will be required to both carry out and manage the production process
- what range of skills and experience will the workers need to offer
- what production system or method will be used
- how will the product be packaged
- how many units will be produced, and over what time period
- how will production be controlled?

## Purchasing

Buying for the whole of a large organisation (rather than allowing each department to buy its own requirements) usually keeps costs down, as items may be bought in large amounts (buying in bulk). Buying in bulk usually means that prices are much lower.

Being a specialist buyer also leads to them becoming experts in a particular resource. They can then use this knowledge to approach the best suppliers and obtain the best deals. For example, a chain of clothing shops is likely to employ a specialist fashion buyer; a catalogue retailer will employ a number of specialist buyers for electrical goods, clothes, or toys etc. Often buyers can make or break other small businesses. A tea grower, for example, would be keen for the buyer from a business such as Tetley's Tea to agree to buy his or her crop.

Purchasing may also be spread throughout the business. Computer Services may know what computer equipment it is best to buy; Administration may be expert in office equipment; Logistics and Transport may be in charge of buying vehicles.

## Processes

Businesses may produce goods through a number of processes, all of which will involve the Operations area. The most common of these are

- **manufacturing** – this is another word for 'making' and refers to the process of taking raw materials and turning them into finished or part-finished goods
- **assembly** – this is another form of manufacturing, in which component parts are put together to make a finished item
- **processing** – this involves taking raw materials and subjecting them

**HOMEWORK ACTIVITY**

Choose a service carried out by a small business near to where you live. Describe the inputs, process and output for it.

### For your portfolio

Which resources does each of your chosen businesses need to carry out its activities? List them under the headings of land, labour, capital and enterprise.

True or False answer

**True.** TQM means that it is everyone's responsibility to make sure that quality is maintained, not just one department.

**Figure 13.3** *Raw materials include anything extracted or grown, in this case, tea*

to a process that changes their nature in order to produce a finished good; eg iron ore may be smelted in order to produce steel
- **refining** – this involves taking impurities or unwanted parts from a raw material in order to obtain a finished product; eg petrol is refined from crude oil

## Quality

It is the job of the Operations functional area to make sure that perfect goods are produced. In some businesses, this is the responsibility of a separate quality control department, in others, it is a responsibility that has been extended to everyone at the business.

Quality controls have developed, in most modern businesses, from quality checking systems – where goods were checked once they had been produced and any faulty ones thrown away – to a system called total quality management (TQM) where everyone is responsible for ensuring that their own part in operations is carried out perfectly. In the old system, there would be a lot of waste, as the parts used in production that were discarded as not being up to standard, could not usually be recovered. The new system tries to make sure that mistakes don't happen – or, if they do, they are corrected straight away.

## Production control

The Operations area is also responsible for the various tasks which have to be carried out in order to make production run smoothly. Apart from quality control, these include maintenance, stock control and efficiency.

Maintaining machinery and equipment is necessary to ensure that break-downs and faults do not interrupt the production process. It is also part of quality control – making sure that each unit of production is correctly manufactured. **Stock control** makes sure that there are enough raw materials, components etc. for manufacturing to continue. Traditionally, stock control meant keeping a store of materials and topping it up when necessary. Nowadays, it is more likely to mean being able to order stock so that it arrives precisely as and when it is needed (called just-in-time).

## CITIZENSHIP

*Production of some products takes place using cheap and child labour, in parts of the world where there are no laws to protect workers. Use the internet to research into a major name product which is produced abroad, and find out the conditions under which it is produced. You could start by using 'globalisation' as your search term.*

## ACTIVITY

✦ Production involves the input–process–output model. Take the job of cooking a dinner, and write out exactly what is required for successful production. What are the inputs, the processes and the output? What labour is involved, what tools or machinery, and what power?

✦✦ Cost the process – including the costs of all the inputs.

✦✦ Explain how a restaurant might go through the same costing process.

✦✦✦ Explain how your example could be used to explain the prices of a restaurant meal.

In retailing (particularly food retailing), stock control means ensuring that stock is used in strict rotation, always using the oldest stock first. Shelf stock in a supermarket, for example, is pulled to the front of the shelf so that new stock can be put behind. Efficiency may mean the efficiency of workers, or of machines, or of transport, or of any other system vital to operations.

## Automation

The introduction of new technology means that, in many businesses, machines have taken over many roles that used to belong to the operations area. Examples include computerised stock control and quality control, as well as the use of machinery instead of people to carry out certain jobs. Using machines to help with production is called **mechanisation**. When the whole process is mechanised, this is called **automation** (see figure 13.2).

In some manufacturing cases, production may be totally computerised, with robots carrying out production and a minimum of human interference. Industrial robots can work all day, do not need breaks, can perform repetitive tasks perfectly, and can be set to check their own quality. This does not mean that people are not needed at all, just that their role will change. People will still be needed to plan, for example, or to maintain the machinery. Specific uses of new technology include:

- CAD – Computer Aided Design (products can be seen and 'tested' without even one being produced)
- CAM – Computer Assisted Manufacture
- CIM – Computer Integrated Manufacturing (where the whole production process is controlled by computer)
- MRP – Manufacturing Resource Planning (by which a complete process can be modelled).

## Services and small businesses

Some businesses produce a service rather than a good. In such businesses, production, as such, will not take place and many of the processes described above will not be needed. However, there will

**FACT FILE**

The inputs used in production are called the _factors of production_ and are usually remembered as land, labour, capital and enterprise (the organisational skill to put them together). The mixture of factors needed will be decided by the nature of the business. A farmer, for example, is likely to need a lot of land, some machinery and some labour to operate it. A modern car manufacturer will need land for the factory, but may need very little labour. If the manufacturing process is totally automated, the car producer will need many machines, but only enough manpower to operate and maintain them. A hairdresser, on the other hand, is providing a service which has to be labour-intensive.

## KEY TERMS

Automation – when new technology and computerisation takes over the production process

Bulk buying – buying in large numbers, usually to obtain a lower unit price

CAD – Computer Aided Design

CAM – Computer Assisted Manufacture

CIM – Computer Integrated Manufacturing

Factors of production – the inputs used for production

Manufacturing – making a product from raw materials or components

MRP – Manufacturing Resource Planning

Total Quality Management (TQM) – where quality is everybody's responsibility

## EXTENSION EXERCISE

Find out who introduced the idea of TQM. Find out how many 'points' s/he said there were to TQM, and write down the five which you think are most significant.

still be a need for certain inputs (which may be mainly the skill and tools of the person providing the service), there will be a process, and there will be a final output, once the job is complete.

Many small businesses provide a service, and their owners carry out their own 'operations' and 'operations control' within the business. A hairdresser, for example, needs the inputs of skill, scissors and other cutting equipment, dyes, lotions, gels and the premises where the service is carried out. The process is the actual hair-cutting and styling, the output is the finished haircut. The hairdresser still needs to control operations – s/he will need certain stock, will need to manage stock, and will certainly need to manage quality if s/he wants customers to come back!

### What you need to do:

- To achieve Level ❶      you will need a description of some of the purposes and activities of each of your chosen organisation's functional areas.
- To achieve Level ❷      you will need a detailed explanation of the purposes and activities of your chosen organisations' functional areas; you will need to explain how the functional areas relate to the aims of the business and how they support each other.
- To achieve Level ❸      you will need a thorough account of the purposes and activities of your chosen organisations' functional areas; you must analyse how effectively functional areas work together.

CHAPTER 14
# Marketing and Sales

Marketing and Sales may be a single organisational area within a business, or they may be divided into two separate departments. Marketing and Sales is in charge of finding out what the customer needs and wants through market research, analysing and interpreting that information, and then making sure that the products the business produces are actually sold, through advertising and other promotional techniques.

*Figure 14.1* *Advertising is everywhere*

## Roles

The jobs that have to be carried out in Marketing and Sales give a good idea of what this functional area is responsible for. The jobs can be grouped together in four main areas:

1 Jobs which involve analysing the market. In this category are people such as market researchers and interviewers, who design the means of collecting data and also carry out the collection. There are also statisticians and market analysts, who take the data and turn it into usable information, from which conclusions can be drawn.

2 All the jobs involved in the creation of advertising, from the creators and designers of advertisements (such as graphic artists, copy writers and creative consultants) to the people involved in making them (producers, directors, printers etc.).

3 Jobs which involve buying; eg media buyers who buy advertising space or slots in publications and in broadcast media. These jobs also include spending money on promotions or public relations.

4 Jobs involving sales. These range from the shop sales assistant to people who seek new sales outlets or clients for large businesses.

**Figure 14.2** *A car salesman completes a sale with a customer*

## Market- or product-orientated?

Some businesses may be described as 'market-orientated', some as 'product orientated'. Market orientated businesses try to develop and sell products which are a response to changes in the market. Such businesses would look at market trends and then produce a product to fit with those trends. For example, if there is a trend towards healthier living, a chocolate manufacturer might start to produce

**True or False answer**

False. Data is the set of raw figures that have not yet been interpreted or presented. Information is when the data has been turned into a useable format – usually by statisticians.

more 'healthy' versions of its products. Such businesses are said to be **looking for gaps** in the market.

Product orientated businesses are those which have created something new or different, and then want to try to persuade people to buy it. New technology businesses tend to be in this category – mobile phone businesses, for example, are continually developing and upgrading their product – not as a result of consumers asking for changes; but because they think they can persuade the consumers to buy the new models. Such businesses are said to be **creating gaps** in the market.

## Market research

Marketing and Sales will be in charge of market research. Market research is the collection of information from and about customers and potential customers (the customers which the business would like to have in the future).

Information is either new (because it is being collected for the first time) or 'second-hand' (information that has been published before). New information is called **primary** market research. It is collected through field research – ie actually talking to customers in various ways. Research that has been previously published (eg in books, journals, and magazines or on the internet) is called **secondary** information. This is collected through **desk** research (because it is possible to sit at a desk whilst obtaining the information).

In some small businesses, market research may be carried out by word-of-mouth – the owner asking customers what they want and what they are happy or unhappy with. In other businesses, market research may be so important that it takes place in a whole separate, specialised, department.

### Desk Research

The most likely sources of secondary information are newspapers and magazines, books and business and government reports. The government produces statistics on all aspects of life in the UK, much of which is freely available, either as leaflets, or on the internet. The biggest sources of information are the annual reports and accounts of limited companies which must, by law, be made available to the public. Secondary data may not be as good as primary data because it may:

- be out of date
- be expensive to buy
- be in the wrong format for what the business needs
- not be exactly what the business wants
- not be complete.

---

## TRUE OR FALSE?

*The cost of advertising is always passed on to the consumer in higher prices.*

*(see foot of page for answer)*

---

## Classwork activity

**You are working for a business that is selling portable, personal DVD players. Draw up a guarantee card for this product with ten questions designed to find out the most about your customers. It should find out information like:**

- **What are their tastes?**
- **What other products might they buy?**
- **How do they like to pay?**
- **How often do they shop?**
- **Where?**

**Try it out on ten members of your class. Explain how the Marketing and Sales area of the business could use the results.**

---

### Field research

Such research gathers data that has not been collected before, so is being collected for the first time – therefore 'primary' research. The main methods of collecting information are through

- questionnaires and other types of survey
- in-depth interviews
- observation and counting – this includes methods such as traffic counts and footfall counts. For example, a researcher could count how many people pass a particular shop window, and, out of those, how many actually go in, in order to measure the effectiveness of the window display
- focus groups – asking panels of people to comment on a product, advertisement etc.
- tasting and testing – inviting people to comment on a product after they have had a chance to try it.

**Figure 14.3** *Observation – a form of field research*

## Market segments

Marketing will also target particular parts of a market. Markets are divided up into various parts, or segments. Segments may be defined according to where people live, their hobbies and interests, age or gender, or even race or religion. They may also be defined according to the income and educational group that a household is considered to be in; these are called **socio-economic** groups. This use of different market segments means that the Marketing area can target particular groups of consumers with products and the promotion and advertising for those products.

## Advertising expenditure

Marketing and Sales is also responsible for advertising and promotion. Advertising is both letting people know that a product is available (informative advertising) and trying to persuade them to buy it (persuasive advertising). The spending of the business on advertising and promotion is usually called either 'above the line' or 'below the line' expenditure.

- **above the line** expenditure is direct expenditure on advertising such as buying media space (space in newspapers and magazines, or slots on television and radio), or the production costs for the making of advertisements
- **below the line** expenditure is indirect spending such as on promotions, competitions, sponsorship and product placement

## Promotion

Marketing and Sales will be responsible for the promotion of the products of the business. Promotion includes the ways by which the business tries to persuade customers to buy its products. It includes publicity, persuasion and value-added promotions, and encourages loyalty and repeat trade. Publicity related promotions include:

- point of sale material – cards, displays etc used where the goods

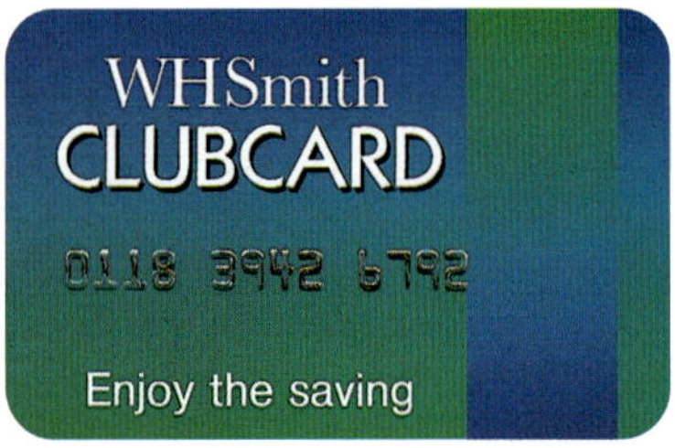

**WHSmith**
**CLUBCARD**
0118 3942 6792
Enjoy the saving

*Figure 14.4*

are displayed in a shop or where they will be paid for (eg at checkouts)
• shop signs telling the customer what the shop sells.

Value-added promotions are where the customer gets more (extra value) for their money than previously. These include:

• free gifts – products will sometimes contain such things as small toys, games or other gifts
• banded promotions – goods may be physically 'banded' together: eg a brand of toothpaste sold with a brand of toothbrush
• money-off coupons – published in the press, delivered direct or as part of the packaging of goods (to encourage repeat purchases)
• special offers such as 'buy one, get one free'
• price reductions – when products are offered at a lower price than before.

Some promotions are designed to persuade people to return again such as:

• customer loyalty cards – customers collect 'points' electronically every time they make a purchase that can be redeemed against selected products instore. Through mailings customers are also rewarded with money off or occasionally cash coupons
• joint promotion – where two businesses agree to promote each other's products because they are aiming at similar markets. A breakfast cereal aimed at children might, for example, promote children's toys or a children's magazine.

## Sales

No amount of marketing can help a business to succeed if it does not have good sales staff. Sales staff are a direct link between the customer and the business, so should always be polite, well-mannered, smart and knowledgeable. This requires training – both in product knowledge and in dealing with customers.

Figure 14.5

**ACTIVITY**

♦ Listen to two different commercial radio stations (eg Classic FM and a pop or rock station) and log the advertisements that are carried in one hour.

♦ List the products that are advertised.

♦♦ Describe the type of message being put across (funny, serious, educated...)

♦♦♦ What does this tell you about the audiences for each radio station? How would this help a marketing area?

**FACT FILE**

*One of the most important sources of secondary data is the Census. Every ten years, on the year ending in '1' (1971, 1981, 1991, 2001) the government holds a National Census of Population. This not only counts the population, it also collects a vast quantity of information about family size and structure, shopping habits, incomes, spending patterns and so on. There is a whole government office that collects and publishes this information. It is called the Office of National Statistics (ONS). The use of Information Technology means that results are now available much more quickly and accurately than they have ever been in the past.*

The importance of sales staff can be seen by the way they are often encouraged to make sales by being rewarded for them – through commission or special rewards such as holidays. Sales outlets also play a part in successful selling. The business itself has the job of creating the right atmosphere for its products. A business will want to project an image that will attract its target customers. A young person's clothes shop, for example, will have a very different atmosphere from one selling gentlemen's suits. In the first, there is likely to be loud music and bright colours, while the second will be quiet and soberly decorated.

## Using Information Technology

Market research and analysis is one field where the use of information technology has meant that results are both much more accurate and available much faster. The use of databases to target particular consumers or types of consumer can also mean that marketing is much more effective than it used to be. Spreadsheets can be used to make statistics more presentable, meaningful and easier to cope with, and the use of mail merge (where the advertising material appears to be directly addressed to the recipient) to

## KEY *TERMS*

Advertising media – the ways (TV, radio, posters) that advertisements are carried
Desk research (also called secondary research) – looking at information that has been previously published
Field research (also called primary research) – finding out new information
Market orientated – developing products to respond to market changes
Product orientated – developing new products, then convincing the market that it needs them

## EXTENSION EXERCISE

Look on the internet to see what marketing information you can find out about your local area. One good place to start is www.upmystreet.co.uk. Explain how a Marketing and Sales department could use this information.

personalise direct mail drops can make both the research itself and its presentation more efficient.

Direct mail is used to target particular customers. Consumers may have filled out questionnaires, guarantee cards or credit agreements, which have revealed preferences and lifestyle details that can be targeted by advertisers. Computerising such records can give businesses a really good idea of the tastes of their target customers, so that they can market products to match the tastes.

## What you need to do:

- To achieve Level ❶    you will need a description of some of the purposes and activities of each of your chosen organisation's functional areas.
- To achieve Level ❷    you will need a detailed explanation of the purposes and activities of your chosen organisations' functional areas; you will need to explain how the functional areas relate to the aims of the business and how they support each other.
- To achieve Level ❸    you will need a thorough account of the purposes and activities of your chosen organisations' functional areas; you must analyse how effectively functional areas work together.

## CHAPTER 15
# Customer Service

Businesses cannot exist unless they have customers to buy the products which they have on offer. It is therefore extremely important to keep those customers happy, and loyal to the business. What the business wants is a satisfied customer, who will not only come back and buy more of a product, but who will also recommend the business to friends and associates. Loyalty to the business also means, of course, that customers are using this business – and not that of any of its competitors. Customers will not demonstrate such loyalty, however, unless they are well looked after. This means that the business must make sure that what it is selling is readily available, safe, reliable and, perhaps most importantly, gives the customer value for money.

**Figure 15.1** *Stores may take credit cards or provide other 'easy' ways to pay*

## Range of services

Customer Service, like many other functional areas, may not be in a separate area, but be carried out by different parts of the business. For example, Sales staff may carry out the Customer Service function of giving advice; a Transport and Logistics department may carry out the Customer Service function of distribution.

Customer services covers a range of different services, all of which help to make the customer happy with the business and loyal to it. The main services which a customer would expect are:

- the provision of information
- the ability to give advice
- financial services such as the provision of credit facilities
- delivery or easy availability of products
- the provision of after-sales service.

## Providing information

Customers need to know a range of information about the products that they might buy, and it is the job of Customer Services to provide this information.

Imagine that a customer was going to buy a new car. Think about what s/he would need to know. One of the first pieces of information needed might be the price, but customers will also want to know many other details: what colours does it come in? what extras are available? what is the performance like? what servicing does it require? who would do the servicing? are there special, easier, ways in which payment can be made? Customer services staff would answer all these questions (and others). Some information may be provided in a standard form – such as a leaflet or sales brochure; some may be provided by outside organisations (such as the fuel consumption figures for a car) and some questions can only be answered by properly trained Customer Service representatives.

## Giving advice

Customers will often expect businesses which sell products to be knowledgeable about them and to be able to give advice on the product. In business to business transactions, this is even more important. A builder may want to hire machinery to carry out a particular job, but not know which machine is best to have. S/he will expect to be able to describe the nature of the job to a business which contracts out machinery, and to be advised on which machine is the best for the task.

Customers will expect advice when buying products about which they may know little. As businesses expect a range of customers, this means a range of different advice which could be as simple as what type of screw to use for a particular fixing, or as complex as how to achieve the best performance out of an aeroplane!

Advice is not, however, always free. Some businesses are set up with the purpose of giving specialist advice – such as lawyers, architects and designers. A customer would expect accurate advice

### Classwork activity

Work with a partner to write a role-play between a customer service assistant and an angry customer. The customer has telephoned to complain about the late delivery of an item, which is the wrong size. Your role-play should show how the situation is resolved so that everyone is happy.

### True or False answer

**False.** Physical distribution describes how a product is physically transported from the manufacturer in one place to the customer in another. Channels of distribution show the stages that a product travels through to reach the final consumer.

**HOMEWORK ACTIVITY**

Write down five types of customer service that you would receive in a large supermarket.

Would you receive all of these services in a small shop? Explain why?

## For your portfolio

You should be able to say how the Customer Services function (whether or not it is in a separate department) in each of your chosen businesses interacts with other functional areas. Which areas is it most

involved with? Explain why.

from such businesses, but would expect to have to pay for it. They would also expect to be able to recover payments or gain compensation if the advice was not accurate. Many businesses of this nature require qualifications; many are also governed by professional bodies, so that if inaccurate advice is given, the professional body can act against the business.

## Providing credit facilities

Customers could expect businesses to provide easy ways for them to pay. Sometimes this is because there are large amounts of money involved, sometimes it is just for convenience. A car retailer would provide the customer with the option of paying over a number of months (or years) because the car is expensive (customers pay for this sort of service through interest payments). On the other hand, a newsagent may only bill a customer once a month – and at no extra charge – just to provide a convenient service. Credit cards are another way of allowing customers to pay later, so are accepted by many businesses. Some large businesses (particularly retail outlets such as high street clothes stores) have developed their own 'in-store' credit cards

There may also be informal credit agreements between customer and retailer. It might be common, for example, for a customer to have a 'tab' or 'tick' at a local shop. The shopkeeper would keep a record of purchases and these would be paid for at the end of the week.

## Delivering goods

Products need to be delivered to customers directly and also to the outlets where customers are going to shop for them. This will be the responsibility of a distribution area. Distribution may be a separate department or area within the Customer Services area. It may also be a part of the Production area in some businesses, as it is to do with distributing the goods once they have been produced.

Goods are not usually sold in the same place that they are produced. There is therefore a need to get the goods to the **point of sale**. The point of sale may be a market or a shop, where the customer comes directly; or it may be a warehouse or similar storage centre, from which customers can order goods. Either way, it is important that customers can easily obtain the product. If not, then they will not buy, but will go to a competitor who provides better service.

Distribution to the customer involves either delivery or collection. Some goods are delivered directly to the customer; eg milk deliveries still take place in most of the UK, sand and cement is delivered to a building site. Customers may also order goods from catalogues or

**CITIZENSHIP**

*Customers have certain rights under consumer protection laws. Find out about your consumer rights. Under which laws are you protected? How are you protected? Explain why these laws are necessary.*

**Figure 15.2** *In many cases, the customer expects delivery. In some cases (like building materials) it may be the only option*

advertisements, or online over the internet. These will all be delivered to the customers home.

In other cases customers collect goods – from shops, markets, stores etc. In the case of services, it is the nature of the service that decides how it is distributed. For a personal service, such as a haircut, it is obvious that the hairdresser and customer have to be in the same place. This place could be a shop, or the service could take place in the customer's home. Some services can take place remotely (eg you can ring an information service to find out the times of trains), whereas others must take place where the service is being delivered (you can't paint a wall or cut a lawn without actually being there!)

Goods have to be transported, either directly to the customer, or to a warehouse or retail outlet. Many large retail businesses, such as supermarkets, have their own distribution centres (called Regional Distribution Centres – RDCs), which act as 'hubs' for the distribution network.

**Figure 15.3** *Waitrose's regional distribution centre*

**ACTIVITY**

✦ **For one business say how it carries out the following:**

- **greeting customers**
- **finding customer needs**
- **meeting customer requirements**
- **taking payment**
- **after sales service**
- **dealing with complaints**

✦✦ **Suggest a possible improvement to three of these areas.**

✦✦✦ **Write a letter to the business to explain how these improvements will make their customer service better.**

## ⬡ KEY *SKILLS*

## FACT FILE

*Many smaller service industries rely on keeping their customers happy rather than on advertising. A plumber or electrician, a solicitor or accountant, may not bother advertising any further than an entry in a phone book and their name on a plaque or the side of a van. (Lawyers were actually barred from advertising at all until quite recently.) They rely on doing a good job and their customers recommending them to friends.*

## Providing after-sales service

Customers may expect various forms of service from a business for a long time after they have bought the goods. Cars will need servicing; electrical goods may need parts or service; customers may need more advice.

Sometimes, after-sales service is almost instant – a bag-packing or carry-to-car service at a supermarket, for example, is taking place after the sale has been made. In other cases, after-sales service is available through guarantees or warranties (promises to provide service, or to replace or repair as necessary) which may be free, or may have to be bought by the customer. Home delivery, information and updates about new products and dealing with customer complaints may all be considered as part of after sales service.

In some cases, after-sales advice is not only not free, but can be very expensive. Examples include advice on using new technology goods such as digital cameras, video-recorders and computers, where technical advice may only be available on payment of a premium rate telephone fee such as £1 or 50p per minute.

## Customer loyalty

The main reason for good Customer Service in a business is to encourage customer loyalty. This means that customers will come back to that business in preference to a competitor. Good customers will also recommend the business to friends (or, in the case of business to business transactions, to other businesses). Personal recommendation through 'word of mouth' is often a much more effective way of advertising and promoting a business than the use of expensive advertising techniques.

## ⬡ KEY *TERMS*

Credit facilities – allowing customers to buy now but pay over a period of time
Customer loyalty – customers who return to use the same business because it provides a good service
Point of sale – the place where goods are actually sold; examples include catalogues and shops
RDCs – Regional Distribution Centres
Word-of-mouth recommendation – when a customer learns about the strengths of a business from a friend or colleague

## EXTENSION EXERCISE

Supermarkets encourage customers to collect their own items from the shelves and take them to a till. Find out how people would have shopped 50 years ago. Which method do you think is better for the customer? Which is better for the business? Explain your reasoning.

The working of Customer Services affects all the other functional areas of the business. Good Customer Service means more customers, fewer complaints, more repeat trade and a greater chance of success for the business.

---

## What you need to do:

- **To achieve Level ❶**   you will need a description of some of the purposes and activities of each of your chosen organisation's functional areas.
- **To achieve Level ❷**   you will need a detailed explanation of the purposes and activities of your chosen organisations' functional areas; you will need to explain how the functional areas relate to the aims of the business and how they support each other
- **To achieve Level ❸**   you will need a thorough account of the purposes and activities of your chosen organisations' functional areas; you must analyse how effectively functional areas work together.
- A detailed study of customer service is required as part of the assessment for Unit 2.

---

CHAPTER 16

# Research and Development

Some businesses are successful because they introduce new products and new technologies. Sony is a good example of this – the Sony Walkman was an innovative product that was immediately successful.

James Dyson allocates a large proportion of his budget to research and development, the result being that Dyson 'bagless technology' vacuum cleaners have become the industry leaders. The 3M Corporation is another example, which allows its research staff to use company facilities to work, for 15% of the time, on their own projects. This has resulted in many new innovations and products, perhaps most notably the invention by employee Art Fry of a glue that sticks many times and yet leaves no trace when removed – allowing the development of the 'Post-it' note.

**Figure 16.1** *Research into car safety uses crash test dummies*

## The department

Good Research and Development (R&D) concentrates on:
- the design of the product – how attractive it is to the consumer, how efficient it is
- lengthening the product life cycle – having a product around (and successful) for as long as possible
- good communication with market research.

## Classwork activity

With a partner, design and make a paper aeroplane, and give it a test flight.

Now write down comments about its performance – what was good about it, what was not so good. Suggest improvements to make it better and test it again.

Continue this process until it is the best you think it can get, then compare it with those of other pairs.

In a large business, there may be a separate Research and Development department. In smaller businesses, it may be a part of the Production functional area. Many businesses may have no research and development formally taking place at all. Large R&D departments will be common in businesses that are concerned with new technology, or which are in highly competitive markets. In both cases, it is important for the business to try to stay ahead of competitors with new or improved product lines. Even in the smallest business, however, there will usually be some research and development – such as businesses trying out new lines or products, or developing different services or varieties of existing services.

### Outside the department

Much research and development is of such a technical or scientific nature that it actually takes place away from business. Current research into genetic engineering, cloning, genetically-modified crops and new medicines and drugs, all takes place in academic institutions such as universities. Some of this research is directly funded by big business; others are bought in by business as being cheaper than running their own R&D department.

## Jobs

Jobs in Research and Development include designers (draughtsmen and women and technical drawing experts), engineers who can build models and prototypes, mechanics, technologists and IT and computer specialists. There may also be experts who are responsible for making sure that new innovations and developments are

**Figure 16.2** *Research may take place in educational institutions like universities*

protected from the competition. New technology can be protected by the use of patents. If a process or development is completely new, and has never been tried successfully by anyone before, it can be registered at the Patent Office. It is illegal to copy or try to copy a registered design.

In many industries there will also be scientists, safety experts and statisticians. Just think of what is needed for the design and development of a new car, for example.

## Research

The first distinct area of the department is research, either market research or product research. The Marketing area will usually carry out market research, but researchers will need to work closely with R&D and Production. It is pointless for market researchers to find a gap in the market for a particular product, if R&D say that the product cannot be developed, or Production that it cannot be made!

Product research will be carried out by R&D. Researchers will look at which products can be developed, or what improvements can be made to existing products. Again, there will have to be close communication with the Marketing department. It is just as bad for R&D to develop a product that nobody wants, as it is for marketing to ask for a product that cannot be made!

## Testing

New products have to be tested at all stages of development. This used to imply a very expensive process of building models and then testing them. Some of this testing may now be done much more efficiently using IT. Computer programmes can show how a design would look, and simulate some of the forces that might affect the design. This saves much of the time and expense in the initial stages of development.

There comes a point, however, when computer testing is no longer good enough, and physical testing has to take place. One example is the way that chairs are tested. A mechanical 'seat' is set up to sit on the chair with the force of a person's weight. Researchers find out the average number of times a chair is used in a year, and the mechanical seat then copies this in a much shorter time period. From this researchers can work out how long a chair ought to last, and marketing can then offer guarantees. 'Guaranteed to last five years' is a claim that will only be made after research like this has taken place.

Physical testing is usually the last stage in a product's development. Cars are tested for safety, washing machines for efficiency, vacuum cleaners for power, furniture for wear, glue for strength, and so on. Many test facilities exist as businesses in their

### HOMEWORK ACTIVITY

Choose three products that you have at home and suggest, for each, a cosmetic improvement that might lead to more sales.

Explain, in each case, why people might buy more of the product.

### For your portfolio

Look at the products produced by your chosen businesses. Describe how those products were initially developed, tested and then produced. What changes – cosmetic or real –

could you propose to increase sales?

## True or False answer

**True.** This is called 'testing to destruction'. The reason for such testing is so that researchers know the absolute limit of a product's strength.

**Figure 16.3** *Cheaper to test it than to build it and watch it sink!*

own right, and a business wanting to test a product would pay to use their specialist testing facilities.

Even products which do not need to be tested in this way are still test marketed – ie tried out on a small section of a market before being launched on to the whole market. Again, this requires close cooperation with the Marketing area.

## Prototype

Part of the testing process, near the end of the development phase, will be to build a prototype. A prototype is a working example of the new product. It may be a scale model (eg a prototype ocean liner which would be tested in a storm tank), or a full-sized version (eg a prototype car, tested on a racing circuit). The use of prototypes allows designers to see how a product will behave under certain 'real' or realistic conditions.

In some cases, the worth of the prototype is proved by its success – and the product can go into production; in other cases, the worth of the prototype is proved by its failure. The failure of a prototype which sends designers 'back to the drawing board' is better than for a good prototype which is already in production to fail.

## Not all brand new

Not everything developed in R&D is brand new, or technologically better. In many cases, small changes are made to make a product look new or different. Sometimes these are no more than 'cosmetic' changes (such as a different colour, or package size), which do not affect the product at all. R&D may also suggest slight changes which Marketing can then promote. How often have you seen products advertised as 'new', 'improved', 'better' etc? While it is the job of R&D to develop new or improved goods and services to replace existing ones, it must also work closely with Marketing to see what is possible, and what customers actually want.

## Product life cycle

Most products have a natural product life cycle, from the initial launch of the product, through its development and finally to decline (see Figure 16.4). R&D will try to either maintain the product's sales

**ACTIVITY**

Wow! You've just had a brilliant idea about a new product that you want to bring to the market!

+ Describe the stages that the product will have to go through before it finally reaches the shops.

++ Describe what other functional areas will be involved along the way.

++ Explain which of these functional areas you think is most important, and why.

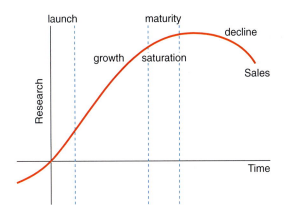

**Figure 16.4** *Product life cycle*

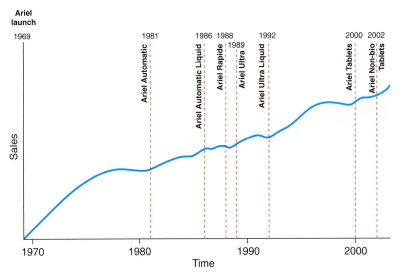

**Figure 16.5** *Ariel's product extension strategies*

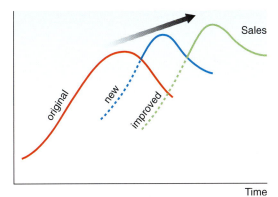

**Figure 16.6** *Riding the wave*

## KEY *TERMS*

Cosmetic changes – slight changes used to lengthen a product's life cycle
Product extension strategies – ways of extending the product's life
Product life cycle – the natural cycle that a product passes through from launch to decline
Prototype – a working example of a new product, for testing
Test marketing – marketing a product in a particular area to test its popularity
Testing to destruction – testing a product to the limit

## EXTENSION EXERCISE

Find out how the Consumer's Association tests products and reports on them.

by using (with Marketing) product extension strategies, or will try to 'ride the wave' by producing new products to replace existing ones. A product extension strategy is when the life cycle of a core product (the original product) is lengthened by various changes which make it 'new', 'improved' or in some way better. Look at the way that Ariel has maintained its market position since it was first launched in 1969 (see Figure 16.5). Whenever there has been a fall in sales, indicating that the product was going into decline, the company's R&D department has produced a new innovation that has revived sales again. Figure 16.6 shows how a product can be timed to 'ride the wave'. In other words, it is timed to be establishing a good market position just as the previous product goes into decline.

## What you need to do:

- To achieve Level ❶    you will need a description of some of the purposes and activities of each of your chosen organisation's functional areas.
- To achieve Level ❷    you will need a detailed explanation of the purposes and activities of your chosen organisations' functional areas; you will need to explain how the functional areas relate to the aims of the business and how they support each other.
- To achieve Level ❸    you will need a thorough account of the purposes and activities of your chosen organisations' functional areas; you must analyse how effectively functional areas work together.

# CHAPTER 17
# The use of IT

Information and Communications Technology (usually shortened to IT or ICT) has become a vital tool in making businesses effective and efficient. All functional areas within a business can benefit from the use of new technology. Growth in this area has been extremely rapid, and new developments are happening all the time.

**Figure 17.1** *Computerisation now makes space flight almost commonplace, but computers were not even invented when man first landed on the moon!*

## A Changing World

Remember that man landed on the moon in 1968 without the aid of computers, microchips or even calculators: the beginnings of new technology only date back 30–40 years (not a long time in business terms) and rapid computers, robotics, digital cameras and videos are still very recent. The first calculators were enormous (and very expensive) and could only carry out simple tasks – nowadays they are cheap (or even free). The first computers were room-sized, difficult to use and slow. New developments mean that not only are modern computers fast and efficient, but many products are guided or controlled by computer microchip.

Everything from washing machines to cars has benefited from the new technology. Businesses have benefited in a number of ways, both within functional areas and between them. There are benefits in:

- communications
- data storage and handling
- security
- customer service and support
- reducing transaction costs.

## Software

The main purpose of the use of IT in business is to cut the business's costs, to improve goods and services and to improve

**TRUE OR FALSE?**

*Intranets and networks are the same thing.*

*(see foot of page for answer)*

**True or False answer**

**False.** A network is where computers are linked together and may be able to share files or programs; an intranet is where web pages have been posted up, similar to the internet, but internal to the business.

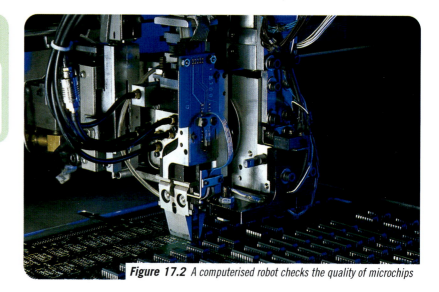

**Figure 17.2** *A computerised robot checks the quality of microchips*

## Classwork activity

Write down three advantages and three disadvantages of using email for communications.

Compare your answers with a partner to see if s/he has different ideas.

Which do you agree is the biggest advantage and which the biggest disadvantage? Explain your reasons.

efficiency. The main software (the programs that actually run on the computer) used in businesses are:

- word processing – documents can be edited on screen, words and phrases can be 'cut and pasted', layout can be altered, and all communications can be personalised
- databases – lists of information can be sorted into different orders and searched very quickly
- spreadsheets – used to store information and carry out calculations
- internet – the huge collection of web pages that can be accessed via a modem
- intranet – a sort of internal internet
- email – messages sent from one computer to another via a modem
- specialist programs – such as design or manufacturing software.

## System management and security

In some businesses there is a separate department to deal with problems and issues of new technology. This not only includes technician support, but also usually an IT expert who is in charge of the business's systems – a systems manager. This person can set passwords and different levels of access, as well as advising on (and often producing) content.

Employees should be able to log on with their own password and to further password-protect files or information that they do not want other employees to have access to. When they have finished for a session, they should log off. System managers will have higher levels of access for themselves and can set levels for various types of employee. These basic levels of security should be common to all businesses using computers. In some cases, it is not just a computer

True or False answer

**False.** Email is quick, but can be very expensive to set up initially. It can also be inefficient – a phone call or face-to-face meeting might be better. It is also possible for email to be 'hacked'.

96

but other computerised systems where people need to log in or out. For example, an employee might have to log on to an electronic till before recording a transaction.

Systems can also be protected by being regularly backed up. The most usual format is called 'grandfather – father – son'. Today is 'son' of yesterday's backup ('father') which is itself a backup of the day before ('grandfather'). Data is doubly protected in this way. IT support may be seen as a specialist part of the Administration function.

Security is also important to protect the business's systems from outside interference. This could come in a number of ways:

- **hacking** – when an outsider tries to break into a system in order to alter or steal information
- a **virus** – hundreds of computer viruses and variations on them are released each year; some are fairly harmless but many can cause enormous damage to machines and entire systems. Many are rapidly spread by email

Businesses protect themselves from such interference through the use of 'firewalls' to prevent outsiders gaining access, and through the use of virus protection software.

## Communications

New technology helps with the speed and efficiency of communications, both within a business and with external contacts. The most common form of modern communication between and within businesses is via **email**. There are many advantages to the use of email, but also quite a lot of criticisms:

- Email allows messages to be passed instantly and for many people to receive the same message simultaneously.
- It is, however, criticised as leading to communications being less formal than with traditional methods, and for taking away the personal contact between people.
- The widespread use of email within a business may mean that a worker emails a colleague even when they are in the next office (or even the same office) rather than talking to them.
- This can actually mean that using email is more inefficient.

Internal information can also be passed via a business **intranet**. An intranet is where a company has linked its computers together and built pages of information (as if they were linked to the internet) for the machines to access. It is an internal internet and, of course, the systems manager has complete control over the content – unlike if the computers were linked to the internet.

Businesses can also communicate more efficiently with customers, using new technology such as the internet to advertise, market and sell goods and services (see Chapter 18).

## Data storage and handling

IT can be used to make both storing and manipulation of data more efficient. In each functional area, there is a use for data storage or handling.

### HOMEWORK ACTIVITY

Traditionally, a business kept records, sent communications, held meetings and gave presentations without the help of IT. Describe how each of these would have been carried out without IT and how they can now be carried out using IT.

### For your portfolio

Visit the website of your two chosen businesses and compare them one against the other. Which is more effective? Why?

If your business does not have a website, write a letter to the owner explaining the benefits that s/he could gain from one.

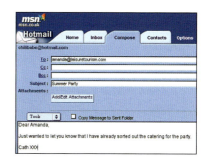

**Figure 17.3** *Using email has become commonplace*

- Human resources can store employee records on a database, making it easier to deal with issues of promotion, discipline, payroll, pensions, holidays and many other issues.
- Production can keep records of inputs, records of stocks of components parts and raw materials for example, and records of output. It will therefore know when to re-stock (some computer programmes will even do the re-ordering of stock themselves).
- Finance can keep all of the financial data regarding the business. Because it can be made available in a format such as a spreadsheet, it makes it easier to extract information from it and to make good use of the figures.
- Customer Services can keep a record of orders and also of dealings with customers. Often, if you ring a telephone helpline, you will be told that the call is being recorded – this is for security and training reasons, but also so that a record of calls is kept.
- Administration can keep records of stock, maintenance, mail in and out, meetings and health and safety issues such as when fire extinguishers have to be checked. The keeping of electronic diaries can also be more efficient than keeping paper-based ones.
- Marketing and Sales can keep customer records and also use computer programs such as databases to manipulate and present market research data.

## Customer Service and support

Computer applications can be used to track the progress of customer orders. One example is the Post Office service, by which a parcel can be traced along its route so that the sender can always know exactly where it is. The use of email enquiries can allow Customer Service departments to respond accurately and quickly to customer queries. In many cases, this is even more efficient than a telephone response, as the Customer Services representative can receive any expert advice or up-to-date information before responding.

## Reducing transaction costs

When a product is passed through a bar code reader in a supermarket or shop, a number of things happen. The barcode tells the till what the item is and the till can then retrieve the price from

## KEY TERMS

CAD – Computer Assisted Design

CAM – Computer Assisted manufacture

Databases – lists of information that can be sorted into different orders and searched very quickly

EDI or Electronic Data Interchange – passing data from one computer to another

EFTPOS – Electronic Funds Transfer at Point Of Sale

Hacking – illegal entry into a computer system

Internet – the huge collection of web pages that can be accessed via a modem

Intranet – a type of internal internet

Spreadsheets – used to store information and carry out calculations

## EXTENSION EXERCISE

Suggest the types of businesses that would have specific uses or needs for:

• CAD
• CAM.

How else could computer applications be used in design and production? Find out what other programs might be used.

its database; at the same time, the system informs the stock room that an item has been sold and, if stock has fallen below a certain level, the system will order new stock. Once all the items have been processed, the till prints out an itemised bill for the customer.

The customer can then pay using cash – or a number of electronic means. Electronic payment systems (such as the use of debit cards) mean that funds are transferred automatically from the customer's bank account to that of the shop, making the transaction both efficient and secure. This is often known as EFTPOS – Electronic Funds Transfer at Point Of Sale. Any data that is passed electronically within a business is called EDI or Electronic Data Interchange.

## Specific IT applications

Businesses may take advantage of specialist IT applications. Websites are used to put information – text, pictures, even sound and video – together in a format that is easy and attractive to use. The business can use the site for advertising, demonstrations and to publish catalogues and price lists. Businesses can use websites to advertise their services and to provide e-commerce facilities for customers. Visitors will be able to buy or order goods; competitors can check prices and ranges; other businesses can easily 'shop around' for the best suppliers. The biggest advantage is that the business is actually addressing a global market and has the possibility of gaining customers from anywhere in the world.

*Figure 17.4* Buying consumer goods via a website – in this case Tesco's

Research and Development can use Computer Aided Design (CAD), while production can use Computer Assisted Manufacture (CAM). R&D can also use computer programs to simulate the way that new products will behave. Production can also make use of robots and automated procedures to make manufacturing cheaper and more efficient.

## What you need to do:

- To achieve Level ❶    you need a basic description of the main techniques of internal and external communication used in your businesses, including IT.
- To achieve Level ❷    you need a clear and coherent description of communications between functional areas, including by IT.
- To achieve Level ❸    you need a detailed examination of how good communications, including IT, supports the work of the business. You should suggest improvements or developments in It that might help the business in the future.

CHAPTER 18

# Business communication – internal and external

Good communication is vital to the efficient functioning of any business. Communication basically consists of four parts: the sender, the message, the medium and the receiver. The choice of medium – the way in which the message will be sent – depends on who is sending the message, who s/he is sending it to, and on its content. In particular, businesses need to ask themselves what is most important about a particular communication. For example, does it need to be quick, or cheap, or confidential?

*Figure 18.1* Networking – informal business meetings and decision-making – is often more powerful than formal meetings

## Internal oral channels

Some communication takes place inside the business, both within functional areas and between functional areas. Channels of communication are either formal or informal. Formal channels will take place within a framework that has already been laid down. They will probably include keeping a record of whatever has taken place. Informal channels can take place at any time and almost anywhere. They may be spoken (oral) or written channels, or may make use of technology to send, for example, graphs or pictures. Internal informal oral channels means, essentially, conversation; eg an instruction or request may be made. These channels include:

- presentations, lectures and speeches – often these take place in formal surroundings, such as a conference. They have the benefit to the presenter of being able to address a number of people at the same time and to use various display methods – such as slides, hand-outs, figures, graphs, charts and video to attract and maintain the audience's attention
- business meetings – these may be between different functional areas or within a functional area. The format for such meetings usually follows a set pattern.

## Internal written channels

**Formal** written channels include

- a memorandum (usually shortened to 'memo') – this may be written or typed but will usually contain a specific request or piece of information
- letters – examples include letters of enquiry, responses to enquiries and letters of invitation (eg to a meeting, conference or exhibition). Letters have traditionally been a fairly formal way of communicating, laid out according to set rules and essential in certain circumstances (eg a letter of resignation)
- reports – in general, a report should contain an introduction outlining the purpose of the report, a brief summary of the report, the main body (laid out in paragraphs and using sub-headings) and a conclusion

---

### TRUE OR FALSE?

*Networking is often a more efficient way of communicating than meetings*

*(see foot of page for answer)*

---

### Classwork activity

Choose the most appropriate method for each of the following communications:

- a request for a day's extra holiday from your boss
- a request for payment from a customer
- an order for goods or services
- a request for the times and fares for a journey from Exeter to Aberdeen – you need to know the cheapest option and the fastest option
- a confirmation of an order received.

In each case, suggest whether oral, written or IT would be best, and why.

---

**MEMO**

For the attention of all departments


**The fire alarm will be tested at 4pm today.**

This is a test only;
you do not need to follow procedures.

**Figure 18.2** *A formal business memo*

True or False answer

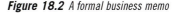
True. Many decisions and negotiations take place through informal networking.

101

## HOMEWORK ACTIVITY

Add three other communications to your classwork list, and say whether each should be oral, written or IT, and why.

- contracts – such as contracts of employment, or agreements with a supplier
- official communications – such as health and safety rules, invoices and customer accounts
- official notices (and noticeboards) – containing text such as safety rules.

**Informal** written channels include:

- notes taken at a meeting, conference or presentation
- informal memos and reminders – these are usually hand-written and short
- newsletter – many large businesses use an internal newsletter to give news of the business's developments and successes. They are also used to let people know what is happening in other parts of an business, to advertise social functions and internal appointments, and to provide a forum for staff to give their opinions
- notice boards – these can carry informal messages aimed at everyone
- email (see below).

## External oral channels

Businesses need to communicate with other businesses, with suppliers, with customers and with local and national government. Any communication which takes place between the business and an outside body is called an **external** communication. Again, these can be written or oral, formal or informal.

Informal oral channels include telephone calls, informal meetings and networking. Networking is the informal interaction and conversation that takes place between people at the start of a conference or meeting, or at coffee breaks or meal times. Networking may also take place on social occasions such as dinners, or even on

---

**MEMO**

Hi Jack,

Don't forget, the final report needs to be presented at the meeting tomorrow.

Jill

---

*Figure 18.3* An informal, one-to-one memo

the golf course. It is often a much more powerful method of communication and decision-making than any formal methods. Discussion can take place in private and without a record being taken. This may be important in reaching an agreement, which can then be confirmed through more formal channels.

Formal oral channels of communication can take various formats. They will be used where an official record needs to be kept. For example:

- interviews – when a panel or individual asks questions of a person (usually an applicant for a job, but other interview situations are possible, eg in a criminal investigation)
- presentations – these often take place when a business tries to sell its products to other businesses
- meetings – formal meetings could be arranged so that discussions and negotiations can take place
- conferences – these may involve listening to speakers or taking part in activities and discussions.

## Email

Informal written channels used to be rare, as it was not usual to write between organisations if no record needed to be kept. Even invitations between organisations tended to be formalised. However, the increasing use of email has tended to make this informal, written channel perhaps the most widespread way of communicating, both within and between organisations.

Email messages tend to be short and to the point, can be sent to many people at one time, are quick, and are not bound by the sorts of rules of formality that accompany formal letter writing or other documentation. Using email also means that a record is kept. However there are two major drawbacks of e-mails:

1 They are so easy to use that people use them far too much, when other methods of communication would be more efficient. There is also no guarantee that the receiver actually reads or deals with emails – especially if there are a lot of unnecessary communications in the 'in-box'.
2 Emails are not secure. Other people both within and outside the organisation can read them if they have the skills to get into the system.

**Figure 18.4** *Computer applications have become essential to the modern business*

### For your portfolio

You should have a section in your portfolio headed 'Communication'. Look at the communications that are used in your chosen businesses and describe what makes a method appropriate. Use these questions:

- Does it need to be quick?
- Does it need to be cheap?
- Does it need to be accurate?

- Does it need to be formal or informal?
- Does it need to impress the receiver?
- Is the security of the message an issue?
- Is it going to one person or many?
- If many, do they all need to get it at the same time?
- Also what sort of a reply should be expected, how, and when?

### CITIZENSHIP

*The local community does not always know what is going on in your school or college, and schools or colleges do not always know what is going on in the local community. Discuss ways by which communications between educational establishment and community could be improved. Put some of the ideas into practice.*

**FACT FILE**

The people in a business meeting are:
• a chairperson, who opens and closes the meeting, decides who is to speak, when votes should be taken, and generally has control of the meeting
• a minute-taker (which may be a secretary) who records the discussions and decisions
• members.

The format for a business meeting is usually as follows:
• An agenda is issued for the meeting – this is the list of items to be discussed.
• The agenda will start by recording who is present and the apologies for absence.
• The next item will be the 'minutes' of the last meeting – this is the written record of who took part and what decisions were made. People who were at the meeting must agree these minutes as a true record. Sometimes these are called 'action' minutes. The discussion which led to decisions is not recorded, just the decisions that have been made and, more importantly, who is to carry them out.
• Matters arising from the minutes, ie discussion that comes directly from the last meeting, will then be discussed.
• Agenda items are then discussed in order.
• The final item on the agenda is usually 'any other business' (aob). This means that the meeting is free to discuss any other items.

## ACTIVITY

Communication flows are

Horizontal – across from one level to the same level

Vertical – up – from one level up to a higher level

Vertical – down – from one level down to a lower

♦ Give one example of each type of communication in your school or college

♦ Give one example of each type of communication in a chosen business.

♦♦ Which of the three is most efficient in school or college?

♦♦ Which of the three is most efficient in the business.

♦♦♦ Explain what problems might be caused due to the most inefficient method of the three in both the educational establishment and the business.

♦♦♦ What solutions would you suggest for these problems?

## External written channels

Much external communication is carried out using formal documents. This is due to one or more of the following reasons:

• An official and formal record of a transaction or communication needs to be kept.
• A particular format or layout is necessary. Often a pre-printed form has been designed to make sure that no vital information is actually missed out.
• A format has been designed to work with certain machinery (such as computers or printers).
• Many copies of a document may be needed; it therefore needs to be standard. (A job application form is a good example of this.)

The main types of formal documentation used between businesses and from business to customer include the following:

• letter of enquiry – a formal letter requesting information, catalogues etc
• the catalogue, information leaflet or price list
• order – a list of requirements properly signed and authorised by a member of staff
• bill or account – notice of the amount to pay and a request for payment, often with itemised details of the items ordered
• invoice – request for payment for work done or goods delivered, sent by the business or individual who did the work.

There are also many formal documents specific to particular trades or industries. A person importing or exporting goods, for instance, will have to fill in various forms for government and for the carriers – ship owners, haulage firms or other freight carriers. This is so that the carrier knows exactly what is being carried and any particular problems that might occur with the goods. Any business dealing in goods that may be dangerous, or inflammable, or even alive (eg livestock), will also have to fill in specialist forms.

## Documents and the public

There are also documents that, for certain businesses, must be formally made available to the general public. The main formal external document of this type is the Company Report and Accounts. This must be produced at least once a year and contains details of the company's trading, directorial staff, dividends paid to shareholders, profits and losses throughout the year. The accounts contain a detailed picture of where money has come from and where it has been paid.

These detailed reports will be presented at the formal meeting of shareholders that is held once a year – the Annual General Meeting – so that the company's shareholders have all the details regarding the company's performance. A public limited company must make these details available to any member of the public on request and must lodge them with Companies House.

Businesses which are not companies do not have shareholders (eg sole traders, partnerships and co-operatives) so do not have to provide these documents. They can therefore keep their affairs confidential – one of the reasons why many businesses of this nature choose not to become limited companies (see Chapter 2).

## Neither oral nor written forms of communication

Modern methods of communication, particularly those using new technology, can be used to replace expensive methods such as meetings. Video-conferencing, for example, can be used, or conference calls – where more than two parties can be connected to the same telephone conversation (see Chapters 17 and 18).

## KEY *SKILLS*

Communication. The discussion that takes place about improving communication between the community and you, could help you achieve one of the key skills levels.

## KEY *TERMS*

- Channels of communication – the way in which messages can be passed
- Medium – the method by which a message is sent; the plural (often used of radio, TV and newspapers) is media.
- Networking – informal (but powerful) meetings, usually at or around a more formal meeting

## EXTENSION EXERCISE

Find out what formal documents would be needed for the export of a bulk shipment of powdered fertiliser from the UK to America by sea. Explain why each document is needed.

Businesses may also communicate with both customers and suppliers through exhibitions and trade shows. Major trade shows for an industry attract thousands of visitors (eg the Motor Show, the Chelsea Flower Show, the Ideal Homes Exhibition, the Boat Show) and are used by manufacturers, wholesalers and retailers to display their latest goods. Many of these are in London, or at the National Exhibition centre in Birmingham. Smaller trade shows also take place around the country.

Communication may also employ visual aids such as drawings, graphics and video, although these are likely to be part of other forms of communication such as presentations.

**Figure 18.5** *The Boat Show – a major way for boat sellers to meet boat buyers*

## What you need to do:

- To achieve Level ❶    you need a basic description of the main techniques of internal and external communication used in your businesses.
- To achieve Level ❷    you need a clear and coherent description of communications between functional areas.
- To achieve Level ❸    you need a detailed examination of how good communications supports the work of the business and its functional areas. You should suggest improvements the business could make to communicate with customers, particularly through the use of IT.

CHAPTER 19
# Being competitive

A business will usually face some form of competition. This will be from other businesses which provide the same or a similar good or service. Sometimes this competition is obvious – two florists or two banks next door to each other are in direct competition. At other times, the level of competition – or where it is coming from – is less obvious. There may be only one fishmonger in a village, so it looks like there is no competition. However, the village fishmonger will actually be competing with any shop that sells frozen fish, the local fish and chip shop and supermarkets that have fish counters (and sell frozen fish). It is also competing with anyone who sells meat, or any other foods, which someone might wish to buy in preference to fish.

**Figure 19.1** *Petrol stations are often in direct competition with each other*

# Types of competition

Competitors are one of the groups of stakeholders in a business because they are trying to sell to the same customers. Any action by a business to compete more effectively will have an effect on every other business in that market.

Businesses may compete with each other by charging different prices or by providing different levels of service and other 'extras'. If they compete on price, this is called **price** competition; on anything other than price, it is called **non-price** competition. Businesses may also compete on quality, by offering a better range, better performance, or higher specification of a good or a service.

If, however, the difference becomes too great, then the businesses may no longer be competing with each other. Is a top fashion designer who makes one-off dresses really competing with a high street clothes shop? Although they may be said to be in the same market (clothes) they are so far apart that neither would consider the other to be a competitor. Competing on quality within the same market is really a form of non-price competition.

# Price competition

Price competition means that a business is offering the same good or service at a lower price than a competitor. This is not always as easy as it sounds, as each business is likely to face the same costs. Imagine two competing garages selling petrol. Each buys it at the same price from a supplier. Each has overheads in the form of premises, staff, power etc which are unlikely to be very different. Price competition in this sort of circumstance can usually only take place for short periods of time – or, if it cuts into profits, may not be possible at all.

## Types of competitive pricing

Businesses can use various different types of pricing to try to compete, depending on the product being sold, and the type of market they are competing in (see Chapter 00). The main forms of competitive pricing are:

- **Promotional pricing** – where a temporary price reduction is made, usually flagged up with stickers or advertisements for '10% off' or 'half price' for example.
- **Loss leaders** – where the business charges less for an item than it actually cost, in order to lead people into buying other items (on which the business can make a profit). For example, supermarkets often sell bread at a loss, knowing that customers will buy other things while in the store.
- **Penetration pricing** – when a business wants to break into a new market, so it charges a special low or introductory price. Once it has established a market share, the price is then likely to rise.

## Classwork activity

You have been asked by a major company, which produces a range of products, to create a new logo. It should say everything people want to know about the business. Their image is:
- bright
- new
- fast
- fashionable
- jazzy
- environmentally concerned
- technologically forward looking

Design the logo, remembering that the company do not want you to use their name or initials in it. Write a page to explain to the business how your logo fulfils their requirements.

## True or False answer

**False.** Some businesses may have costs so similar to their competitors that they cannot afford to lower price.

## HOMEWORK ACTIVITY

Find three products at home that are part of a promotion (good places to look are cereal packets and washing powder). Interview the person that bought them to find out if they were affected by the promotion.

What do their answers tell you about the effectiveness of promotions?

## For your portfolio

You should have a section in your portfolio headed 'Competition'. In it you should list

- the main competitors for each of your two businesses

- the 'secondary' competitors for each business

You should explain how your businesses have responded to competition from these competitors in the past, and suggest ways by which they might compete in the future.

- **Skimming or creaming** – when a business is introducing a brand new product, it can sometimes charge a high price for those customers who want to be first with the product. This often happens with new technology; examples include computers, digital cameras, wide/flat screen television and video recorders.
- **Destroyer or predator pricing** – when a business sets a deliberately low price in the hope of driving a competitor out of business.

### Can I compete on price?

Some businesses are in **direct** competition with each other. If there are two butchers, greengrocers, hairdressers or pubs in a village or on a high street, then they will be competing directly for the same customers. The degree by which one business competes with another depends on how closely the products that they each sell can be substituted for each other.

Imagine going to a market where only eggs are being sold by a large number of market traders. All the eggs look the same, and are packaged the same. They are all priced at the same price. (In a case like this, because there are so many sellers, the price will have fallen to the lowest possible level that will allow the sellers to stay in business.) What is going to make you buy from one seller rather than from another? In a case like this, the goods are so alike that there may seem to be nothing to make the consumer buy one rather than another.

But even in this case there are differences that can allow businesses to compete. For example, you may prefer brown or white eggs, or speckled ones, or they may come in different sizes, so that you are not actually buying like-for-like.

There are bound to be other differences. The stallholder nearest

**Figure 19.2** *Head-to-head competition; Lloyds pharmacy and Boots. What advantages are there to the business? To the customer?*

the market entrance will have a competitive advantage – as will the one nearest to the car park or bus stop. The owners of the market are likely to have recognised this, and will charge slightly higher rent for such locations. The sellers will have recognised it, and are likely to charge slightly higher prices. Where would you expect to find the cheapest eggs on the market?

## Non-price competition

Non-price competition is when businesses compete with each other in different ways. Examples of non-price methods of competition include:

- providing a better service than a competitor, such as opening for longer hours
- selling a wider range of products than a competitor
- providing the customer with convenience and extra facilities, such as car parks, bag packing services, extended opening hours and personal service
- adding value – eg with special promotions such as 'buy one, get one free' or 'free x with every purchase of y'
- offering free gifts or other rewards for customer loyalty (often through the use of loyalty cards).

Often, however, there is a cost involved with such 'extras' which mean that, eventually, prices will actually be higher than competitors. Businesses are gambling on customers regarding the extras as more important than the price difference.

### Branding

One of the main ways in which a business tries to make itself different from all the other businesses in a market is through **branding**. This means giving a product a particular brand name and identity. This is usually reinforced through particular colours, slogans, lettering and logos. Even though the brand may have

## CITIZENSHIP

*Competition can mean that businesses exploiting labour in order to keep costs down and market share up. Visit www.corpwatch.org to find out information on how corporations are being competitive in this way. Write a brief outline of your views on the issues once you have looked at the site.*

## **L3 KEY SKILLS**

IT and Communications. Use IT to create a poster or series of overheads for a presentation on global corporate responsibility. You will need the information from the Citizenship task (above).

## ACTIVITY

♦ **Suggest the type of pricing that would be most appropriate for the following**

- **a new portable DVD device which is expensive but runs current DVDs**
- **a new portable DVD device which is cheap but needs special, expensive DVDs**
- **a new flavour of ice cream**
- **a new brand of orange juice, where you really want to build market share**
- **to get rid of old stock before the spring fashions come in**

♦♦ **In each case, suggest why it would be most appropriate.**

♦♦♦ **For at least two examples, choose another possible pricing strategy and explain how the situation would need to change to make this the most appropriate method.**

**Figure 19.3** *A quality product is one that does exactly what it is claimed it will do*

developed in connection with a particular range of goods, businesses will often transfer it to other products as a way of competing. The Nike brand, for example, may be found on many other items than sports shoes. It has been transferred to many types of sports equipment and leisure wear, but also to items that have no connection with sport, such as mugs and pencil cases.

## Quality

A separate area under non-price competition is **quality**. In business, a quality product is defined as one that does exactly the job that the consumer wants it to do. A black bin bag may not be thought of as a 'quality' product but, providing that it holds rubbish without tearing, it is exactly the quality that it needs to be.

Consumers often think of quality in different terms. Many think that quality means that a product has to be expensive. This is not the case. A cheap product can be just as much a quality product as an expensive one – providing it fulfils the function that it is supposed to. It is therefore important for any business to make sure that it is dealing in exactly what its customers want.

## Availability

It is important to customers that the businesses they use provide not only what they want, but where and when it is wanted. Businesses must be prepared to open the hours that customers prefer, or to come to customers' homes, or be prepared to lose custom. For example, the rental business which has the latest blockbuster DVD, in sufficient numbers, available late at night, will win out over the business that does not adapt to its customers wants. It is even better if it can collect and deliver!

## Aims and objectives

How does the level of competition affect the aims and objectives of the business? If there is a lot of competition, a business may find that it is not able to focus on its aims and objectives as much as it would like. A business may have an aim of being more environmentally

**FACT FILE**

A price war is when two (or more) competitors try to beat each other by lowering prices. Each lowers prices further than the other until one is forced out of business. This is good for the customer in the short term as there are lower prices. However, in the longer term, there will be less choice and higher prices. Less choice because there is now only one business where before there were at least two; higher prices as the business tries to recoup the losses it made during the price war.

## KEY *TERMS*

Branding – providing a product (or range) with a distinct and recognisable identity
Destroyer or predator pricing – prices set deliberately low to put competitors out of business
Loss leaders – charging less for an item than it actually cost, in order to lead people into buying other items
Non-price competition – competing through ways other than by lower prices
Penetration pricing – a special low or introductory price to enable a business to establish a market share
Price competition – competing by charging lower prices than competitors
Promotional pricing – temporary price reductions to boost sales
Quality – in business, a product that does what it is supposed to do
Skimming or creaming – a high price for those customers who want to be first with a new product
Stakeholders – any person or group with a concern in the success of the business

# EXTENSION EXERCISE

Find out about recent price wars that have taken place (in the last five years). What was the immediate effect of the price war? What was the long term effect? What does this tell you about price wars?

aware and want to change its production process so that it causes less pollution. Competition may mean that it cannot now afford the change, as it has to put resources into advertising or promotion instead. It is also possible, however, for competition to force a business to achieve its objectives (one of which is often to be more competitive), by making it more efficient so that it can better compete.

## What you need to do:

- To achieve Level ❶     you will need a description of some of the main external influences on each of your chosen organisations, including their main competitors.
- To achieve Level ❷     you will need an assessment of the impact on each of your chosen organisations of market competition.
- To achieve Level ❸     you will need an example of how competition has, or might, affect each business.

CHAPTER 20

# Building customer profiles

Products are very carefully targeted by businesses. A good business has not only a particular market, but also a particular sub-section or segment of that market in mind when it produces a good or service. In many cases it has developed a picture of an ideal customer. For example, a car may be aimed at a 25–30-year-old working mother, who needs it to take children to school and herself to work in town traffic. Another may be aimed at a 55-year-old company director, who needs it to impress other company directors and clients. These may be one and the same car, but have different features emphasised for the different targets! Each customer 'picture' like this is known as a customer profile.

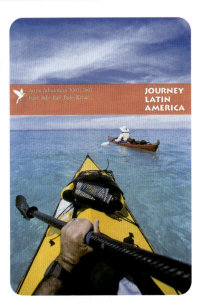

*Figure 20.1* Holiday companies need to appeal to all the different types of customer

## Identifying the customer

To build a customer profile, a business has to know about its own market. It needs to know both the size of the market and its structure so that it can target the precise part of the market that it needs to. Markets are divided up into separate parts or segments, to make it easier for businesses to target products. Market segments can themselves be sub-divided, making ever smaller and more specialist markets. These tiny, specialist markets are called **niche** markets (a niche is a small hole, or gap).

In many cases, the market is divided so many times that it comes down to a market of one, a single individual. Anyone who has had anything custom-made – a wedding dress, business suit, furniture or kitchen worktops to fit a particular space – or received any service that is unique to them – like having a haircut – has actually bought from a niche market of one.

## Market segments

Look at Figure 20.2. It shows how the market for holidays could be segmented (there are many other ways of doing this!). The bold lines show that one particular market would be holidays to the Football World Cup in Korea and Japan; different types of transport and accommodation make up different packages. Even the games which supporters wanted to watch could be pre-booked for them, making each package individualised – a niche market.

Markets are most commonly divided (or segmented) by one or more of:

- age
- gender
- geography
- income and lifestyle.

## Age

There are various well-defined age groups, with particular patterns of spending. Under 12s, for example, have no income but can still be targeted by advertisers. This is because they will use 'pester power' to get parents to buy products. Television advertisements are therefore often timed to be shown when both under 12s and their parents will be watching.

Other important age groups are the average age when couples get married; the time when people are at their maximum earnings; the time when parents have teenage children; and the time when their children have left home (known as 'empty nesters'). The age of retirement will also be a target for certain

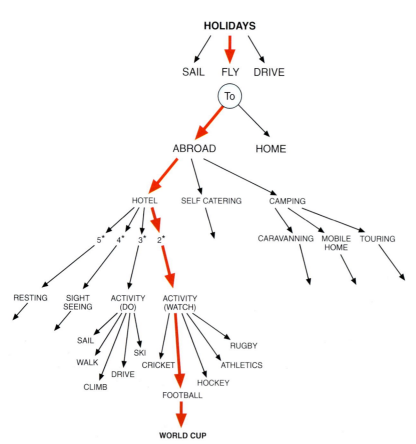

**Figure 20.2** *Market segmentation the holiday market has to cater for everyone's tastes. In this case a World cup supporter in a 2\* hotel*

products. Even though marketers recognise that income is likely to have fallen, they also know that retired people have few debts and much free time, and so can target products accordingly. Look at some holiday brochures in a travel agent or on the internet and notice the difference (in style, content and advertising) between various travel companies.

## Gender

One recent clever advertisement for Fiat Punto was split into two. One half showed all the features of the car that a woman would like (such as safety and style); the other highlighted the sort of features that might attract a man (engineering, speed, performance and electrical 'extras'). The advertisement used stereotypes to make its point that the car would be good for either gender.

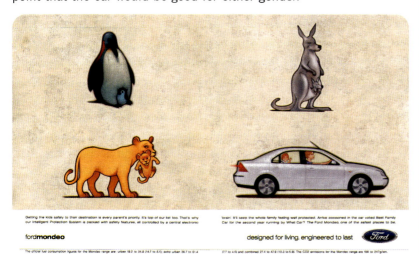

Getting the kids safely to their destination is every parent's priority. It's top of our list too. That's why our Intelligent Protection System is packed with safety features, all controlled by a central electronic 'brain'. It'll keep the whole family feeling well protected. Arrive cocooned in the car voted Best Family Car for the second year running by What Car? The Ford Mondeo, one of the safest places to be.

ford**mondeo**

designed for living. engineered to last

The official fuel consumption figures for the Mondeo range are: urban 19.2 to 34.0 (14.7 to 8.1); extra urban 36.7 to 61.4 (7.7 to 4.6) and combined 27.4 to 47.9 (10.3 to 5.9). The CO2 emissions for the Mondeo range are 196 to 247g/km.

*Figure 20.3* Which market segment or segments is Ford aiming at here?

## Geography

Spending habits vary in different parts of the country. In the South East, for example, many people commute to work in London, making this a major part of their expenditure. There are also different regional tastes – in food, entertainment and leisure activities, for example. Advertising media have recognised this; eg many newspapers publish different regional editions, and television advertising can be limited to a particular television region.

## Income and lifestyle

The population is officially classified into a number of groups according to the job, earnings and education of the head of the household. Advertisers and government use these segments extensively. They are called socio-economic groups.

### Classwork activity

List five of the goods or services produced by either or both of your two chosen businesses. For each, say

> Which market segment – precisely – you think it is targeting

>> Which other market segment could be targeted by the same product

>>> What sort of advertising or promotion you would recommend in order to target the new segment.

### HOMEWORK ACTIVITY

Look at the figure for market segmentation of the holiday market and choose a different way of segmenting this particular market. Draw the diagram. Collect three holiday brochures and say exactly which segment they are targeted at.

### True or False answer

**False.** Niche markets are actually very common, particularly in service industries. Often a particular service *has* to be customised for a customer or small group of customers.

## KEY SKILLS

IT. Look at the websites of at least five different businesses that operate in different markets. What are the similarities between them? What are the differences? Explain how the websites reflect the market segment that the business is targeting.

### For your portfolio

Which market segment does your chosen businesses target? Build a customer profile for each of your businesses to show the market segment and type of customer that they are targeting. You should add an

explanation of how they ensure that their target market is as unique as possible, and compare this with the target market of competitors.

## CITIZENSHIP

*Visit the site of the Office of National Statistics (www.statistics.gov.uk) to see how government statisticians divide the market. Do you agree with the way this is done? For exampe, is it fair to include single parents, retired people and students in the poorest social group? Won't some of them be quite wealthy? Suggest a fairer way of dividing a society.*

## ACTIVITY

♦ Watch one or two sets of commercial television advertisements at four different times during a weekday:

- between 7.30 and 9.00 in the morning
- between 10.00 and 11.30 in the morning
- between 4.00 and 5.30 in the afternoon
- between 8.30 and 10.00 at night.

♦♦ Describe the main or core market segment being targeted at each time.

♦♦ Describe any other market segments that might be targeted.

♦♦♦ Suggest a product that a business might advertise in each slot and explain why it would be a good slot for them.

### Socio-economic groups

The government categorises society as follows:

1 Group A are top earning professional people, eg high court judges and university professors.
2 Group B are people in management, technical and executive jobs such as bank managers, teachers, solicitors and accountants.
3 Group C1 are people in supervisory or clerical non-manual occupations such as sales assistants, filing clerks and secretaries.
4 Group C2 are skilled manual workers (often self-employed) such as carpenters, electricians and plumbers.
5 Group D are semi-skilled manual workers such as assembly line workers, packers and fitters.
6 Group E are low or fixed income groups. This includes unskilled manual workers, the unemployed, single parents, state pensioners and students.

### Other segments

Marketers can target any segment that can be recognised and separated from others. Other ways of segmenting include:

- **race** – certain products will only be useful to certain races, or generally used or eaten by them
- **religion** – certain products will be more usually used or needed by certain religions; good examples are foods that have to be prepared in special ways (such as Kosher or Halal meat); there will also be magazines and other publications which target these groups
- **interest or hobby** – specialist niches exist for hobbies and interests providing the clothing, tools, equipment, publications etc needed for that particular pastime
- **behaviour** – businesses can target people who buy in particular ways: many businesses aimed at young people, for example, deliberately encourage impulse buying (buying on the spur of the moment).

## Customer profiles

Everyone in the population will be in several different market segments, helping marketers to more clearly target through customer profiles. A magazine such as Heat, for example, is targeted at

1) girls
2) 14–16-year-olds
3) interest areas of television soaps, show business personalities and gossip.

Compare this with Hello! magazine – targeted at much the same interest area, but obviously at women rather than girls, and at a much older age group. Looking at the advertisements in a magazine will give a very good idea of the customer profile that the particular business is building.

## Marketing and Sales

The job of deciding which market segment to target with a particular product belongs to the Marketing and Sales area. It is this area that will build up the customer profile – essentially a picture of the ideal customer – and then make sure that all advertising and promotional material is targeted at that 'ideal'.

Information is available from specialist publications, websites and government figures (such as the national statistics office at www.statistics.gov.uk).

## Small businesses

Small businesses may not have a specific marketing area to carry out the marketing function, but will still target a particular market. Sometimes this comes from local knowledge (eg the corner shop that knows which products its customers like) and also by looking at what the competition offers. Small businesses are often established on the back of particular market trends. Since garden makeover programmes started trends in decking and water features, businesses have sprung up to provide just these services. Just because a business is small doesn't mean that it is not perfectly capable of forming its own customer profiles and targeting accordingly.

| Group | are.................... |
|-------|-----------|
| A | professional |
| B | management |
| C1 | supervisory |
| C2 | skilled manual |
| D | semi-skilled manual |
| E | fixed income |

**Figure 20.4** *Magazines cater for many different socio-economic groups. Which is this one aimed at?*

**FACT FILE**

*Marketing people have special shorthand for particular target market groups. A young couple with no children would be called 'DINKYs', standing for Dual Income No Kids. Perhaps the best known abbreviation was YUPPY, standing for Young, UPwardly mobile, Professional.*

## KEY TERMS

Customer profile – a picture of the 'ideal' customer
Market segment – a part of a market
Niche market – a very small market segment
Pester power – term used by marketers to describe the way that younger children can persuade parents to buy for them
Socio-economic groups – how government and statisticians divide the population by income and education
Target market – the market segment that the business is aiming at

## EXTENSION EXERCISE

Suggest three ways in which a local, small business could extend the range of customers that it is appealing to. Explain whether or not it would be worthwhile for the business to do so, and why.

## Branding

The use of brand names is another way in which businesses target particular groups. Modern brands are not always linked to a particular product, but are aimed to portray a particular lifestyle or way of doing things; eg the Coca-Cola 'image' is youth and freedom. Some brands are so linked to the lifestyle idea of branding that they don't actually produce anything. Tommy Hilfiger underwear is made by Jockey, its Tommy shirts are made by a firm in Oxford, its jeans by a business in London and its footwear by the Stride Rite Corporation of America. The brand is what provides all these goods with an identity, which can then be linked to a particular 'lifestyle' market segment.

## What you need to do:

- To achieve Level ❶     you will need a description of some of the main external influences on each of your chosen organisations, including their main competitors.
- To achieve Level ❷     you will need an assessment of the impact on each of your chosen organisations of market competition.
- To achieve Level ❸     you will need an example of how competition has, or might, affect each business.

CHAPTER 21

# Coping with competition

Another external influence which businesses have no control over is their competitors. Only a business which sold an absolute essential and had the complete monopoly on a market could be said to have no competitors. As the only essentials are air, water, food and shelter, it is not possible for such a monopoly to exist. Even businesses which may look like they have complete control usually face some form of competition. The Microsoft Corporation, for example, still faces competition from other operating systems (such as Unix) and other platforms (such as Macintosh).

*Figure 21.1* *There is fierce competition in the market for computer games*

## Markets

Competition takes place in a market. This does not mean that the market has to be a collection of stalls, like a second-hand market; it does not have to have a 'physical' existence or a specific location at all – it is anywhere that businesses compete.

Nowadays this may be in a village, town or city high street, or it is just as likely to be internationally, over the internet. Think about the market for insurance, for example. If you wanted to insure a car, or needed travel insurance, where could you go? You might go to a car sales showroom or a travel agent, who might be able to help you. Or you could ring up one of the businesses that provide insurance by telephone, or you could log onto the internet and search for insurance – you could even look through a telephone directory for an address and write for a quote. You might use Teletext or Ceefax on television to get a contact, or respond to an advertisement. But where are all these businesses in the insurance market? Some are on the high street, others tucked away in telephone call centres, and others – accessed through web sites – may not even be in this country at all! They are still all part of the same market.

## The size of market

Think about the market for fast food. It is itself part of the market for food (and only a fairly small part of it). This market can first be divided into hot and cold food. Competing in the hot food market are traditional fast foods such as fish and chips and hotdogs; next to them are imported ideas such as burgers, pizzas, curries and kebabs. In each of these markets different businesses compete – in the burger market it is McDonald's, Burger King and Wimpy; in the pizza market it is Domino's, Pizza Hut and supermarkets making pizza to order. Each business will try to divide the market even further – do you want to sit and eat your pizza here, or take it home? Do you want to take it yourself, or have it delivered? What size would you like it? Thick or thin crust? What toppings would you like on it? What would you like with it?

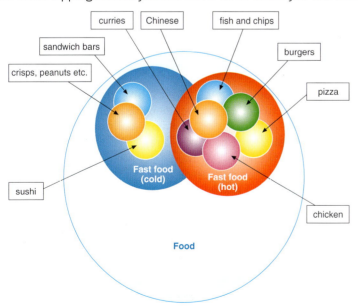

**Figure 21.2** *Segmenting the food market*

**Classwork activity**

How has the market for telephones changed over the last 40 years? Draw up a table, and for each of the factors of income, time, technology and tastes say how the market has changed for households, businesses and individuals. Choose one of the changes for each group which you think has been the most significant, and give a reason for your answer.

# CITIZENSHIP

*Find out about the work of the Competition Commission. Do you think that it is right that a government-appointed body should decide what is best for consumers? Discuss whether you think consumers would be better to make their own decisions. Look at the politics of the last 30 years. Do you think that government should intervene in the market, or should markets be 'free'?*

## For your portfolio

You should find out what sort of online competition faces each of your chosen businesses. Look at the main goods or services which they produce and see how many other businesses you can find competing based in the UK, or internationally.

The main UK search engines are www.freepage.co.uk; www.Google.co.uk; www.searchuk.co.uk; www.ukdirectory.co.uk; www.ukindex.co.uk;

www.ukplus.co.uk; www.yahoo.co.uk; www.yell.co.uk.

The main worldwide search engines are: www.Altavista.com; www.excite.com; www.google.com; www.hotbot.com; www.infoseek.com; www.lycos.com; www.northernlight.com; www.webcrawler.com; www.Yahoo.com.

The market for food is a huge market, known as a **mass market**. As providers become more and more specialised, markets become smaller and smaller, eventually becoming a niche market. If you wanted an apple-flavoured pizza with extra custard – and a pizza seller was willing to make you one – you would have just created a niche market of one.

## Types of market

Markets are usually defined by the number of businesses that are in the market. In some markets there are many competing businesses, in others only a few. In some cases, there may be said to be no real competitors. The main types of market are:

- **Competitive** – when there are a lot of businesses, usually of a similar size, competing for customers. Examples could be a local newsagent, opticians or garden centres.
- **Oligopoly** – when the market is dominated by just a few businesses. Internationally, the oil market is dominated by half a dozen companies; in the UK, banking is an oligopoly – with HSBC, Lloyds, NatWest, Barclays and Halifax being the major players. Another UK example is the supermarkets, where the big four are Tesco, Asda, Sainsbury's and Safeway.
- **Duopoly** – a market which is dominated by just two businesses. One example in the UK is the market for soaps (soap, soap powders, washing up liquids etc) where most of the market is in the hands of Lever Brothers and Procter & Gamble.
- **Monopoly** – a market which is dominated by a single firm. These can even exist on a worldwide basis, one example being the Microsoft Corporation. This company has the monopoly over the 'Windows' trade mark and operating system used by almost all personal computers.

## Competition Commission

Because competition is regarded as healthy, encouraging businesses to be more efficient and to produce new ideas and products, governments are usually against monopolies. In America, anti-trust laws mean that Microsoft has been taken to court in an attempt to break its monopoly. In the UK, the Competition Commission looks at proposed **mergers** between businesses to see if the new business (with less competition) will be 'in the public interest'. It can block mergers if it thinks that the lack of competition will be bad for the consumer. In Europe, the European Commission can do the same job.

## Identifying competitors

Any business should try to identify its possible local, national and international competitors so that it can compete more effectively. It will always be in the interests of a business to know who its competitors are, and how powerful they are in that particular market. Sometimes this is obvious (a sweet shop on the high street can see if there is another sweet shop down the road) but sometimes less so. There are a number of ways in which a business can find out about its competitors.

- **Observation** – even the sweet shop owner mentioned above will not know exactly what sort of competition s/he has unless s/he visits the other shop to find out. Businesses can often observe what competitors are doing, eg what new lines are being sold, and introduce their own competition in response.
- **Company reports** – public limited companies must publish annual reports and accounts for their shareholders; these, of course, can be read by competitor businesses, giving them a good idea of how competitors are performing.
- **Business Directories** – these may be general, eg for a particular geographical area, or specific to types of business, eg a directory of timber or building suppliers.
- **Yellow Pages** – businesses are grouped in this free publication by what they do or produce; it is easy to find where the local competition is situated.
- **Search engines** – using a search engine to look for competitors on the internet. This will show a business where both national and international competitors are competing online.

It is also important for a business to see how easily a competitor's product could be substituted for theirs, ie how similar it is, and to try to make theirs different (see Branding, Chapters 18 and 20).

## Changing markets

A number of factors has a direct effect on competition in a market. These factors will cause a market to change either its size or its structure. Sometimes a market will increase as more customers are convinced (or able) to buy a product. At other times, markets will shrink as customers leave. Changes in structure could mean changes

*Figure 21.3* Observation

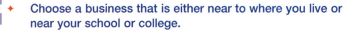

**HOMEWORK ACTIVITY**

Write down who makes the food you buy for your own pet, or that which is bought for a friend's pet. Bring this back into class. You can then collate the information to give you an idea of how many businesses there are in the food market, and which companies dominate it.

**ACTIVITY**

- ✦ Choose a business that is either near to where you live or near your school or college.
- ✦ Identify all the competitor businesses within a three mile, five mile and ten mile range.
- ✦✦ How far do you think that people will be willing to travel to buy these types of goods? Who are therefore the most significant competitors?
- ✦✦✦ What on line competitors does your business have? How ever many it is (and in some cases it will be none) explain why you think this is.

*Figure 21.4* There is not much call for gas lamps any more

# ⊏Ξ KEY *TERMS*

Blue sky market – a new market with no competitors
Competition Commission – government body that monitors takeovers and mergers, and prevents those it thinks will be against the public interest
Competitor – any business selling similar products, to similar markets
Duopoly – markets dominated by two businesses
Monopoly – markets dominated by one business
Niche market – the smallest market segment
Oligopoly – markets dominated by a few businesses

# ⊏Ξ KEY *SKILLS*

IT. Put the results of your search for competitors (using the search engines given) into a database. From this you should be able to draw conclusions about which search engine is the most/least effective.

## FACT FILE

*One of the reasons for taking some businesses into public (government) ownership was so that they could never be owned by a private monopoly. Since businesses like water, gas and electricity were put into the private sector, they have been encouraged to compete with each other. This means that you can now get electricity from a gas company, gas from an electricity company, or water from any of the water companies anywhere in the country!*

in the type of customer, or in the number of businesses competing. The most common influences causing change in a market are:

- **Income** – as the general level of income increases, customers are more likely to buy more expensive goods and services, and to cease buying cheaper ones. If a customer can afford, for example, to eat in an expensive restaurant, they are unlikely to choose to go to a burger bar instead. This causes one market (for the expensive good or service) to expand and another (for the cheaper good or service) to contract. Of course, this can also happen in reverse if incomes are falling – perhaps in a period of high unemployment, for example.
- **Time** – being first into a new market, before anyone else, can often give a business a huge advantage over its competitors. Launching a new product into a market is often called entering a 'blue sky market'. However, entrants know that, even if their product is protected by patents, competitors will be along sooner or later. An example can be found in computer games: the PlayStation 2 had new features which meant it was launched into a blue sky market; the X-box took some time to catch up with its own launch, but has then immediately provided strong competition.
- **Technology** – new technology replaces old, changing the market for both; eg gas lamps were replaced by electric light, which meant that all the businesses that produced gas lamps, or parts for them, had no market any more. A more modern example could be the technology of Dyson vacuum cleaners replacing old technology.
- **Tastes** – these change over time; they may include markets in food, fashion and furniture. Current trends in each include healthier eating, tattoos and piercing, and leather. Trends were different five years ago, and will be different again in five years' time.

Usually it is not just one of these factors that affects a market, but a combination. Often one factor can be stronger than the others. For

# EXTENSION EXERCISE

Find out who or what the Seven Sisters represent. Do you think that they are still as powerful as they ever were? Give reasons for your answer.

example, people may get more income but still *prefer* (taste) to go to a burger bar rather than an exclusive restaurant.

> ## What you need to do:
>
> - To achieve Level ❶   you will need a description of some of the main external influences on each of your chosen organisations, including their main competitors.
> - To achieve Level ❷   you will need an assessment of the impact on each of your chosen organisations of market competition.
> - To achieve Level ❸   you will need an example of how competition has, or might, affect each business.

CHAPTER 22

# Business and economic conditions

The general economic conditions in which businesses operate change from time to time. Sometimes, economies are 'booming', ie it is easy to get a job, there is a lot of consumer spending and the atmosphere is right for the successful launch of new products and businesses. At other times however, the economy is not in such a good state; there is high unemployment, much business failure and consumers unwilling to spend. The government of a country will try to solve these problems by using various policies to affect consumer spending and business confidence. The government's aim is to make sure that the economy of the country is managed in such a way that both customers and businesses can plan for the future with confidence.

It is important for businesses to be flexible enough to be able to respond to any changes that affect them. To do this, they need to recognise which changes are more important than others to them. It is also important for businesses to be able to predict possible changes so that they can plan for the future. One set of changes takes place through the operation of the business cycle.

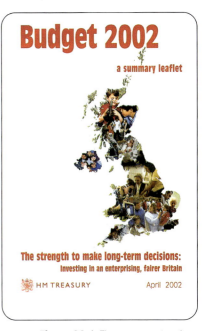

**Figure 22.1** *The government makes the case to support its planned taxation and expenditure*

## The business cycle – recession

The economy passes through cycles of growth and decline (see Figure 22.2). When the economy is in decline, this is called a recession. Usually this means that consumers are not buying as many goods, which, in turn, means that businesses either have to build up stocks, or cut down on production. If businesses are reducing the amount that they are producing, this will lead to less employment. Businesses may have to cease employing new workers, and also to make redundant existing ones or, at the very least, cut down on extras such as overtime.

This means that people's incomes are falling and there is likely to be a further reduction in the amount that people can afford to buy. People are also likely to have to draw on their savings, if their

## CITIZENSHIP

*Find out about the institutions which make up the government – at local level, the operation of your local council; at national level, how a law is passed and who is involved; at international level, about the institutions of the EU and how the EU affects business. Which level of government do you think is the most important? Why?*

incomes are falling. This means that the banks do not have so much money to lend, so interest rates (the cost of borrowing money) tend to rise. This also affects business decisions as to whether or not to borrow money for equipment, expansion etc. Because both customers and businesses are not spending so much, prices tend either to stay the same or fall – there is no pressure put on them to increase.

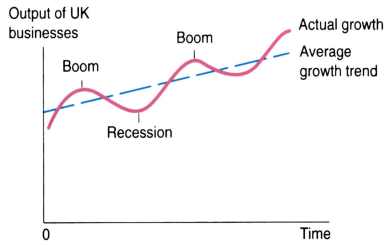

**Figure 22.2** *Cycle of growth and decline*

## The business cycle – turning points

At the bottom of the cycle, a number of things happen to cause it to turn. Businesses run out of the stocks that they have been holding and have to produce new items to stay in business; this means that they will have to increase employment. This, in turn, means that people are earning more money and will therefore spend more.

One of the main reasons for the turn is called 'expectations'. This means that consumers and businesses believe that the situation can get no worse and therefore expect it to get better. Because of this, businesses start to invest again and consumers start to buy. Banks will lower interest rates to try to persuade people to borrow money, and many businesses will offer special 'deals' to convince customers to buy – such as low or no interest credit.

## The business cycle – boom

As customers start to buy more goods and services, businesses need to produce more and therefore employ more workers. This means that people are earning more money and spending it. Wages tend to increase, as businesses need to pay more to attract labour. There will be little unemployment, so it is necessary for businesses to pay higher rates. As the 'boom' continues, prices will be pushed up and so will interest rates.

At the top of the cycle comes another turning point. People think things can get no better (expectations), borrowing has become

**Figure 22.3** *Some important industries will, in time, go into decline*

expensive and business costs are high. It only takes one or two major businesses to stop expanding, for others to soon follow suit.

## Government policy

Governments will try to use various policy tools in order to counteract the worst effects of the business cycle. These include changing the patterns of public spending – so that when businesses aren't spending or employing, the government is, or by using changes in taxation or interest rates.

### Interest rates

The level of interest rates affects a business by making the cost of borrowing money either cheaper or more expensive. Businesses borrow money for three main reasons:

1 To start up the business – raw materials must be bought and paid for before the business is earning any income.
2 For expansion in either size, the introduction of new products or for new or replacement machinery. Money will need to be borrowed to update plant and machinery.
3 To allow trade credit for its customers. Many business customers will not want to pay for goods straight away, but will expect to be able to receive an invoice from the business, and to pay later. Funds are needed to cover the time that this takes (often as long as three months).

The government no longer sets levels of interest rates; this power was given to the Bank of England in 1997. This is because governments have been known to change interest rates for political reasons, rather than economic ones. The Bank's Monetary Policy Committee meets once a month and decides, after looking at all the indicators in the economy, whether interest rates should go up or down. Sometimes the change is as small as a quarter of a per cent – but this can still have an effect on businesses. Changes in interest rates may particularly affect business expectations – if interest rates start to rise, however slowly, this could be enough to reduce business confidence.

True or False answer

**True.** Probably, based on the fact that the majority of the UK's foreign trade is with the other countries of the European Union.

## Prices

Businesses are concerned with both the general level of prices in an economy, and with the changes to that level. The general level of prices in the economy is important to businesses because it affects their ability to pay for raw materials or to plan for the future. A rise in the general level of prices is called **inflation**.

Perhaps more important is the direction in which prices are moving. Price rises can cause uncertainty for businesses. Uncertainty means that a business is not able to plan for the future. Changes in the general level of prices are measured by government through the retail price index (RPI). This takes a typical week's shopping for a family and tracks the changes in prices over a period of time. In this way, a business can see whether prices are generally rising and at what rate.

## Exchange rates

Businesses may also be affected by the prices of goods or services that they buy from overseas. These prices are changed by changes in the exchange rate. For example:

- If the exchange rate is $2 to £1 and an order from America costs $100, then the business will have to pay £50 to buy the dollars to buy the goods.
- If the exchange rate then changes so that £1 is worth less, the goods become more expensive.
- If the exchange rate is $1 to £1, then the business now needs £100 to buy the dollars to buy the goods.

This is an extreme example, but, when businesses are dealing in large orders, even a tiny change can be significant.

## FACT FILE

Another policy tool which can be used by government is that of regional policy. Governments can support particular regions which are suffering from, for example, industrial decline or unemployment (see Chapter 7 on the location of businesses). The European Union also has a Regional Fund which means that support can be directed to businesses both in particular industries (like the fishing industry) or in particular geographical regions.

## ACTIVITY

The 2002 Budget included the following major measures:

- a planned increase in spending on the NHS of over £35 billion over five years
- a one per cent increase in National Insurance Contributions
- a cut in the corporation tax rate for small companies (this is the tax on company profits)
- increases in child allowances, income support and the Working Families Tax Credit
- a freeze in fuel duties and road tax
- a freeze in duties on spirits, wine and beer
- an increase in duties on alcopops and tobacco.

✦ Find out what each of these measures means.

✦✦ Explain how you, personally, will be affected by these measures over the next five years – in particular, how your spending might be affected.

✦✦✦ Choose two businesses, in different markets, and explain how they are likely to be affected by each measure.

Changes in exchange rates affect customers as well, changing their spending. If the UK currency is strong, this makes exports more expensive and imports cheaper. This means that

- home customers are more likely to buy imported products than home-produced ones
- overseas customers are less likely to buy products from UK businesses.

However, this has to be balanced against the problems of a weak currency. If the UK currency is weak, exports are cheaper (good for businesses that are trying to sell products in overseas markets); but imported products are more expensive. Many UK businesses import raw materials from abroad, so a weak currency is bad for their business.

**Figure 22.4** *How much is that in 'real' money?*

## Managing the economy

The government uses various tools to manage the economy so that businesses and customers do not face too many uncertainties and can plan for the future. The major tools used are

- fiscal policy
- monetary policy.

### Fiscal policy

Fiscal policy involves changes in taxation and government spending. An increase in personal tax means that people have less money to spend. This will have an indirect effect on business. An increase in tax on business income or profits will directly affect businesses. For example, in the 2002 Budget, the Chancellor of the Exchequer promised to spend huge amounts on the National Health Service over the following five years (rising from £23.1 billion in 2003/4 to £105.6 billion in 2007/8). At the same time, however, taxation was put up at the same time (through National Insurance Contributions).

### Monetary policy

This involves using various instruments to change the amount of money in the economy. Money is not just notes and coins, but

## KEY TERMS

Business cycle – the general cycle of 'boom' and 'bust' that an economy passes through

Fiscal policy – changes in taxation and government expenditure

Inflation – a rise in the general level of prices

Monetary policy – changes in the amount of money and credit available in the economy

Recession – a period of falling demand, employment and business growth

RPI (Retail Price Index) – a measure of changing prices in an economy using a 'basket' of typical purchases

Trade credit – one business allowing another business to have goods and services now, and pay later

# EXTENSION EXERCISE

Look into the history of the trade cycle. When was the last time the UK was in a 'boom'? What were the effects on business?
When was the last time the UK was in a 'recession'. What were the effects on business?

includes credit. Changes in interest rates are the major factor in this, although governments can also affect money supply through their own borrowing and spending.

## What you need to do:

- To achieve Level ❶   you will need a description of some of the main external influences on each of your chosen organisations, including the underlying economic conditions in the country and the industry.
- To achieve Level ❷   you will need an assessment of the impact on each of your chosen organisations of current economic conditions.
- To achieve Level ❸   you will need an example of how changes in economic conditions has, or might, affect each business.

CHAPTER 23

# Businesses and the environment

Businesses can bring both benefits and disadvantages to the communities within which they operate. Some businesses may be noisy, or require heavy transport; some may deal in dangerous products or produce unpleasant waste products. Many businesses are able to regulate themselves, to make sure that the bad effects of their business do not upset the local community.

However, the government has also passed laws to make sure that businesses do not damage the environment or present a danger to communities. There are so many advantages to businesses of being environmentally responsible, that many do much more than government legislation makes them. The advantages include greater efficiency and lower costs, as well as the increased custom that comes from a better reputation. Being seen as environmentally friendly may be one of the main objectives of a business.

**Figure 23.1** *Industrial pollution: the various colours indicate the type of waste product that is being burnt off. The site itself presents a huge amount of visual and light pollution*

# External costs

The main problems are external costs – these are costs which are paid by the whole community, rather than by the business. The main external costs created by businesses are:

- **Air pollution** – in the form of fumes, smoke, smell or other waste products released into the air. Some of these can have a devastating effect; eg sulphur from UK power stations has been accused of damaging forests in Scandinavia.
- **Water pollution** – usually in the form of waste products, not properly treated, and released into streams and rivers.
- **Noise pollution** – this could be from the operation of the business (eg the use of heavy machinery, or the noise that is inevitable from an airport) or from the transport required to take raw materials in or finished products out.
- **Visual pollution** – many business sites (particularly factory sites, or those involved in heavy industry such as steelworks or oil refining) damage people's visual amenities by spoiling views, or just by looking ugly and unpleasant.
- **Safety hazards** – from increased traffic, or because of the nature of the business itself. The Sellafield nuclear waste recycling plant has been deliberately sited away from areas of dense population because it is dangerous.
- **Waste products** – apart from waste discharged into the air or water, many businesses produce other waste products that are either dangerous or difficult to cope with. For example, much plastic packaging does not break down and rot (bio-degrade) easily; used car tires are difficult to dispose of; refrigerators have to be disposed of so that the harmful chemicals in them are not released into the atmosphere.

# International environmental concerns

Global concerns about the environment have hit the headlines in recent years. Amongst the most reported are

- pollution concerns – the use of pesticides, insecticides and weed killers has proved fatal to much wildlife and even human populations
- the build-up of waste materials which cannot be easily destroyed or disposed of – particularly toxic waste
- holes or gaps in the ozone layer, caused, in the main, by the use of CFC gases in refrigerators and aerosols
- global warming the causes of which include the emissions of carbon dioxide from industry, the felling of large areas of rain forest and CFC gases.

In many cases, although there are laws in the UK to prevent further use or damage (such as on pesticides and CFCs), these do not always apply in the rest of the world, so the problem may still continue.

## TRUE OR FALSE?

*It is possible to consider even light to be a pollutant.*

*(see foot of page for answer)*

## Classwork activity

Draw a circle of one-mile radius from your school or college and from your home. Now see how many environmental problems you can find within the circle. It could be problems of emissions, noise, unsightly buildings, traffic, litter, waste etc. Mark them as 'hotspots' on your map. Choose the three worst hotspots and say what you think should be done about them.

## HOMEWORK ACTIVITY

Following on from the classwork activity, write a letter to a local councillor, pointing out the problems that you have found and recommending a course of action.

**True or False answer**

**True.** Light pollution refers to the artificial light that is used by industry (and households) in such amounts that it becomes difficult to see the night sky.

### for your portfolio

ISO 140001 is a management commitment to an environmental policy. The environmental policy will include the following:

- clearly defined environmental objectives
- a programme of activity including a management structure

- areas of responsibility and training
- regular reviews and audits to continue improvement.

If either of your businesses has ISO140001 (or EMAS), find out what they had to do to achieve it. If they don't have it, write a report to let them know how they could obtain it.

## CITIZENSHIP

As a class, write a letter to your MP about the five environmental hotspots that you agree are the worst.

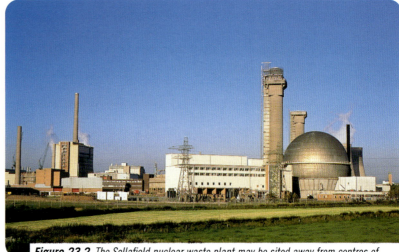

**Figure 23.2** *The Sellafield nuclear waste plant may be sited away from centres of population – but this means that it can be seen by visitors to the Lake District National Park*

## Sustainable Development Strategy

The Government has published a set of measures which it calls the Sustainable Development Strategy. Sustainable Development means that businesses should take no more out of a system than they put back in. An example would be to make sure that at least one tree is planted for each that is cut down. The Strategy involves preventing pollution, taking advantage of the new 'knowledge driven' economy and the efficient use of resources. Major initiatives include the:

- Green Fleet Certification Scheme – for owners of car or lorry fleets who convert them to cleaner fuels
- European Eco-Efficiency Initiative – designed to raise awareness of which businesses are doing best at eco-efficient operation so that other businesses can learn from them (called 'sharing best practice')
- Environmental Technology, Energy Efficiency and Construction Best Practice Programmes – practical help and advice to businesses wanting to become more environment friendly but cut costs at the same time
- Environmental Management Systems – formal schemes to show that a standard has been reached such as the ISO 14001 Standard or the European Union Eco-Management and Audit Scheme (EMAS).

## Government recommendations

The Government has recommended a number of ways in which businesses can help. Some of the things businesses can do are to:

- look at how operations are impacting on the environment, possibly through formal management systems (such as ISO 14001 or EMAS)

- work towards 'producer responsibility'. This means taking responsibility for every aspect of production – from the use of raw materials to the eventual disposal of a product
- design for sustainability – taking environmental concerns into account at the design stage
- be socially responsible: a 'good neighbour' to local communities, a good employer, a green producer
- be an 'ethical trader' – in other words, not using products made under poor conditions, like child labour, or which exploit people or environments
- communicate green standards to customers – through clear and accurate labelling and other publicity.

## New regulations

The Government is always looking at current problems, and ways in which laws or regulations may be introduced to reduce them. Some of the methods used are:

- tax incentives (lower taxation) for those businesses which are prepared to invest in energy saving technologies
- duties on cleaner fuels such as ultra-low sulphur petrol and diesel have been reduced in comparison with other fuels; special reductions in duty are planned to promote sulphur-free fuels
- the freezing of car road tax (properly called Vehicle Excise Duty) and introducing a lower rate of duty for those cars which are most fuel-efficient and least polluting.

# Environmental policies for businesses

Many businesses have recognised the effect that their business can have on the local, national and international environment, and have taken steps to reduce the impact. Many businesses also take advantage of these steps in their marketing – letting customers know of their environmental concern in the hopes that this will increase sales. The most common methods are:

1 Recycling paper and packaging, and using recycled paper for packaging (look for the recycling logo).

**Figure 23.3** *The FSC trademark identifies timber or other forest products from independently certified well managed forests.*

ACTIVITY

+List the environmental problems which your school or college causes. Think about waste, noise, traffic, visual pollution, use of resources etc.

++Write a policy for the school to follow that gives them five key points to look at, to improve their environmental standing.

+++Explain why you think that these points are important, and how easy it would be for the school to follow them.

## KEY *SKILLS*

IT and Communication. Go to www.environment-agency.gov.uk/business/and find out which regulations and legislation affect businesses. Use the information as the basis for a class discussion.

2 Only using timber or other forest products from sustainable forests – those managed in an environmentally appropriate, socially beneficial and economically viable way.
3 Fitting pollutant controls (such as smoke filters) wherever possible.
4 Transport – using 'green' fuels in transport that has high performance in terms of miles per litre, and fitted with pollution reduction devices such as catalytic converters.
5 Energy-saving policies; eg double glazing, insulation and lighting systems that switch on and off only when areas are in use.

### Residential areas

Businesses located in residential areas have to follow regulations concerning areas such as noise, dirt and operating hours. Businesses will not be allowed to operate between certain times and, in some cases, may be refused permission to operate at all because of noise or dirt issues. Businesses need planning permission to operate, and planning officers will look at areas such as transport, parking, noise, dirt and waste disposal before granting planning consent. Residents can object at any stage and, if they feel that businesses are not complying with planning regulations or consents, report them to the local planning officer, environmental health officer (for health and safety concerns, including excessive noise) or highways (for problems with traffic). Local councils and council officers operate the regulations.

### Current anti-waste laws

There are laws concerning specific waste items (eg the disposal of car tyres, building waste or waste motor oil) and often a charge is made for their disposal. The government also run a landfill tax scheme – businesses that need to dispose of waste in landfill sites are charged a tax. The money collected from this tax is used to benefit local communities directly through environmental improvement schemes.

### FACT FILE

*Pollution and environmental control can often help a business to achieve other objectives, such as reducing costs or increasing profits. Clark's, the shoe company, had to comply with a new law that said they must reduce the pollution caused by its use of solvents. It actually chose to invest in new machinery to get rid of the problem altogether at a cost of £250,000. However, the new machinery was so much better than the old, that they recovered the extra cost in a period of just six months. At the same time, of course, the move improved the image of the company with customers.*

## KEY *TERMS*

EMAS – European Union Eco-Management and Audit Scheme
Ethical trading – not trading with countries/businesses with unethical labour or trade practices
ISO 140001 – International standard for environmental business practice
Sustainable development – not taking more out of an environmental system than can be replaced

## EXTENSION EXERCISE

Using the information at www.environment-agency.gov.uk/business/, write an advice leaflet for both of your chosen businesses which concentrates on forthcoming legislation.

## What you need to do:

- **To achieve Level ❶**   you will need a description of some of the main external influences on each of your chosen organisations, including the environmental restrictions, concerns and legislation.
- **To achieve Level ❷**   you will need an assessment of the impact on each of your chosen organisations of environmental restrictions, concerns and legislation.
- **To achieve Level ❸**   you will need an example of how changes in environmental restrictions, concerns and legislation has, or might, affect each business.

# BUSINESS

## People and Business

# CHAPTER 24
# Internal stakeholders

If you have an interest in something then you have a stake in it – you are a stakeholder. Businesses have a number of groups of people who have stakes in them – in other words, who are concerned with the success of the firm. These are known as the *business' stakeholders*. One group of stakeholders may be considered as 'internal' – a part of the business. These are the owners, managers and other employees. 'External' stakeholders are customers, suppliers, competitors, government and the local community in which the business operates. Not all stakeholders necessarily want the same things out of a business. This means that there are often conflicts between the different objectives that stakeholders have.

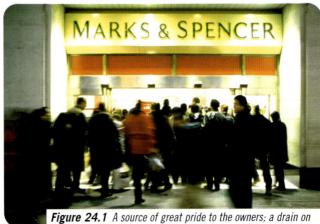

**Figure 24.1** *A source of great pride to the owners; a drain on capital to the managers; a place of employment to the workers*

## Owners' expectations

The owner of a business may be a single person (a sole trader), two or more people (a partnership), a group of people (a co-operative, the shareholders of a limited liability company) or the government (public sector ownership). There are likely to be different sets of aims for owners, depending on the type of business ownership. For a sole trader, partnership or co-operative, this may be the achievement of survival, independence or break-even; other forms of ownership may have their sights set on profitability. The one thing that all owners have in common is that they desire success of some description.

## Owners' influence

The owners of a business are likely to be the group that is most concerned with the success of the business. Their influence, ultimately, is greater than any other single group. They started (or bought) the business; they can close it down or sell it if they wish.

Owners are often entrepreneurs – the people who take the risk and, in return, get the rewards of business. It is likely that they have a lot of their own money (and hopes and ambitions) tied up in the business, so they will be very motivated to see it succeed. Even with this huge stake in the business, not all business owners are successful; 50% of all small business start-ups end in failure within two years of being established.

## True or False answer

**True.** Workers who do not feel that they are being properly rewarded can produce shoddy workmanship or even sabotage output.

**Figure 24.2** *Share trading used to take place on the floor of the stock exchange, so that scenes like this from the Financial Times Exchange were common. Now most dealing is done via computer*

## Shareholders

Shareholders are a special case of owners. In a small private limited company, the few shareholders are likely to behave much like any other owner – wanting success for the business and supporting it in achieving that success. In such small companies, the owners may well also be the managers of the business. The shareholders in larger (especially public) limited liability companies often have nothing to

### Classwork activity

The class should be divided into four groups, to represent:
- employees
- shareholders
- managers
- owners

Each should write down one way in which their group could influence the others, and one aim that they would be seeking.

Display this information so that you can choose the group that your group will most come into conflict with.

Suggest ways to resolve the conflict?

What does this exercise tell you about stakeholder groups?

**HOMEWORK ACTIVITY**

What do you think is meant by the term 'empire building' in a business? How might this make internal appointments more or less effective?

## For your portfolio

Using your chosen business, identify what the stakeholders expect from it – different stakeholders will have different expectations. You should list each stakeholder in a table and put in the next column what

their expectations are likely to be. In a third column write how each internal stakeholder can influence the business and how the business can react to these influences.

## CITIZENSHIP

*What rights and responsibilities do employers and employees have? Explain how these rights are upheld.*

### KEY SKILLS
**Information Technology 2.x**

Communication. Look through recent newspaper and magazine reports and find examples of stakeholder disputes. You could also search through news sites on the internet. Use the information you collect to make a display.

do with the business apart from the ownership of shares – in other words, they take no part in its management. These shareholders are likely to be mainly interested in getting a good return on the money they have spent on shares. They have two ways of getting a return:

- through dividends – their share of the profits of the business
- through an increase in the value of a share due to an increase in the value of the business

However, the price (and dividend returns) of shares does not always reflect how well or badly a business is doing. Prices could change due to actions that have nothing to do with the success of the business. For example, a business could gain a large new order; this success could see its share price rise; a major shareholder could decide that, with the shares at this new high level, it is going to sell in order to make a profit. The sale of so many shares could lead the price to fall below what it was before the order. The result of a success has, in this case, led to a fall in the price of a share.

## Shareholders' influence

The actions of shareholders will be in the best interests of the shareholders – this is not always in the best interests of the business. While some shareholders are interested in the businesses that they own shares in, others are not. There are speculators in the share market, who buy and sell shares in the hope of making a profit out of price movements.

The buying and selling of shares does not affect the internal finance of the business. (The shares are not being sold back to the business.) However, this can, through changes in share price, affect the **value** of the business. Perhaps more importantly, changes in share price can affect a business's reputation. This can affect its ability to get orders and have a real effect on its success.

Many shares are owned by what are called 'institutional' shareholders. This means that insurance companies, pension funds and other large financial institutions hold the shares. Such businesses are not interested in risking their members' money, so would be unlikely to support a struggling company. Institutional

## ACTIVITY

In the past, people have often complained about buying what they termed a 'Friday afternoon' car. This was a vehicle that had many faults, and had to be returned time and again for service or repair. In many cases, the owners have given up trying to get problems put right and demanded their money back.

✦ Which stakeholders are involved in or affected by a 'Friday afternoon' car?

✦✦ Which group of stakeholders do you think is most responsible and why?

✦✦✦ Explain which group of stakeholders you think is most affected, how, and why.

shareholders often lead the way in making a particular business, or business sector, popular or unpopular with other shareholders. Their influence is thus very great.

## Employees' expectations

Employees want a fair day's pay for a fair day's work. They will also want job security, to know that their job is safe for the foreseeable future, and they may be entitled to proper training for the job. They will also expect, and are entitled to, comfortable and safe working conditions.

Another expectation, linked to all of these, may be to have some part in negotiating all of these things. When an employer makes a decision regarding pay, or working conditions, employees would like to feel that they could have some influence on the decision. As a result, there are employees' organisations (trades unions) and, where there are a lot of employers in the same industry, employer associations.

## Employees' influence

The employees are responsible for the quality of the output of the business and can therefore have a great influence on the success or otherwise of it. Employees who are happy, well-motivated, well-trained and well-rewarded for their work will try their best to produce quality products. It is therefore in the best interests of the business to make sure that its workforce does not feel undervalued. Many businesses have tried to influence the efficiency of their workers through good basic pay and conditions, but also through:

- training opportunities
- promotion opportunities
- profit sharing schemes and bonuses
- 'perks' such as discounts
- social activities, such as trips.

## Managers' expectations

Managers are a special group of employees, who may have different objectives and influence to the other employees in a business. Managers may share the same aims as owners – especially if they are entitled to rewards arising from the success of the business, such as free shares, bonuses, higher salaries, or profit-sharing schemes. If

**FACT FILE**

*The owners of Marks and Spencer plc are the shareholders. The directors of the business still include some of the family of the original founders. When Marks and Spencer was going through a period of crisis, part of the management solution was to consider selling off Marks and Spencer's most expensive branch, on Oxford Street, in London. The owners, however, did not wish to consider the sale of such a 'flagship' branch.*

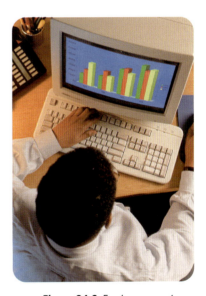

**Figure 24.3** *Employees expect a fair day's work for a fair day's pay*

## KEY TERMS

- ACAS – Advisory, Conciliation and Arbitration Service (ACAS) – which will work with both sides to solve industrial disputes
- Dividend – a share of the profits of a business, divided between shareholders
- Entrepreneurs – the people who take the risk and, in return, get the rewards of business.
- Institutional shareholders – large bodies, like pension funds and insurance companies, who hold a lot of shares
- Stakeholder – any group or individual with a stake in the success of a business

# EXTENSION EXERCISE

Imagine you are a major shareholder in your chosen business. What would be the main aims that you think the business should have? What would be your main aims as a shareholder? Explain whether these aims conflict and why (or why not).

they do not receive such direct rewards then they may seek rewards in other ways. For example, managers could be interested in increasing their status.

## Managers' influence

Managers are responsible for the efficient running of the business. In small businesses, the owner and the manager may be the same person; in large businesses, the ownership may be with thousands of shareholders, who trust the managers to run the business on their behalf. (This is called the **divorce of ownership from control**.)

Managers thus have the power to be innovative, or efficient, or not. They can be much more responsible for the success or failure of a business than the owners. It is therefore important to owners that they are appointed with great care, and properly rewarded for their management abilities. This is why some senior managers can attract very high salaries, regardless of the business or industry that they are managing.

## Conflicts of interest

Typical conflicts between internal stakeholders are:

1 Between employer and employee. Unfortunately what each thinks is a fair day's work for a fair day's pay may be different. The employee will be seeking to maintain or increase his or her standard of living (often in the face of other external changes such as tax changes or inflation). The employer is likely to want greater efficiency. Because conflicts are so likely to arise between employer and employee, there are special measures and bodies – such as the Advisory, Conciliation and Arbitration Service (ACAS) – put in place to help to deal with them.
2 Between shareholder and worker. Shareholders want more profit; workers do not want to work harder or more efficiently unless their rewards also reflect the profit that they are receiving.
3 Between owners and managers. Owners often have a different set of objectives to managers. For example, an owner may be so close to a business, having established it and watched it grow, that they cannot see what needs to be done to manage it. On the other hand, managers – in seeking efficiency – may change the whole nature of the business from that originally intended.

## What you need to do:

- To reach Level ❶    you need to identify the stakeholders in the business you are investigating and describe how the business affects them.
- To reach Level ❷    you need to explain the influence of the stakeholders on the business.
- To reach Level ❸    you need to explain how there might be conflicts of interest among different stakeholders in the business you are investigating and suggest how these conflicts might be resolved.

CHAPTER 25

# External stakeholders

Businesses have a number of groups of people, or institutions, which have a stake in the success of the business. The external stakeholders are those which are outside the control of the business. These are the customers, suppliers, competitors, government and the local community in which the business operates. Not all stakeholders necessarily want the same things out of a business. This means that there are often conflicts between the different objectives that stakeholders have, and mechanisms have to be established to resolve those conflicts.

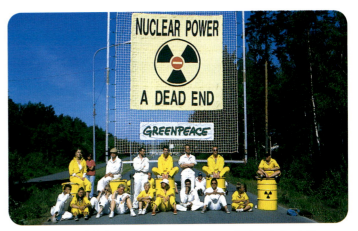

**Figure 25.1** *Protesters represent one group of external shareholders – the public*

## Customers' expectations

The main thing which customers want is value for money. This means that they want quality products – ie ones that do the job that they are supposed to do efficiently – at reasonable prices. If a good or service falls outside the price range that a customer thinks is reasonable, then it will not be bought. A few people may think that a bar of soap, or a tube of cleansing lotion, is worth £100, but not enough to make it worthwhile for the Body Shop to sell these goods in this price range.

There are also internal customers in a business; eg when one functional area needs a product or service from another. Keeping internal customers happy is also part of the efficient running of a business.

Customers also have increased expectations of businesses' ability to provide a range of goods and of new services, such as shopping via the internet.

### TRUE OR FALSE?

*A quality product is an expensive product.*

*(see foot of page for answer)*

**True or False answer**

False. A product can be cheap, but do the job it is meant to do, making it a quality product.

## Customers' influence

Obviously, without customers, no business could exist. Customers influence businesses by their spending patterns, ie by what they do or do not buy. It is up to businesses to try to spot what customers want and make sure that they supply plenty of it; and to spot what customers no longer want, and stop selling it.

Businesses go to great lengths, through market research, to find out why customers buy particular goods, and why tastes have changed or are going to change. If a business can correctly predict what customers are going to want, this can contribute to its success.

## Suppliers' expectations

A supplier is any business which supplies another business with raw materials, components or services. All businesses need central suppliers of services such as power and telecommunications, but many also need specific suppliers of raw materials. A fish and chip shop is dependent on a supply of potatoes, cooking oil, eggs and flour for batter and, of course fish.

Suppliers want regular orders from a business as this helps them to be a successful business themselves. They want businesses that are reliable, who are going to pay on time.

**Figure 25.2** *There are many inputs to even a simple business, so suppliers always have influence*

## Suppliers' influence

Suppliers can influence a business through prices, through quality and through efficiency. The cost of raw materials will be a major part of the cost of many businesses; should this increase, the business then has the choice of either letting profits fall, or of passing on the increase to the customer in the form of higher prices.

The quality of supply is also a major consideration. Businesses will rely on receiving a consistently quality product from suppliers. Breaks in supply, or changes in quality, can affect the success of the business. It is also important that delivery is regular and reliable.

Some businesses can also influence suppliers, because they buy so much of a product. A burger bar chain, for example, may buy all of the beef produced in a certain region. This means that this business can have control over price and even over how the meat is produced.

## Creditors' expectations

Creditors and other financial backers are any group or individual to which the business owes money. This could be money which the business has borrowed to set up, eg from a bank. It could be credit for goods and services – often businesses allow other businesses to take goods and services but not pay for them until they have been paid themselves. It could be money given by local or national government in the form of a grant.

In all cases, creditors expect the business to be careful with their money and to repay it when it is due and including any interest that is due. (Even if the money has been given as a grant, there are likely to be certain conditions attached to it to help the business be a success.)

## Creditors' influence

Governments (or other bodies which give grants) can attach conditions to the grant so that a business uses it for a specific purpose, or in a specific way. For example, it could be a grant to upgrade a plant so that it is more environmentally friendly; the business would not be allowed to use this grant on, for instance, market research instead. Finance providers can also vary the terms on which they offer a business finance. They could:

- change interest rates – banks will charge a higher interest rate to a business which they feel is a greater risk
- want some form of control – banks may insist that, if they have lent a business a lot of money, the bank has a say in how it is spent, perhaps as a member of the board of directors, or as a partner
- change the length of time that credit is allowed – if a supplier thought that a business was going to be unable to pay its debts in the future, it could call all of them in for immediate payment. On the other hand, it could give extended credit to a favoured business.

## Local community expectations

Businesses need to operate within the community where they are situated. Small businesses provide a service to the local community. In many cases this is retail, such as corner shops, newsagents and grocers. In other cases, small local businesses provide trade services such as carpentry and plumbing. Larger local businesses will provide employment; much of the money earned may then be spent locally.

Businesses may also attract other businesses – eg suppliers – and this will create more jobs. It may also create problems, like extra

*Figure 25.3* Local communities benefit from employment opportunities, but may lose out in other ways

## CITIZENSHIP

*Look up, either in the library or on the internet, a recent issue involving a pressure group. Write down points for the pressure groups stand and points against. Who, in the case you are looking at, do you think is in the right? Why?*

traffic. Sometimes there are laws to cover this – such as not operating noisy machinery between certain hours, or not polluting the air or water. Sometimes it is left to a business to regulate its own activities; eg through parking with consideration for others in the community. The local community will expect a business to care for its local environment and the community in which it is situated. Businesses may even contribute directly to local communities through sponsorship or other activities.

## Local community influences

The local community can welcome businesses which it feels are bringing benefits, perhaps by way of jobs. It can also oppose those businesses that it feels are harming the community. Communities can take legal action against polluters, and can refuse to buy products from businesses that cause problems.

## Government expectations

The government expects businesses to provide the goods and services that the economy needs, and also to provide employment. The goods and services should be sufficient, and of sufficient quality, to allow the country to trade with the rest of the world and the economy to grow. Government also relies on businesses to provide employment which is fair, safe and fairly paid. Employees, of course, provide the government with income through taxation.

## Government influences

Local, national and international (in the form of the European Union) governments affect businesses through laws and regulations which they pass. Governments collect taxes from businesses and in return provide them with services, for example, transport systems. Government also runs its own businesses in the public sector, as well as services such as education and the National Health Service. Laws affect the way that businesses can operate. The main groups of laws affecting business are:

## ACTIVITY

External costs are costs which are caused by business but paid for by the community.

+ List five local businesses or developments that are generating external costs to your community.

++ Choose the one which you think is generating the highest costs. How do you think it could help to pay for these costs?

+++ What other stakeholder groups could you join with to persuade it either to reduce or pay for these costs? Which do you think would be most effective, and why?

- fairness and equality laws – making sure that there is no discrimination (see Chapter 29)
- other employment laws – such as to ensure the payment of a minimum wage, or to ensure trades union rights
- health and safety laws – not just the Health and Safety at Work Acts, but also laws to prevent pollution, congestion and dangerous practices, such as the use of materials such as asbestos
- Consumer protection laws – to protect consumers from businesses trying to trade unfairly.

Government also affects businesses by providing financial incentives, such as lower taxes, and, in some cases, grants (see above).

## Pressure groups' expectations and influences

Pressure groups are groups of people who have come together in order to agitate for change – to try to sway public opinion or government policy on particular issues. Pressure groups are likely to be:

- single issue groups – eg a group wishing to ban hunting would achieve its aim when the law is passed
- general groups – such as Greenpeace and Friends of the Earth, with very wide aims.

Pressure groups can influence government and business by direct action such as demonstrating, by publicising information or by going through legal channels. One example is the two protestors who started to demonstrate against McDonald's by issuing leaflets outside burger bars. McDonald's took them to court, but they then defended their own case and publicised the defence widely when they were found not guilty of any wrongdoing.

## Conflicts

There are numerous conflicts that can arise between external stakeholders, and between external and internal stakeholders.

### KEY SKILLS
**Information Technology 2.x**

Communication. Give a presentation on the problem business that you identified in the Activity. Explain what benefits it brings to the local community and what costs and how you think that these balance out. You should include images in your presentation.

### FACT FILE

Stakeholder auditing, also known as social auditing, is when a business carries out an audit (measurement) to see how well its stakeholders think it is doing. The Body Shop carries out such an audit to include over 5,000 franchisees, shareholders, customers, employees, suppliers and Fair Trade partners. It also audits the local communities in which it operates, in all parts of the world. The information collected allows the management to make informed decisions about where changes to the business can most effectively be made.

### KEY TERMS

- Creditor – anyone to whom the business owes money
- External stakeholders – those with a stake in the business but outside of its control
- Pressure groups – groups that agitate for change or improvement

## EXTENSION EXERCISE

Add the internal stakeholders to the list of external ones used in the classwork activity. Decide which two groups are likely to be most opposed to each other (and therefore most often in conflict), and explain why.

Conflict arises whenever one group wants something that another group doesn't. For example, customers want low prices, the business wants higher profits; workers want more pay, employers want to pay less; managers want to save money by delaying payments, suppliers want payment on time.

Situations often affect a number of groups at once. For example, a government passing an anti-pollution law could lead to:

- improved life in a local community
- increased business costs
- business failure
- higher prices to consumers
- the disbanding of a pressure group.

## What you need to do:

- To reach Level ❶    you need to identify the stakeholders in the business you are investigating and describe how the business affects them.
- To reach Level ❷    you need to explain the influence of the stakeholders on the business.
- To reach Level ❸    you need to explain how there might be conflicts of interest among different stakeholders in the business you are investigating and suggest how these conflicts might be resolved.

CHAPTER 26
# Organisational structures

All businesses need to be organised. The best structures help a business to meet its objectives. This does not mean that all businesses will be organised in the same ways. The actual structure will depend on a number of factors including the size of the business, the number of staff, the types of jobs, and the type of goods or services being produced. Most medium to large businesses usually employ a pyramid structure which shows a clear chain of command. Some organisations have tried to flatten out these structures to reduce the links in the chain and improve communication. Whatever the structure, the chart will help to show basic job roles and responsibilities.

*Figure 26.1*

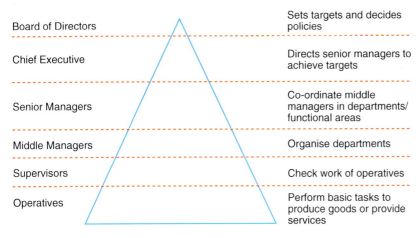

| | |
|---|---|
| Board of Directors | Sets targets and decides policies |
| Chief Executive | Directs senior managers to achieve targets |
| Senior Managers | Co-ordinate middle managers in departments/functional areas |
| Middle Managers | Organise departments |
| Supervisors | Check work of operatives |
| Operatives | Perform basic tasks to produce goods or provide services |

**Figure 26.2** *Pyramid structure*

## Pyramid Structures

A typical pyramid structure for a company is shown above. This helps to show that the company has a tall structure. This hierarchical structure clearly shows the chain of command. The Board of Directors has immediate authority over the Chief Executive, while the senior managers are responsible to the Chief Executive for their various departments or areas or work.

This diagram can also show how decisions are passed down the chain from one level to the next. Information will also be passed back up the chain. The number of levels will vary with the size of an organisation. The fewer the number of levels, the easier it will be to pass down instructions and to communicate between staff.

## Organisation Charts

Many businesses show their organisational structure in a vertical chart. In a large business this may be very complicated, but a simplified example is shown here to illustrate the basic idea.

The chart on page 146 shows that there are six levels within the business. Typically it will have a large number of people working at the bottom level, and relatively few at the top. This leads to the description of a 'pyramid' organisation. Some businesses turn the chart through ninety degrees to make it a horizontal chart. This is supposed to suggest that the organisation is less hierarchical, and highlights the need to co-ordinate activities at each level.

### For your portfolio

Your description of how your chosen business is organised needs to include both notes and a chart. You could link this with the descriptions of job roles which is explained in Chapter 27, 'Key job roles and working arrangements'.

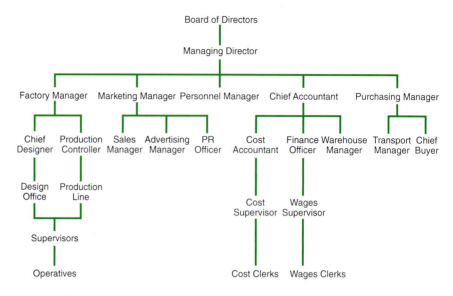

**Figure 26.3** *Organisation chart*

The diagram shown organises the business in departments or functions. There are other ways of organising:

1 Other businesses may choose to draw up their organisational chart on a product basis, especially if they have a number of clearly separate products.
2 Some businesses prefer to organise by divisions or groups with each subsidiary company having its own organisation chart.
3 Other businesses choose to organise on the basis of the markets they sell to, while another method is to use a project-based approach which is sometimes preferred by construction firms.

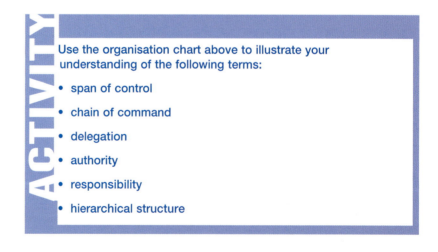

**ACTIVITY**

Use the organisation chart above to illustrate your understanding of the following terms:

• span of control

• chain of command

• delegation

• authority

• responsibility

• hierarchical structure

There is no best way of organising a business. The structure is likely to need to change as the business develops and as new ideas influence the understanding of those managers leading the business.

## Organisational Terms

When considering why a business has chosen its organisational structure and whether there might be a way to improve it, you will need to consider a number of terms and concepts.

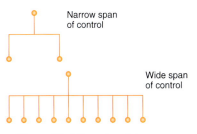

**Figure 26.4** *Span of control*

### Span of control

This measures the number of workers directly controlled by one person. A narrow span of control might be said to be between two and six people, while a wide span of control might be seven or more. The actual width of the span will depend on such things as the nature of the work, the degree of supervision needed and the skills required. Communication and decision-making problems may result if spans are not right.

### Chain of command

This is the way power is passed down through the organisation. In a small business, workers may be directly supervised by the owner or manager, but in larger firms the chain of command is more complicated and longer as it goes through several layers. Each layer has a certain status and shows who takes decisions, and to whom the decisions are passed.

### Delegation, responsibility and authority

The Board of Directors will take the major decisions in a business. They will then pass on or delegate the responsibility for day-to-day decision-making to the managing director and the department heads. Delegation of decisions and duties requires staff to be given the authority to make these decisions. The authority to make these decisions will be written up within an individual's job description.

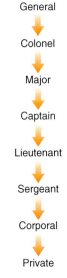

**Figure 26.5** *Military chain of command*

# EXTENSION EXERCISE

Use your school or college to practise drawing up an organisational chart. Discuss this with your teachers and lecturers as it may be more complicated than you realise.

### Internal communication

There are many ways of communicating within an organisation, but perhaps the key thing to focus on is the direction of communication. Downwards communication means that a manager is communicating with an employee at the next level below and may want the communication to be passed on down the chain to finally reach operatives. Upward communication refers to messages and information being passed up to more senior staff in the organisation. At each level, it would also be expected that communication would be passed between different departments to help co-ordinate and control the work of the whole business.

## What you need to do:

- To reach Level ❶    you need to describe how your chosen business is organised.
- To reach Level ❷    you need to explain why the organisational structure of your chosen business is appropriate.

# CHAPTER 27

# Key job roles within a business

It might be quite useful at this point to consider the reasons behind a person's decision to work. A basic reason is to obtain money to pay for both essential goods and services and life's more desirable luxuries. Other more complex factors include achieving status, being given responsibility, enjoying friendship and self-fulfilment through work. All of these factors influence us as individuals, and they can affect our behaviour and performance at work. They, therefore, are likely to have an impact on workers' attitudes both to their job roles and to the working arrangements within the business.

*Figure 27.1*

## Types of job roles

There are literally thousands of different types of jobs ranging from factories to offices, from shops to transport, from construction sites to farms, and from garages to hospitals. Each job in each occupation involves a range of different duties, activities, skills, responsibility and problems. While it can be argued that each job is completely different or unique when compared to others, the main job roles in most organisations can be broadly grouped as directors, managers, supervisors, operatives and support staff.

## Directors

In a company, the highest level of management is the Board of Directors. This body is responsible for setting broad targets for the company, and will decide on broad policies to achieve these targets. By law they have to look after the shareholders' interests and decide how to share out company profits.

**Figure 27.2** *Board of Directors meeting*

Some directors work full-time and take part in the day-to-day running of the company. They are usually known as Executive Directors. Others directors might be part-time, attending board meetings but not taking an active part in running the business. They are usually known as Non-Executive Directors. Many directors will also be shareholders in the company but some, especially Non-Executive Directors, are invited in and paid for bringing broad, independent ideas and views to the business.

The Managing Director, sometimes called the Chief Executive, has specific duties including:

- providing leadership and taking urgent decisions
- appointing senior staff
- making sure policies are carried out
- maintaining and improving staff morale
- taking part in key negotiations with customers, suppliers and trade unions
- overall supervision, control and co-ordination of the day to day operations
- chairing key meetings.

## Managers

In a company, the Managing Director and the Board of Directors fills the top level of management. Below this level, there will usually be senior and then middle managers. Finally there may be junior managers.

In many firms, all of these managers are organised in departments, with each department carrying out specific functions. Managers need leadership and communication skills, and they have to plan, organise and co-ordinate the work of the departments. Senior managers also have to decide how much responsibility to give to managers in the level below them.

In other firms with lots of branches (especially in retailing), a manager might control a single workplace, with deputy managers then carrying specific jobs to run the business efficiently. Whatever the structure, managers will be aiming to ensure that staff work efficiently. This will involve taking operational decisions, setting targets, solving day-to-day problems, monitoring progress and communicating with all staff both in their sections and in others.

## Supervisors

These staff are likely to combine both a management role and an operational role. Supervisors are sometimes called first-line managers because they are responsible for supervising the activities of either production operatives or business support staff. This will involve checking that the operatives are working correctly and efficiently, and dealing with immediate problems. They will be expected to refer more serious matters up to the next level of management.

As well as carrying out this management role, they are likely to be directly involved in the work of either the operatives or the support staff. A supervisor in a shop might spend some time on the till or

# EXTENSION EXERCISE

- Divide your class into groups of three or four students.
- Collect a large range of job advertisements from newspapers.
- If you have a whole page of advertisements, cut them into single job adverts.
- On a large desk or table, spread out the separate job advertisements.
- Place the jobs into groups by identifying similar levels of responsibility and importance.
- Write a description of the similarities and differences between the jobs at each level. Do not compare between levels.
- Re-organise the jobs using another set of criteria: eg by industry or by pay.
- Compare the similarities and differences as before.
- Draw up and write a report giving an analysis of five job roles and their typical characteristics using the job advertisements and your earlier descriptions.

# KEY *TERMS*

Directors – senior managers usually elected or appointed by shareholders to represent them on the Board of Directors, setting key targets and policies

Managers – a person responsible for the control and supervision of an activity or group of activities

Supervisors – an employee who manages operatives carrying out the production process. It is the most junior form of manager and will have limited decision-making, but will be expected to check that work is being done correctly and that targets are being met

Operatives – individual employees who are directly involved in producing the goods or providing the services

Support staff – people who are not directly involved in the production process but support those who are

Job security – the extent to which a person is 'safe' from being made redundant because the business no longer needs that employee

stocking shelves, while in a manufacturing factory the supervisor might be expected to spend a certain amount of the working day directly involved in making the product.

## Operatives

In the past these were more commonly called 'shop-floor workers'. Their main role is the direct operation of machinery and equipment to produce the goods or provide the services. Increasingly they are being given responsibility to check for quality at their stage of the production process. Some firms try to build in team-work so that operatives feel an important part of the business and can contribute ideas to improve production.

Their job roles involve supporting the internal working of the organisation as a whole and the individual parts that contribute to it. Typical job titles include receptionists, clerks, security guards, cleaners, maintenance engineers and caretakers. There will also be staff whose job roles support the external operations of the business. These might be van drivers, service engineers and customer service staff.

## Support staff

In some organisations, assistants might be used at various levels of management. A typical example is where a managing director might have a personal assistant who performs clerical and administrative duties. Bricklayers and plumbers often have assistants or 'mates' who carry out basic tasks such as mixing cement and holding radiators in position. Whatever the level and type of of assistance, these workers are filling the role of support staff.

## Analysing job roles

In your investigations, you need to find out the main responsibilities of each of these categories of staff. At the higher levels, managers will have broad and major responsibilities. At lower levels in a business structure, the responsibilities become narrower and more

**Figure 27.3** *A telephonist at work*

specific. You could also find out how many staff each person directly controls. This is called the span of control. This clearly links to the type of decisions each member of staff is allowed to take and how far they are expected to personally solve problems in the workplace.

### Tasks and activities

You also have to find out the main tasks and activities of typical workers at each level. For some this might be quite specific and quite clear. A telephonist will be expected to make and receive telephone calls for staff, and take and pass on messages as necessary, each working day. Other staff may have a wide range of ever-changing tasks and activities. A headteacher will have a variety of tasks and activities to carry out, but may find that the tasks on two consecutive days are completely different.

### Job security

Job security refers to the likelihood of someone being made redundant. This is quite difficult to judge and certainly varies both from one occupation to another and within an occupation. Much will depend on the effects of new technology, the success of the individual business and changes taking place in the whole industry. It might depend on how much competition the business experiences from foreign business and, of course, changes in consumer tastes can have a big effect on orders, profits and finally employment levels.

### Qualifications

In many businesses there might be quite formal and rigid qualification requirements. Certain skill levels might be fixed for each level of job. Personal qualities such as the abilities to work independently, to work as part of a team, and to be a good communicator are more likely to vary from one business to another. As well as asking questions in your chosen business about these, you could also look at job advertisements to see examples of requirements in similar occupations and businesses.

### Be discreet!

Finally, when you try to find out about levels of pay and other benefits, you need to be very sensitive and discreet. Do not ask a member of staff how much they are paid and what benefits they directly receive. Rather, you need to ask the rates of pay and benefits for a type of job. These may vary according to experience, skills and qualifications, and you will probably find that the wage or salary for a job ranges from a minimum to a maximum.

## What you need to do:

- To reach Level ❶     you need to investigate job roles and working arrangements within your chosen business.
- To reach Level ❷     you need to analyse job roles and working arrangements within your chosen business.
- To reach Level ❸     you need to produce a detailed analysis of the job roles and working arrangements within your chosen business.

CHAPTER 28

# Employment contracts and the rights of employees and employers

The relationship between employers and their employees is very important. Whether this is a happy and successful one will depend to a great extent on the way the rights and responsibilities of both parties are put into action. Both sides will have certain key expectations.

**Figure 28.1** *A contract protects both employer and employee*

## Expectations in the workplace

Employees might expect:

- a fair wage for the work done
- to be treated fairly by the managers and everyone else in the organisation
- to work reasonable hours in a clean and safe environment
- to receive some paid holidays
- to receive appropriate training for the job
- to join a trades union or staff association
- to be able to access their confidential computer records kept by the business.

In return, employers might expect employees to:

- be punctual and co-operative
- obey all reasonable instructions
- treat facilities and equipment with care and respect
- be loyal and trustworthy and perform a fair amount of work each day
- notify them if they cannot attend work
- dress in appropriate manner.

These lists of expectations need to be turned from a 'wish list' into a legally binding agreement. Most will be included but a few may not be part of the agreement. This agreement is called an **employment contract**.

> ### TRUE OR FALSE?
>
> *An employment contract must always be written to be legally binding.*
>
> *(see foot of page for answer)*

True or False answer

**False.** A verbal agreement is legally binding on the parties who make it. It must be replaced within two months by a written contract, however.

**For your portfolio**

To reach both the level 1 and level 3 requirements, you also need to read and use Chapter 27, 'Key job roles within a business'. To reach the level 2 requirement, you also need to read and use Chapter 30 'Resolving disagreements'.

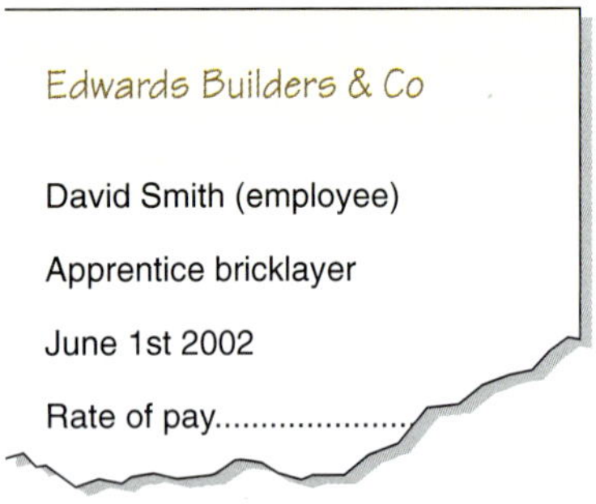
Edwards Builders & Co

David Smith (employee)

Apprentice bricklayer

June 1st 2002

Rate of pay.....................

***Figure 28.2***

## Employment Contracts

As far as the law is concerned, a contract exists once a person has agreed to work for an employer and the employer has offered to pay wages. The basis for the contract is that someone has made an offer (the employer) while someone else has accepted (the employee), and both are benefiting from the agreement. This means that a contract is legally binding, even if it is only a verbal agreement. The problem then would be in dealing with any disagreements. So, each employee hired by a business must be given a written contract of employment.

The Trade Union Reform and Employment Rights Act 1993 (TURER) states that an employee must be given a written statement of the main terms and conditions of their employment within two months of starting a new job. Any changes to the statement must be notified in writing within one month. The details to be included in a contract have been set out by the Contract of Employment Acts, 1972–82.

The main details include:

- employer's name and employee's name
- job title
- date the job started
- rates of pay; eg a wage of £6.50 per hour or a salary of £15,000 per year
- frequency of payment; eg weekly or monthly
- hours of work; eg seven hours per day Monday to Friday, between 0800 and 1600 with an hour allowed for meal breaks
- holidays; eg 25 days per year plus bank holidays with dates subject to agreement with management
- place of work; the address of the normal place of work including offices, retail outlets, tele-working, mobile and home-based working
- sickness benefits, stating that the employee is entitled to time off with pay
- grievance procedure; how to deal with problems at work
- agreements with trade unions that are legally binding on the employer
- disciplinary rules
- period of notice required to leave the employment, both by employer and employee
- pension rights, if any, with details of contributions.

Sometimes a business will include some of the information that applies to all employees in a 'conditions of service' booklet. The contract may then be a shorter and clearer document. Both employer and employee would still be expected to abide by the terms. Employment contracts are required for all workers, whether they are full- or part-time, permanent or temporary.

## Why change the terms of these contracts?

Nearly every industry and every business organisation expects to have to make changes if they are to remain competitive. We live in a sophisticated country that is part of a global economy. Many businesses expect to compete against foreign-produced goods and

## Classwork activity

1   Create a word processed blank employment contract including all the main sections for an imaginary business of your own choosing. Save the blank, using a sensible filename.
2   Print out a copy of the blank contract. Use this to draft a contract for a new employee to your imaginary business.
3   Once you are happy with your draft, load the file of your blank employment contract. Type in the details from your draft and, when finished, save under a new filename.

services either at home in the UK or in worldwide export markets. If we are to compete successfully, our businesses need their workers to change their ways of working, just as the companies themselves change the way they are organised. If employees have to change their working arrangements they will need a new employment contract.

There are five broad reasons for a business changing the working arrangements of its employees and therefore its employment contracts.

## The business needs to increase productivity

This means the business wants to increase the output from each of its resources at work in the firm. This may mean operating machines for longer periods of time. It may mean introducing more and better machinery. It certainly may mean increasing the average output of each employee.

The productivity of employees in a business manufacturing wooden toys may be measured by calculating the total output of toys made by all the workers over a day and dividing this by the number of workers. To improve the productivity of the workers, changes might have to made for example to their hours, the time of day worked, the type of tasks expected and even their place of work. All of these changes will require changes to be made to employment contracts.

## The business needs to improve the quality of products

Customer tastes are constantly changing and a business may find the only way to maintain sales levels is to increase the quality of its

## CITIZENSHIP

Look at the list of expectations for both employers and employees.

Are there any missing items?

In small groups, discuss how far you think the two lists are **fair** to both employers and employees.

Explain how your group has interpreted the word 'fair' in each case.

## KEY TERMS

Contract of employment – a written document detailing an employee's terms and conditions of employment
Productivity – a measurement of the quantity of goods produced by a worker or other resource over a period of time.
Working Practices – the expected way for workers to carry out a job, possibly written down in formal written rules and regulations

products. For employees in the wooden toy factory, the introduction of a total quality management system to produce better quality toys might mean that all workers are expected to check for quality as production takes place. Again, this might need a change to the employment contract.

## The business needs to introduce new technology

Sometimes a business will find that its plant and machinery needs to be replaced either because it is worn out or because it is out-of-date. New machinery may mean that workers have to be re-trained and

**Figure 28.3** *New technology has replaced both this printing press and the skills needed to use it*

may have to work in different ways. Wage rates may have to change to reflect the different types of work and levels of responsibility required. Hours of work may also change. Any of these changes will require employment contracts to change.

## The business needs to introduce new working practices such as team-working and multi-skill practices

As new technology has been introduced to many industries, the old ways of working have changed drastically. In the newspaper industry the introduction of computers and desk top publishing software completely changed the way newspapers were printed. Many highly skilled jobs were lost, and replaced by the need for multi-skilled employees. Other businesses have organised employees into teams to encourage worker motivation and the likely achievement of higher production targets. In many cases these changes will require major alterations to be made to employment contracts.

# EXTENSION EXERCISE

Think about your school or college.
What are the expectations in your educational establishment for both students and teachers or lecturers?
Draft a contract suitable for students being accepted on to your course of study.
Share your ideas with others in the class and discuss the issues.

## The need to be more competitive than other businesses

To some extent, the above four reasons are all linked into this final reason for change. To survive and to grow, all businesses need to become more competitive. This often means re-organising and re-structuring a business which in turn means changing the way it uses all of its resources. As employees are often the most important and the most expensive resource at work in a business, they are the first resources that will be reviewed. Changes in the type of work, the pay rates, hours, training and benefits will almost certainly result and require all workers to agree new employment contracts.

## What you need to do:

- To reach Level ❶      you need to describe the rights of the employer and its employees using examples from the selected business. You also need to describe the roles of **three** people who have different responsibilities within their chosen business.

- To reach Level ❷      you need to explain the content of the Contract of Employment for one of the three people chosen for level 1. This should include terms and conditions of employment and working arrangements. For your selected business you also need to explain how it resolves disagreements with its employees over rights of employment and working conditions.

- To reach Level ❸      you need to evaluate, using examples, how well the contract of employment meets the needs of the business and the employee. You also need to recommend and justify suitable changes to the Contract of Employment. Finally you also need to evaluate the extent to which your selected business ensures that a good working relationship exists between the employer and its employees.

CHAPTER 29

# Employment legislation

In many businesses, managers set out the rules and regulations that derive directly from these laws and directives in a comprehensive policy. This policy will often stress its importance for both employer and employee and will show what is expected from each group of people in the workplace. This may be illustrated by the following extract from a message to its employees by Remploy. Remploy states that it believes that:
'All employees have a part to play; Everyone is important; Each job has a part in the overall structure.'
The company develops this in a number of policy statements including its equal

*Figure 29.1*

opportunities policy. Remploy state that, '. . . all employees will be given encouragement and equal opportunities to progress in the organisation.` The company expects everyone to take the responsibility to make the policy happen and is particularly keen to promote it in job applications, interviews, training opportunities and promotion.

The company's safety policy is very detailed, involving risk assessment, safety committees, the use of advisory bodies, strict rules and regulations, safety officers and safety audits. These more than obey the various laws, but again Remploy emphasises the role of all workers when it states, 'All staff and employees have a duty to take personal care of themselves and other persons who may be affected by their acts or omissions.'

## Legal protection for employers and employees

When a business is operating, it must expect to obey many laws. Four key legal areas in the employment of people are

1  health and safety
2  equal opportunities
3  employment rights
4  access to personal information.

In all of these cases, either the UK and/or the EU has created laws and directives that businesses must follow, together with the penalties that will result if they are broken. Many businesses may choose to operate their own rules and regulations that protect the worker by more than that required by law.

### For your portfolio

To help you reach level 2 you also need to read and use Chapter 33 'Staff Development and Training'.

# Health and Safety Laws

There are a number of general laws covering health and safety in the workplace. In addition, in some industries – such as coal mining and chemicals – there are special health and safety codes. Some firms and industries add to this through their own voluntary regulations often as a result of negotiations with trade unions.

The main general laws covering health and safety are:

## Health and Safety at Work Act 1974

This stresses that both employer and employee have a responsibility to keep safe conditions at work. The employer must take all reasonable practical steps to ensure the health, safety and welfare of all employees. The employee is expected to take reasonable care to look after his/her own safety and the safety of others in the workplace. If the rules are not obeyed, the employer could be punished by a court of law. To check that the rules are being obeyed, the Health and Safety Executive have the right to inspect the premises and will enforce the Act.

## Reporting of Injuries, Diseases and Dangerous Occurrences Regulations 1985

Any injury that results from an accident at work which causes an employee to be unable to work for three or more days must be reported to the authorities. Listed diseases must be reported, as must any accident involving work equipment.

## Control of Substances Hazardous to Health Regulations 1988

An employer must identify any task which is likely to be harmful. The risks have to be minimised, and workers dealing with hazardous

*Figure 29.2*

substances must be given both detailed information and appropriate training.

### Noise at Work Regulations 1989

Employers are now expected to reduce the risk of hearing damage to employees. This might be greater noise insulation around machinery, or more simply providing ear protectors.

### Workplace (Health, Safety and Welfare) Regulations 1992

These regulations replaced some earlier laws and now affect virtually all employers, employees and the self-employed. There are six main areas for new rules and these include:

1 Employers are expected to have a highly organised system for dealing with health and safety.
2 All equipment should be suitable, safe, in good working order and staff should be trained in its use.
3 Strict rules are applied to manual handling operations such as lifting, pushing, pulling, carrying and the moving of loads.
4 Conditions in the workplace are rigidly controlled from ventilation and lighting, to cleaning and the provision of basic facilities such as toilets and rest areas.
5 Protective equipment must be supplied to staff where it is necessary and staff must be well-trained in its use.
6 Regular users of display screen equipment are helped through the identification of risks from repetitive strain injuries and are entitled to free eye tests.

## The effect of these laws

In the majority of firms, the workplace should now be a much safer place for employees. It may increase costs in some firms, although some of this ought to be offset if the number of accidents falls and therefore there is less disruption to the production process. Few firms are keen to risk the punishment and bad publicity that would result from a court case for infringing the regulations. In general, it has made both employer and employee more health and safety conscious, with all organisations employing five or more people having to produce a written safety policy. This policy:

- sets out who is responsible for workplace health and safety
- must set out all the arrangements made for health and safety in the workplace
- must be communicated to everyone in the workplace
- must be backed up by training of employees, by inspections of the workplace, and in large organisations, by an active health and safety committee.

# Equal opportunities in the workplace

A lot of people mistakenly believe that this is simply about making sure that females have a fairer chance of getting a job. Equal opportunities is much wider than this, and aims to give all individuals identical rights and opportunities regardless of:

- gender
- racial group
- age
- physical characteristics
- sexual orientation
- other features.

From a business's point of view, it ought to be in its interests to provide equal opportunities since it should only gain from getting the best person for each job. For the employee, it should at least guarantee that he or she is treated in an identical way to everyone else.

There are many equal opportunities laws which apply to the workplace:

## Sex Discrimination Act 1975

As the name suggests, this act tries to prevent any sex discrimination in the workplace. It is illegal for an employer to discriminate in:

- selection procedures
- employment terms
- training and development opportunities
- fringe benefits
- selection for redundancy.

Under the terms of the Act, discrimination could be direct. For example, if one of the criteria used to judge the suitability of a manager was that he was male, then this would be direct

**Women. Men. Different. Equal.**
Equal Opportunities Commission

*Figure 29.3*

# KEY TERMS

- Health and safety policy – any policy introduced by a firm to meet the country's laws and its own regulations in ensuring the health and safety of its employees
- Equal opportunities policy – a policy written by a firm to meet the law and to set its own rules so that all individuals have identical rights

**HOMEWORK ACTIVITY**

Try to word a law that would prevent discrimination in the workplace on the basis of age. Display your main points on a card for display in the classroom and use this as a basis for discussion about the merits of such a law.

discrimination. Another example would be stating that a post was only open to an unmarried person.

Indirect discrimination is also illegal but is more difficult to prove. For example, the criteria for appointment might clearly state that the job is open to both sexes; but by the nature of the job it might have been traditionally filled by a male and fewer women feel able to apply for it.

### Race Relations Act 1976

Under this Act, nobody should be discriminated against on the basis of their race.

### Equal Pay Act 1970

A man and a woman in a company or organisation, doing the same work or work of equal value, should be paid the same amount. To make a claim that you are not being paid an equal amount, you must be able to compare yourself with a person of the opposite sex who is doing exactly the same work. This is where the problems might occur as it is often difficult to find someone who is directly comparable to you.

### Disability Discrimination Act 1995

Past Acts have stated that employers of more than 20 people should employ 3% of the workforce who are disabled. Many employers do not meet this quota and few prosecutions have been made. This new law makes it unlawful for employers with 20 or more staff to discriminate against current or prospective employees because of a reason relating to their disability. They must not be discriminated against in recruitment and retention, in promotion and transfers, in training and development, and in the dismissal process. In some cases, employers must adapt the workplace for the disabled so that they are not disadvataged.

You can see from this list of Acts that not all discrimination is illegal. For example, no law has yet been passed preventing discrimination by age. It might be quite difficult to word such an act, because young, middle-aged or old people might all claim that they have been discriminated against at some time or other.

## Employment Rights and working hours

### Employment Rights Act 1996

This brought together much previous legislation. The main rights for workers will include all employees being entitled to a statement of their employment details. In addition, employees should be given an itemised pay statement, a minimum notice period, a written statement of the reasons for their dismissal, the right not to be unfairly dismissed and the right to redundancy payments.

## Working Time Directive 1999

The introduction of this directive is the result of EU legislation. The Directive limits the working week to 48 hours and the working day to 13 hours. It sets down minimum rest periods and limits overtime in hazardous or stressful jobs.

# Data Protection laws

Data Protection laws are quite complex but generally are based on the following principles:

- Personal information must be obtained legally.
- It may be used only for the purposes for which it was collected.
- All reasonable steps must be taken to protect this information from being stolen or misused.
- The owner of the information has the right to check the information, and insist it is corrected if it is wrong.

The first Data Protection Act came into force in the UK in 1984 to protect individuals who had information on them held on computers. This obviously applied to businesses which held records both on customers and employees. Such organisations had to register with the Data Protection Registrar. They had to agree to levels of accuracy and security. The Act gave people the right to see their personal file.

The most recent Data Protection Act of 1998 was introduced because the previous Act did not apply to written data, individuals had little control over the use of personal data, and there many exemptions that were not included, such as pensions and payroll data. The new Act regulates the way personal data is collected, stored, processed and used. It applies to all data stored in a computer system and paper-based or manual records that are stored in a structured

**Figure 29.4** *Each business will have access to a large amount of data and it must handle this correctly*

# EXTENSION EXERCISE

One of the problems for the content of this chapter is keeping up to date with all the changes taking place. For each area of employment legislation described above, carry out research to find out if new UK laws and new EU directives have been introduced. You could start on the internet by carrying out searches on the laws named above. You could also use your local library. During your investigations for your portfolio, you could also ask for advice from the contacts at your chosen business. For the area of data protection, talk to your ICT teachers.

way. Within an organisation a person, called the Data Controller, should take charge of the storage of all personal records. The Information Commissioner, appointed by Parliament, will ensure that the Act is carried out and will keep a register of all Data Controllers.

### Data Protection Act 1998

The Act of 1998 set out eight data protection principles:

1. Data must be collected and processed fairly and lawfully.
2. Data must be collected for specified purposes and cannot be used in ways that are not compatible with those purposes.
3. Data must be adequate, relevant and not excessive for the purpose.
4. Data must be accurate and kept up-to-date.
5. Data must not be kept longer than necessary.
6. Data must be processed in accordance with the data subjects rights under the Act.
7. Data must be protected against unauthorised access and against accidental loss or damage.
8. Data must not be transferred to a country that does not have appropriate data protection legislation.

Within a business organisation, the Data Controller must make sure that these principles are carried out. If the Information Commissioner became aware of any problems, a thorough investigation would be started and action could be taken. This may include stopping access to and processing of data, correction of inaccurate data, and compensation to an individual person if he or she has suffered damage or distress.

## What you need to do:

- **To reach Level ❶**    you need to describe the main laws which protect people at work. You also need to identify health and safety risks at work and explain what your chosen business does to prevent accidents.
- **To reach Level ❷**    you need to explain how training people in your chosen business to maintain a safe and secure working environment.
- **To reach Level ❸**    you need to suggest and justify alternative or additional procedures to improve the safety of the working environment.

# CHAPTER 30
# Resolving disagreements

Disagreements at work can occur over the treatment of individual employees or groups of employees. Some of these disagreements may be disciplinary issues, others may be forms of grievances, while others may come under the heading of industrial relations problems. Most disputes will be dealt with at a local level and will be kept within the business. Some disputes will become national issues and will have to be solved by national organisations. In a few cases, the dispute may involve international organisations and require the intervention of a body such as the European Court of Justice.

**Figure 30.1** *Disagreements at work can lead to major disputes*

## Types of Disputes

### Disciplinary disputes

All firms will have a set of rules and regulations that they expect their employees to follow. If these rules are not followed correctly or perhaps deliberately ignored and broken, an employee may face disciplinary procedures. In some cases disciplinary procedures may take place if it is felt that an employee is not carrying out his or her duties satisfactorily.

### Grievance disputes

These occur when a worker or group of workers feels unhappy about their treatment at work. The workers may think the firm has acted unreasonably or failed to take their interests into account. Sometimes grievances can lead to complaint and may even lead to disputes.

### Industrial relations disputes

Some of these disputes are linked to situations where workers are wanting improvements in their pay and conditions. Other disputes may be linked to disciplinary or grievance matters. They all become forms of industrial relations disputes when employees use their unions to support their cases. In a few cases, if disputes cannot be solved through negotiation, a union may ask its members to take industrial action in support of those workers affected by the dispute. Such action may include the withdrawal of goodwill, go slows, work to rules, selective and all out strikes.

**Figure 30.2** *Most disputes are resolved through negotiations*

*Figure 30.3*

# Resolving disputes

In the majority of cases, disputes will be settled before such action is taken. Most businesses have quite formal and detailed procedures to deal with disciplinary, grievance and industrial relations problems. Examples of such procedures are described below.

## Handling disciplinary and grievance procedures within the business

Most businesses follow advice from the Advisory, Conciliation and Arbitration Service (ACAS). The details of the procedures should be written down and understood by both management and employees. The advice from ACAS also expects discussions to take place between the complainant and his/her immediate supervisor or manager within 24 hours.

The second stage would be to reach an agreement within three days. If an agreement cannot be reached, the dispute might require the involvement of more senior managers and perhaps trades union representatives for the employee. Evidence would need to be collected and presented. Once again it would be preferable to all concerned if the dispute could be settled by negotiation. It may take a few meetings to achieve agreement.

## Settling disputes outside the business

Some disputes cannot be settled within the business, and either side may decide to try and find a solution from an external agency. There are three routes.

### Negotiation through ACAS

This independent organisation offers employers, trade unions and individuals the opportunity to obtain unbiased assistance in solving disputes. As the name suggests, ACAS can offer advice to all sides in the disputes. It can also try to bring the sides together as it tries to conciliate and suggest ways to move towards a solution. Finally, ACAS can act as an **arbiter**, which means listening to evidence from both sides and then providing a solution. ACAS will insist that both

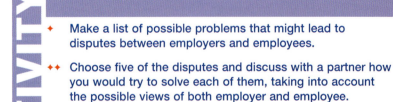

**ACTIVITY**

◆ Make a list of possible problems that might lead to disputes between employers and employees.

◆◆ Choose five of the disputes and discuss with a partner how you would try to solve each of them, taking into account the possible views of both employer and employee.

◆◆◆ Choose one of the disputes and create a role play with your partner. One of you should take the role of the employee and the other should take the role of the employer.

**Figure 30.4** *A few disputes end up being settled in court*

sides agree to abide by its decision before starting the **arbitration process**.

### Employment Tribunals

Most of the disputes dealt with by an employment tribunal are for unfair dismissal. The employee must first ask ACAS whether the case needs to be taken to an employment tribunal. The tribunal is made up of individuals who have specific knowledge of employment law. The chair of the tribunal is either a barrister or solicitor. The other two are independent lay people. All three have an equal say, and after listening to the evidence presented, will make a decision by simple majority verdict. Individuals who have had their complaint upheld are entitled to compensation, reinstatement or re-engagement.

### Court action

Appeals on points of law made by an employment tribunal can be referred to the Employment Appeals Tribunal. Some cases can be taken further to the Court of Appeal, and sometimes up to the final court of appeal in the UK, the House of Lords. Since the UK is part of the European Union, individuals and employers can take their cases to the European Court of Justice.

## EXTENSION EXERCISE

Search the internet to find:

- examples of the work of ACAS
- examples of people who have recently been involved in an employment tribunal
- any examples of appeals that have taken place against the ruling of employment tribunals.

## What you need to do:

- To achieve Level ❶   you need some knowledge and understanding of procedures to deal with disputes within your chosen business organisation.
- To achieve Level ❷   you need to give a clear and coherent description of procedures to deal with disputes.
- To achieve Level ❸   you need an in-depth evaluation of the procedures for addressing industrial disputes.

CHAPTER 31

# The recruitment process

Recruitment and selection is the process by which the business finds the best candidate for a job. Before doing this, however, the business must identify exactly what the job is: what skills or special qualities are needed, and how it can best attract the right type of applicant.

**Figure 31.1** *Every job needs a unique set of abilities and experiences. How do businesses identify who has them?*

## TRUE OR FALSE?

*Businesses can insist that their staff are all non-smokers.*

(see foot of page for answer)

**KEY SKILLS**
**Information Technology 2.x**

IT, Communications – Create a job advertisement using an IT application. Use an image (such as a logo) to make it more attractive. Perform a presentation to say how successful you think it will be in attracting applicants.

## What is the recruitment process?

A business needs to fulfil the following tasks in order to recruit an employee:

- identify that there is a vacancy
- carry out a job analysis to create a job specification
- draw up a person specification
- advertise the vacancy
- short-list applicants
- interview applicants
- select and appoint the most appropriate candidate for the job.

These are all part of the Human Resources function of a business. In a small business, a single person, such as the owner or one of the partners, may carry these out. In a larger business, a specialist HRM department will carry them out.

True or False answer

**False. Businesses can insist that staff do not smoke at work, and can also have special arrangements regarding insurance and pension funds, as smokers may die earlier and be a greater drain on these. In most circumstances, a business cannot insist that workers do not smoke when they are away from work.**

# Identifying that there is a vacancy

It is up to the Human Resources function in a business to see if there is a vacancy, and, if so, what sort of person would be the best to fill it. This is not always as straightforward as it sounds. Someone leaving could create a vacancy – in this case HRM needs to confirm that the job still needs doing. Even if it does, it may need additional duties as the nature of the job may have changed. In other cases, it may be a change in technology, or in production, or in the range of products made that means a new job is created. Once HRM has identified that there is, indeed, a job that needs to be done, they will have to analyse and describe it in order to get a picture of exactly the right sort of person for the job.

# Job analysis

Job analysis is the breaking down of a job into its component parts in order to identify exactly what the job requires. This means that a business can then advertise for staff that exactly match the detailed job requirements. It will include the tasks that need carrying out, the skills needed to carry them out and the relevant qualifications and experience that will be necessary. The analysis will be used to draw up a detailed description of the job and of the type of person wanted for the job.

## Job description

The job description will say what the job entails and what qualifications and experience are wanted. It will include the job title and the purpose and main duties of the job. It may also include an idea of working hours and conditions, who the person appointed will be responsible to, and other necessary details such as where the job is located.

# Person specification

The person specification is written to fit the 'ideal' candidate for a job. It is usually presented in three parts:

- the essential characteristics that a person applying must have – this could be qualifications or experience
- the desirable characteristics for the applicant – these are the aspects that will make the candidate more suitable for the job. They could include items such as a willingness to work flexible hours, or to take on extra work when necessary. They could also include skills and qualifications that would be useful. For example, for a person working in a kitchen it might be desirable to have first aid skill; for a person working in an office environment, certain IT

**Classwork activity**

1. There are ways other than interview to get a job. With a partner, explain what you think is meant by:
   - head-hunting
   - personal recommendation
   - personal enquiry
2. Sometimes jobs are not advertised as internal appointments are made. This means that someone from within the business is appointed.
3. Write down three good points of such a system and three bad points.
4. Compare your points with the rest of the class to draw up a master list.
5. Do you conclude that internal appointments are good or bad for a business?

skills might be desirable. (Candidates with the desirable skills are likely to be looked on more favourably than those without them.)

- The additional qualities that the business would, ideally, like the person to have – these could include things like a sense of humour or being a non-smoker.

## Advertising the vacancy

Once HRM are sure that they have the right descriptions and specifications, they need to advertise the vacancy. At this stage, a business may decide to use a specialist recruitment agency. These will carry out the rest of the process on behalf of the business, using their expertise where, perhaps, the business doesn't have it.

**Figure 31.2** *Inappropriate advertising!*

It is important that a business advertises its job vacancies in the right place. This depends on the nature of the organisation and the type of employee that they are seeking. A small trader might only need a card in a newsagent's window; other outlets include 'situations vacant' in local papers and, for better qualified or experienced staff, national job advertising. This could be through the trade press for a particular industry – specialist publications that are aimed at people seeking jobs in that industry. Teachers and other educational jobs, for example, are advertised in the *Times Educational Supplement* on a Friday. It could also be through national newspapers. Many newspapers have particular days for particular types of job. Teachers and other educational jobs, for example, are advertised on a Tuesday in the *Guardian* newspaper.

Vacancies can also be advertised through places provided by the government. Job centres are provided by the Department of Employment and aim to make it easier for people to find jobs by providing a free site for employers to advertise.

## Long-listing and short-listing

Once the business has received the applications, it then has to sift through to see which ones it is going to invite for interview. First the business will draw up a 'long list'. This is when the business takes a general look at applications and weeds out those that do not appear to fulfil the job specifications; perhaps applicants do not have the qualifications, they have produced untidy or illegible applications, or failed to carry out the instructions on 'how to apply'.

The next stage is short-listing. Applications are now read in detail and a list of possible candidates for interview is drawn up. Sometimes all the candidates on the short list are invited for interview; sometimes only some of them. At this stage, the business may also ask for references – from current or former employers, or from educational establishments. These are both to establish that what the applicant says about him or herself is true, but also to get some idea of the character and strengths of the applicant.

**CITIZENSHIP**

*It is important that businesses, through job advertisements, do not discriminate against certain groups. You will study the laws that relate to this. Find out what is meant by 'positive discrimination' and discuss whether or not your class or group agrees with it.*

## Interviewing

Interviewing can take a number of different formats. Examples include:

- the applicant is invited to answer questions by a panel of interviewers or a single person
- simple tests can be given to see if an applicant can do the job
- psychological tests may be carried out – these will usually be carried out by someone from outside the business who is then able to interpret the results to say, for example, whether a person would make a good team leader, or be able to act on their own initiative
- applicants may be asked to give a presentation on a particular subject, or to say how they would deal with a particular situation
- situational interviews can be given – where an applicant is put in a particular situation and asked to show how they would deal with it (a teacher might be asked to take a class, for example).

Interviews are sometimes held by the relevant people from HRM, sometimes by the line manager (the person who will be the successful applicant's immediate boss) and sometimes by a combination of both. Specialist interviewers brought in from outside the organisation may also hold interviews.

**Figure 31.3** *An interview*

**ACTIVITY**

✦ Draw up a job advertisement for a job in your chosen business.

✦✦ Compare this with a real job advertisement produced by your business and say which is better and why.

✦✦✦ Where did the real job advertisement appear (eg newspaper, job centre, message board)? Look at this place and say what features make it a good place to put the advertisement. How do you think the placement of the advertisement could be improved.

**FACT FILE**

*Advertising in national newspapers can be both very effective and expensive. It is therefore essential that a business chooses exactly the right place to put an advertisement. Applicants for particular types of job will only look in particular places; businesses should only be advertising in these places.*

## KEY *TERMS*

Job analysis – breaking down a job into its parts, to see what needs to be done
Person specification – an outline of the ideal qualities of a candidate
Recruitment – the process of finding someone to fill a job vacancy
Recruitment agency – a specialist business that will carry out recruitment on behalf of a client
Situational interviewing – putting interview candidates into situations to see how they cope

## After the interview

After the completion of the interview process, the successful candidate will be offered the job, and a contract of employment. This may happen on the same day as the interview, or could happen some time later, where a job offer is made by letter or telephone call. (Interviews may not all take place on the same day, or even at the same location.) Unsuccessful applicants can also get something positive out of the experience of an interview by asking for feedback from the business. This should answer questions such as how well did they do? what were their strengths and weaknesses? what could they do better next time?

## EXTENSION EXERCISE

Look at some job advertisements and ask for an application pack for at least five different ones. Compare the sort of information that is given by businesses, and the sort of information that they require. What are the most common questions asked? Why?

## What you need to do:

- **To achieve Level ❶**   you need to draw up a CV and complete an application form with a letter of application for a job of your choice in a chosen business. If possible, you should use a real job opportunity and advertisement.
- **To achieve Level ❷**   you need to explain how the application relates to the job description and what process the business might take to make a selection.
- **To achieve Level ❸**   you need to analyse and evaluate the effectiveness of the recruitment process at the business.

CHAPTER 32

# Personal job applications

When a person applies for a job, s/he needs to show him or herself in the best possible light. S/he will need to give the employer a detailed outline of his/her experiences, achievements and qualifications. S/he will also probably have to fill in an application form (or some other kind of detailed written application) and will almost certainly have to attend for an interview. Some of these can be pre-prepared; eg the current record of achievements and qualifications could be on an up-to-date Curriculum Vitae (CV). In other cases it is essential that the application is tailored to exactly what the business wants.

**Figure 32.1** *How important are the other skills and qualifications which people have?*

## Applying for a job

The usual way to apply for a job is by answering an advertisement. This will usually require one or more of the following:

- a letter of application – this could be part of an application form or a separate letter. This is the applicant's opportunity to say, in more detail, what makes him or her the ideal candidate for the post
- application forms – these are designed to give a business a quick reference to certain details of applicants so that they can easily select the ones that they want to look at in detail. Forms may also ask for personal details such as name, address, national insurance number, education, training and qualifications, as well as details of current job and employment history
- Curriculum vitae or resume – this is the 'story of your life' and is used to outline personal details, qualifications, education and experience and job histories.

There are other ways of applying for a job that can also be successful. For example:

- making an informal approach to a business – a telephone call or personal visit
- leaving a CV 'on file' – this means letting a business have a copy of your CV which they can keep and contact you if they have a suitable vacancy
- being headhunted – sometimes a business wants a particular person so badly, that they will offer them extra money or other rewards to tempt them away from their current employment.

### TRUE OR FALSE?

*Making an informal approach to an employer can often be successful.*

*(see foot of page for answer)*

True or False answer

**True.** If a business has a reliable person 'waiting' for a job, then it does not have to go through the time consuming (and expensive) process of recruitment and selection.

## CVs

CV stands for Curriculum Vitae. Sometimes it may be known as a 'resume' – this means a summary. It is designed to be a summary of your achievements and qualifications to date, and has advantages and disadvantages. To the applicant, it has the advantage of being already prepared for an application. To the employer it has the disadvantage of not necessarily being specific to the job being advertised.

CVs will be different, depending on age, qualifications, education, experience etc. Two examples for young people follow:

Jenny is still at school. Her brother Adam is at University. Jenny is applying for a part-time job with a local hotel. Adam is applying for his first full-time job at an electronics company, which has advertised a post in micro-engineering. While their CVs will be similar is some ways, in other ways they will be different. Either of them could choose to use a standard CV from a computer program. There are a number of such programs around, but Adam advised that they should their own CV, explaining that this would look better (as long as it was professional) than one that looked like everyone else's.

An applicant's CV should let an employer know the basic details about the applicant, so must include information such as name, address, age and education. The name should go first, then some personal details. The address and contact numbers can also be put in this first section, so that the employer can easily find them. Jenny's CV starts:

**Jenny Jones**
13 Woodside
Tyketown
YO1 0XX
Telephone 0123 456 789
Email: jen@usp.co.uk
Date of birth: 1st November 19xx
National Insurance Number AB 12 98 34 76
Health: Excellent

and Adam's starts:

**Adam Jones**
42 Student Flats
University of the North
SC42 1LL
Contacts: Term time: 0145 98 654; Mobile: 07777 12345; email adthelad@uninorth.ac.uk
Out of term: Home: 0123 456 789; email adthelad@usp.co.uk
Date of birth: 3rd July 19xx
National Insurance Number XX 98 65 32 00
Health: Excellent

### Classwork activity

Using Jenny as an example, draw up a CV for yourself as you are today.

Now draw up a CV for when you are Adam's age. What would you expect to have accomplished?

How do you think your CV will look in 20 years' time?

### HOMEWORK ACTIVITY

Choose a particular type of job that you would like. Look in a large newsagents for three possible publications where you would expect jobs of this type to be advertised.

### For your portfolio

You will need to collect, from your business, the details of a job. This could be one that is currently being offered or that has been advertised in the past. You then need to go through the process of applying for that job. Show the process in your portfolio – this should include any forms that the business requires an applicant to fill in, a letter of application and your CV. If possible, get someone responsible for HRM at your business to take you through the process of selection and interview.

Jenny and Adam then have different aims and ambitions. This is the next line on the CV. This should be a brief outline to let the employer know why the applicant wants the job, and how it fits in with the needs of the business. To do this, each has looked at what the employer has provided as a job description. It is a waste of time for Jenny to apply for part-time work while she studies, if the business actually wants people who want to make the catering industry into a career.

Jenny's aims and ambitions reads:

I am currently studying for my A levels and am seeking a part-time job while I study at Tyketown Sixth Form College.

Adam, however, is looking for a full-time job that he can make into a career. His ambitions are different:

I am about to complete my degree in electronics. I have developed such an interest in this field that I am looking to make a career in electronics, in particular in the field of micro-electronic engineering.

Each then adds a brief history of his/her education and qualifications so Jenny has:

Tyketown Comprehensive 19xx to 20xx
GCSEs in English Language (A), English Literature (A*), Business Studies (A*), Mathematics (B), French (C), Double Science (BB), Textiles Technology (C), History (A)

**CITIZENSHIP**

*Part of the selection process for some jobs – particularly those working with children and young people – require a police check before an appointment can be made. What do you think this means? Do you think it is necessary or fair?*

True or False answer

- ◆ Give three formal and three informal ways in which a person could apply for a job.
- ◆◆ Describe the process that they would have to follow for one of the formal methods.
- ◆◆◆ Explain what you think are the good and bad points of this process, and why.

And Adam has:

Tyketown Comprehensive 19xx to 19xx
GCSEs in English Language (A*), English Literature (A*), Business Studies (A*), Mathematics (A), German(C), Double Science (AA), Electronics (B), Computer Science (B)
Tyketown Vith Form College 20xx to 20xx
AS levels in English (C), Mathematics (A), Physics (A), Computer Science (B)
A levels in Mathematics (A), Physics (A), Computer Science (B), General Studies (C)
Key Skills at Level 3 Application of Number; Level 3 Information Technology; Level 3 Communications
University of the North, 20xx to 20xx, BSc in Electronic Engineering; first year exams: pass with distinction; second year exams: pass with distinction; expecting degree at upper second or first.

Notice that neither of them has mentioned primary school, or previous achievements such as swimming or cycling awards – these are no longer relevant so have 'dropped out' of the current CV.

Jenny and Adam then detail their work experience. Again, only the most relevant experience is included. For Adam, this means that his first couple of part-time jobs are no longer relevant, but his job last summer with an electronics firm is really important. Jenny's work experience is still relatively recent, while Adam's (at a pet shop) is no longer included.

Both then add their interests and activities. These do not have to be relevant to the job, but sometimes it can help if they are.

## ⬛ KEY *TERMS*

- Curriculum vitae or CV – the 'story of your life'
- Head-hunting – being offered a job by a business, without going through a process of selection
- Resume – similar to a CV

# EXTENSION EXERCISE

Another way of getting a job is through 'nepotism'. Look up this word and explain what it means. Do you agree with this practice? Explain your reasons.

Jenny adds:

I enjoy reading and watching television; actively I enjoy skiing, snowboarding and dancing. I play the cello and have a grade 3 qualification. (National qualifications in areas such as music or sports should always be mentioned; they show commitment and the ability to pass examinations.)

Adam adds:

I enjoy rebuilding computers and other electronic equipment as well as playing computer games; I am President of the University Electronics Society; I am also a keen swimmer (and qualified life saver) and have represented Yorkshire in the County Championships.

## KEY SKILLS
### Information Technology 2.x

IT, Communications. Look at the various different types of CV designs that are available via computer programme or the internet. Choose three of these and create a document which compares them to each other. Explain which you think is the most effective and why.

They then both add the names of two referees. Mr Khan, the headmaster of Tyketown Comprehensive, is named for both (although the reference request is likely to be passed by the school to their form teacher). Jenny also gives the name of a professional family friend, who can say that she is honest and trustworthy, whilst Adam gives the name of his University tutor.

## Application forms

Often businesses want the applicant's details in a particular format, so do not ask for CVs. Instead, they produce an application form that asks for the specific details they need. One of the reasons they may want information of a particular type and in a particular order is that they can enter it onto a computer database. Many businesses now provide application forms online for applicants to fill in.

**FACT FILE**

The government provides job centres and has also set up job clubs, where advice on filling out application forms, writing letters and composing CVs is available, and equipment on which to make job applications such as computers is provided. In certain cases, grants to cover postage costs for applications and travel expenses to interviews may also be given.

## Letter of application

A letter of application may also be required. This is the applicant's chance to say why they think they are the best person for the job – what qualities or experience makes them most suitable. In this letter, applicants can enlarge on their own skills, list any further achievements (including giving more detail of those outlined in a CV) and show their enthusiasm for the job. They can also say what their hopes and expectations are for the future – enlarging on the opening statement of their CV to say what they think they can bring to the job and how.

## Interviews

The final selection process for a job will usually take place through an interview. Jenny and Adam (and all other interview candidates) should always

- dress smartly and appropriately for the interview
- make sure that they are punctual
- be confident (but not over-confident)
- answer questions as fully and clearly as possible
- be able to demonstrate an ability to do the job, if necessary
- ask sensible questions when asked to do so
- only sit down when asked to
- remember not to smoke, chew or swear.

## What you need to do:

- To achieve Level ❶  you need to draw up a CV and complete an application form with a letter of application for a job of your choice in a chosen business. If possible, you should use a real job opportunity and advertisement.
- To achieve Level ❷  you need to explain how the application relates to the job description and what process the business might take to make a selection.
- To achieve Level ❸  you need to analyse and evaluate the effectiveness of the recruitment process at the business.

CHAPTER 33
# Staff development and training

Training and development play an important part in business when a company has recruited new staff, when it reviews problems with its workforce, and when it is managing its human resources. Training and development of the workforce may have a number of purposes, from introducing new staff to the company, to showing existing staff how to operate new machinery and to retraining workers with redundant skills. A number of methods may be used but broadly they may be either on or off the job. While most training will have benefits to both employee and employer, there are also possible costs to both. Training and development of workers is also vital to the improvement of the UK economy.

*Figure 33.1*

## Appraisal

Many businesses operate a system of staff appraisal. This is a way of reviewing an employee's performance, usually on a yearly basis but it can be more frequent if required. Targets may be set and reviewed. In the best systems, employees and managers are able to openly discuss issues and identify how the employee can be helped to improve performance. In this way the business is able to help bring about real staff development. Increasingly, businesses are taking part in formal schemes that recognise and certify the achievement of both the company and its workers in training and development.

The most important part of the process is usually a discussion between the employee and his or her manager. The best schemes will identify both ways for the employee to improve, and the help the business will need to provide for the employee. In this way the employee is able to develop as a more effective member of staff.

## The purposes of training

A business should have a very clear idea of what it hopes to achieve by a training scheme. The purposes will depend partly on the type of business, the nature of its product, the type of workers it is dealing with, and its available budget. Typical purposes will include:

- introducing new employees to the firm, its workplace and the job
- increasing the efficiency of the workers. Virtually all firms are keen to increase the output obtained from their workers; and training may help to achieve this. In the modern workplace, there is a greater need for workers to be able to do a variety of tasks. The process of achieving this is called **multi-skilling** and it allows workers to be used flexibly

**ACTIVITY**

Re-read the descriptions of induction, on-the-job and off-the-job training.

✦ 1. Think of other possible costs and benefits of training to add to this list:

- improving company image
- better quality products
- wage rates may rise
- wasteful motivation
- improved promotion prospects

- the cost of courses
- higher production
- lost production
- improved worker
- workers are more skilled

✦✦ 2. a) Decide whether they are costs to the firm or the employee.
b) Decide whether they are benefits to the firm or the employee.
c) Create a grid to record your decisions for each of the three types of training.

---

## For your portfolio

In your investigation of your chosen business you need to:

1. find out the types and purposes of training given to new employees
2. find out other forms of training available to all employees
3. find out how the business measures the success of the various forms of training given to employees

4. consider how else you could measure the success of the training.

In your report you need to:

1. describe the type and purpose of training given to new employees
2. assess how successful each type of training is for your chosen business
3. suggest other forms of more appropriate training the business might try to use.

---

- helping to introduce new technology into a business, as many employees will need training both in how to use it and how to repair and maintain it. This is often referred to as **upgrading skills** and is particularly important now as information technology is being increasingly used in the workplace
- providing training in health and safety procedures, especially when there are changes in the law
- using appropriate training as a way to motivate workers
- as a way to help some workers to gain promotion, either inside or outside the firm that employs them. This is often referred to as **staff development**
- for an increasing number of employees in an increasing number of industries, retraining is vital so that they can move into new jobs as their old ones disappear.

## The Types of Training

There are three basic types of training:

### Induction

Where this is used a firm usually introduces the new worker to the firm, the workplace and the job. Information will be given to the new worker about the company and its products, the company regulations and important health and safety considerations. If the job is in a large building, the worker may be given a tour and shown the layout of all the facilities. The worker will be introduced to the people s/he will be working with, and will be told about the other key personnel. The firm may also take time to identify the particular needs of the new worker. This information may then be used to help plan the more specific types of training needed.

***Figure 33.2*** *New employees will need a demonstration on the machines they are to use*

## On the job

This type of training takes place within the firm and on the production line. It often means working with an experienced employee who will show you how to use any machinery and will check your progress. Some firms try to improve on this by using specialist instructors. In general, you are 'learning by doing' and you will be making the product or providing some sort of service. So, the firm receives some direct benefit from this training, although new employees may create a lot of waste while they learn the job.

## Off the job

This form of training takes place away from the production line. The trainee will not be making goods or providing services that can be sold. Larger firms may have their own training centres staffed by specialist instructors, while smaller firms are more likely to use

***Figure 33.3*** *A tour of the workplace for new workers*

## Classwork activity

1. In pairs, each student needs to discuss, agree and set objectives or targets for improving the quality of work in your studies. As part of the discussion, agree the length of time between setting and judging the actual achievement of the targets. Also, discuss and decide how to measure the achievment of the targets.
2. At the end of the time period agreed, in your same pairs, discuss how well each of you have achieved your targets. Identify how you personally could have improved your performance and identify the help you need to continue improving.
3. Discuss, agree and set anew set of targets for the next period of time.

Colleges of Further or Higher Education to provide specialist courses. In this case, the trainee will be released from the workplace. This could be for one day a week or perhaps for a whole block of time.

It is quite likely that such training will lead to an external award or qualification; in some cases, the firm may want the trainee to receive a broader training rather than something that would just help him or her directly in the workplace.

## The costs and benefits of training

Most of the costs of training will be paid by the business. The most obvious costs will include the wages paid to any trainer directly employed by the business or the costs of sending workers to a course. The less obvious costs might be the waste generated by employees as they make mistakes while learning how to make the product 'on the job', slower production levels while they are still learning, and poor customer relations if they provide a less than satisfactory service.

The benefits may be shared between both business and employee. The benefits received by a business might be quite clear, including higher production levels and better quality products and service. In a more hidden way, a company might gain a good reputation for training its workers well, while its workers might be more positive and motivated. For the employees, the benefits received from training might be wage rises, better promotion prospects both within and outside the company, the feeling of being more skilled and hopefully more motivated.

## National schemes for recognizing training and development

One of the best known schemes is the Investors in People Standard. Any organisation working towards the Standard must work through a series of steps, setting itself goals and making a plan to achieve them. The staff must be fully involved in these plans and staff development needs to be identified to achieve these goals. The development must then take place, ending up with a thorough evaluation to see how far the investment has been a success. Organisations that successfully work through the steps may then display the Investors in People logo at their premises and on their headed notepaper.

In recent years, a number of training initiatives have been introduced by the Government. These include modern

**INVESTORS IN PEOPLE**

*Figure 33.4* © *Investors in People UK, 2002*

## KEY TERMS

Induction Training – for new staff, an introduction to the company, its organisation, its rules and regulations and to the job
On-the-job Training – methods of training that involve a worker learning the job as s/he works on the actual production line
Off-the-job Training – methods which take place away from the production line so that the trainee is not involved in producing the good or providing the service.

# EXTENSION EXERCISE

Remploy is a national company which was set up to directly employ large numbers of disabled people. It employs over 12,000 people on 96 sites in the UK. Over 10,000 of these employees are registered disabled. One of the factories is at Ashington, in Northumberland, with 105 shopfloor employees – all people with disabilities. The company operates a general induction programme for all new employees. This covers health and safety training in addition to information on the company, company history and all the rules, regulations and benefits offered by Remploy. Once this is complete, any specific skill training is delivered in the factory. Remploy uses what they call the 'buddy system` where a skilled operator is teamed up with the trainee. All training is to NVQ level 2 in Manufacturing, Assembling and Processing skills so that all employees achieve a formal qualification. As Remploy states, "All employees will be helped and encouraged to attain their highest level of ability and a multi-skilled workforce will emerge fully motivated and rewarded."
Read the data and answer the following questions.

1. Explain the possible reasons for Remploy operating an induction programme.
2. What type of job specific training is Remploy using? Explain the possible advantages to Remploy from using this.
3. Describe the possible costs to Remploy from using this form of job specific training.
4. Suggest the possible benefits to Remploy's employees from this training.

apprenticeships which take up to three years to complete. Most trainees are classed as employees and are paid a wage. The Government supports the cost of the training in service areas as well as in the traditional areas such as engineering and manufacturing. National Training Organisations have been set up for specific industries with a Training Standards Council monitoring the quality of the training and the awarding of National Training Awards to trainees.

## What you need to do:

In your portfolio of evidence from your investigation of your chosen business:
• To achieve Level ❶    you need to identify what training you might receive if you were newly appointed and what training you might receive if you were an experienced employee. You also need to describe the procedure for appraisal and performance review, the retraining for the introduction of new technology or new work practices, any national training initiatives affecting your chosen business, and health and safety training.
• To achieve Level ❷    you need to analyse how effective these training and other procedures are in enabling people to perform their jobs.
• To achieve Level ❸    using the analysis for level 2 you need to suggest and justify alternative or additional procedures that might improve the effectiveness of employees.

CHAPTER 34

# Meeting customer expectations

Most organisations today recognise the importance of their customers. They try to understand what customers need and want so that they can try to provide the goods and services to match these requirements. For many businesses this means putting the customers first through the range of goods and services on offer, through the prices charged, and through the customer care and service offered. For many businesses this means they must give their staff extensive training. Staff will need to be aware of customer needs. They will need a great deal of knowledge about the products sold by their organisation. They will also need to develop personal skills to deal

*Figure 34.1*

with the variety of problems and situations likely to arise when dealing with customers.

*Figure 34.2 For Next, quality and choice are key to meeting customer expectations*

## Types of customers

Many businesses will only have external customers. For a business such as a clothing manufacturer, this is most likely to be a retail business buying clothes for sale in its shops. These external customers may have very specific requirements. For example, companies such as Next will order specific designs, sizes and colours from its suppliers and will expect the clothing to meet the highest quality standards. When Next sells its clothing to the public, it will also be dealing with external customers. In this case the customers in a Next store may have less specific requirements but will want to choose from a range of designs, colours and sizes and will be looking for value for money.

Some businesses will have both external customers and internal customers. Those with internal customers are likely to be organised into sections or departments. In a pharmaceutical company, one section may manufacture a basic form of bulk penicillin. While some of this may be sold to customers outside the company, the remainder might be 'sold' to a section within the company that processes the basic penicillin into more sophisticated antibiotic drugs. These type of internal customers are likely to have equally high expectations and may also require appropriate customer care.

## Customer expectations

Today's consumers seem to have ever higher expectations from the goods and services they buy. They also expect customer service and care to match the quality of the products being purchased. Typical expectations are listed and described below.

1. Providing an appropriate range of goods and services. Most people expect a wide choice when they are buying virtually any product. This seems to be the case whether it is for the family's basic food shopping, or for a new season's wardrobe of clothes or for those ever important electrical necessities of televisions, mobile phones and computers.

2. Providing good value products. This clearly links to the first point but brings in the ideas of quality and price. Most goods are available in a range of quality levels. The price of a good is likely to reflect the quality of the good. Generally speaking, the higher the quality, the higher the price. Customers will take this into account when making their purchases and will expect the value of an item to reflect the price paid and the level of quality built into the product.

3. Dealing rapidly with enquiries. Customers become very frustrated if problems and general enquiries are not dealt with quickly. Some firms set targets for dealing with enquiries by a certain amount of time. If customers feel that their questions are at least being dealt with, they are likely to regard the business in a more positive light.

4. Providing clear and honest information. This can be applied to information about the features of a product, its price, its delivery, and the aftercare available once the product is bought and taken home. Customers are more likely to buy from a company in the future if they feel that they have been given the full picture.

5. Having good and clear communication systems. This obviously links with points 3 and 4, but is also important in its own right. Businesses need to provide clear systems whether it is the way telephone calls are received, letters are dealt with or face to face enquiries are handled. Any faults can lead to a customer's opinion of the business being lowered, and a bad reputation can result if this is passed on by word of mouth.

## CITIZENSHIP

*In groups discuss whether 'have a nice day' or the smile and a 'hello' from the supermarket checkout operator really make a difference to customer expectations and satisfaction.*

**Figure 34.3** *One way to give a good impression*

**ACTIVITY**

You are going to investigate customer expectations for a small range of products.

✦ Split into small groups.

✦ Choose five everyday goods or services that people buy.

✦ Create a small questionnaire to discover customer expectations for these five goods or services. Use this chapter to help identify the types of expectations customers might have and therefore the questions you could ask.

✦ Each person in your group should try the questionnaire on four members of the public.

✦ Share your results with everyone else in your group.

✦ Write a report describing what your group has found out about customer expectations for your five goods or services.

6. Building relationships with customers. This might be as simple as dealing in a courteous way with customers. It certainly includes showing care and attention when dealing directly with customers. If two products are identical in every respect, a customer is more likely to buy from the business that has shown the right level of courteous attention to detail in the past. We may laugh at such phrases as 'have a nice day', but they might just make a difference to some customers.

7. Providing after-sales service. Many businesses claim to provide a high level of help, information, maintenance and even repair once the customer starts to use the product. The reputation of many businesses, however, has been lost when the level of service promised has not been delivered. How many people, for example, have had difficulties contacting mobile phone companies when they have had problems with their phones?

**Figure 34.4** *Prompt repairs keep customers happy*

## What you need to do:

- To achieve Level ❶     you need to identify the features in your chosen organisation that contribute towards good customer service.
- To achieve Level ❷     you need to analyse how customer care in your chosen business help to meet the needs and expectations of its customers.
- To achieve Level ❸     you need to suggest and justify how customer service might be improved to better meet the needs and expectations of its customers.

CHAPTER 35
# Measuring customer satisfaction

If a business wants to measure the satisfaction levels of its customers, it needs to carry out market research. Market research can be used to discover the answers to a whole range of questions including what product to produce, what price to charge, how to promote the product and how to distribute it. You should remember in this chapter that we are trying to focus research on the measurement of consumer satisfaction which will normally result during and after the purchase of the good or service.

**Figure 35.1** *Measuring customer satisfaction by market research*

ACTIVITY

◆ Make a grid of the research methods described below, using three columns. In the first column, give a basic description of the research method. In the second column give the main advantages of each method, and in the third column give the disadvantages. Remember that this is research to assess customer satisfaction.

# What is market research?

The process of market research involves six basic steps:

1. Defining the problem to be researched – what do you want to find out?
2. Determining the most suitable research technique – what is the best method to get the most accurate data in the most cost effective way?
3. Selecting the sample for the study – which data set or which groups of consumers should we use in the research?
4. Collecting the data – actually carrying out the research.
5. Analysing the data – what do the findings of the research really tell us?
6. Presenting the results – showing what has been found out and the conclusions that have been drawn.

# Research methods

Most market research uses **quantitative** techniques to discover answers to broad questions that start with how much or how many. In other words, they are trying to collect data that is easily measured and can lead to conclusions backed by valid statistics. **Qualitative** techniques try to discover consumer attitudes and provide answers to broad questions starting with the question why.

Market research information can be gained in two ways – using desk research or field research. Desk research generally collects secondary data which involves the study of existing information. This can be collected from within the organisation by looking at the business's own records of accounts, sales, and customer complaints. Information may also be collected from outside the business from trade associations, government statistics and from the media. Field research generally collects primary data since it usually involves obtaining new information about a firm's products and its market.

Methods suitable for measuring customer satisfaction include:

• Database research: many businesses now create their own database using ICT to collect, store and analyse data about their customers. This data could include names and addresses of customers, how often they buy and how much they spend as customer profiles are built up. Increasingly much of this data is created through the use

*Figure 35.2*

## KEY *TERMS*

- Quantitative techniques – these discover answers to broad questions that start with how much or how many.
- Qualitative techniques – these try to discover consumer attitudes and provide answers to broad questions starting with the question why.
- Desk research – generally collects secondary data which involves the study of existing information.
- Field research – generally collects primary data since it usually involves obtaining new information about a firm's products and its market.

of bar-code scanners and swipe machines for debit and credit cards. Records of communications from customers – whether by post, telephone or perhaps by email – may be kept and analysed to show levels of customer satisfaction.

- Surveys using questionnaires face to face, over the telephone or by post. These are most likely to use quantitative techniques, as questions are created to measure the responses of consumers.
- Interviews, either on a one-to-one basis or as part of consumer panel or focus group, are able to employ qualitative techniques to collect information about consumer attitudes and responses to products. Skilled interviewers are able to question consumers in more depth and can encourage them to think about their responses more carefully.
- Observation of the way consumers act when buying is an underrated but important method. Measuring the time a customer spends in a shop, the direction walked, how products are inspected and whether they appear to be attracted to in-store advertising can all provide useful information.

## EXTENSION EXERCISE

Either as an individual student or in small groups:

Create a questionnaire that could be used to measure customer satisfaction with a local supermarket. Remember to include questions about products, packaging, prices, display, availability, advertising, queues, any other general services available such as car parks, and the quality of the customer service provided by the supermarket. Try to use a mixture of questions that use quantitative techniques and qualitative techniques.
Test your questionnaire out before trying it on the general public. Amend questions as necessary.

Once you are happy with your questionnaire, try it out. If you plan to do this at the actual supermarket, you must get permission from the store management first.

## Other methods of assessing customer satisfaction

A business may try to review its arrangements for providing customer service and therefore achieving customer satisfaction by carrying out its own checks. This might be achieved by managers observing and assessing staff as they deal with customers, they might employ 'mystery shoppers' to assess and report on staff, and they might review their all their procedures for dealing with complaints and sorting out other problems.

### What you need to do:

- To achieve Level ❷     you need to identify and explain how the business finds out about the needs of its customers.

CHAPTER 36

# Features of customer service

Chapter 34 looked at the importance of a business meeting the expectations of its customers, while Chapter 35 explained how a business can measure the satisfaction levels of its customers. This chapter will help you to consider the possible features of customer service that a business might use.

***Figure 36.1*** *All important view for all firms?*

## Different aspects of customer service

The actual customer service features used will vary between businesses, and depends on such things as the size of the firm and the product being sold. A business needs to select the most appropriate customer service features from the following list. It then has to decide how to operate the features, and how to measure their effectiveness. The features are expressed as a set of questions grouped under six broad headings.

## TRUE OR FALSE?

*Providing customer care and service will cost a firm a lot of money and will reduce profits.*

*(see foot of page for answer)*

### The products

- What quality of goods or services are being offered?
- Is the product meeting safety requirements?
- Is the package appropriately packaged?
- Is information about the product clearly presented and readily available?
- Is there a wide enough choice of products?

### The staff

- Are the staff knowledgeable and helpful?
- Are they polite and appropriately dressed?
- Are there enough staff to meet customer requirements?
- Do the staff have good communication skills?

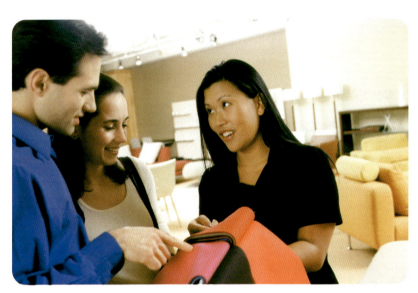

***Figure 36.2*** *Good staff are vital in maintaining customer care*

### The premises

- Are the premises well equipped and offer an appropriate range of facilities?
- Are the premises well signposted?
- Are the premises clean and well organised?
- Are the premises accessible to disabled people?

***Figure 36.3***

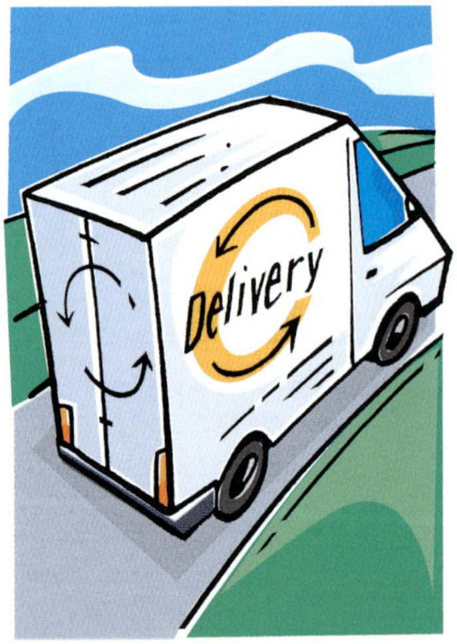

### Delivery

- Is delivery available?
- Is delivery reliable and prompt?
- Is delivery free or at a reasonable price?

True or False answer

True and False. It will cost a business money but, if it helps maintain business reputation, sales and revenue may be increased so that the overall level of profit is unaffected.

## After-sales service

- Is after-sales service available?
- Is after-sales service provided in an appropriate way?
- Are there guarantees on the products?
- Are telephone helplines available?
- Can products be exchanged if they are not appropriate to a customer's needs?
- How will repairs be arranged?
- How will customer complaints be dealt with?

## Other features

- Is there a range of possible payment methods?
- Are there initiatives such as customer charters and mission statements, making promises to customers?
- Are there set ways to deal with customers, eg set words for answering the telephone?
- What training in customer care is given to staff?

This list may not cover all of the possible features of customer care and service, but it should give you a very full flavour of typical features for most organisations. As technology moves on, businesses are likely to make use of email and websites as a way of both providing and measuring customer service.

**For your portfolio**

In your investigation of the customer care and service provided by your chosen business, you need to find out how the business measures customer satisfaction, as well as discovering the key features of that care. To some extent this is covered in Chapter 35, but the following points might act as a reminder of key methods that might be used by the business.

- Is sales performance analysed? For example, are sales records, the number of actual customers, loyalty card records monitored?
- Are there records of complaints and/or returned goods?
- Are there customer panels or interviews?
- Are questionnaires used?
- Is observation used? For example, does a 'mystery shopper' visit?

**CITIZENSHIP**

*Is it right to judge staff using this sort of checklist? Does the use of 'mystery customers' put too much pressure on staff?*

*Discuss these issues within your class.*

### Observation Checklist

Name of staff member.......................................... Date.................
Observer........................................ Time From.........To..............
Counter

| Counter Service | Possible | Actual |
|---|---|---|
| 1. Smiles and gives friendly greeting to customer | 5 | |
| 2. Is attentive when taking customer order | 3 | |
| 3. Informs customer of promotions and possible extras | 4 | |
| 3. Products are collected in correct order to maintain quality | 3 | |
| 4. Asks for and receives payment politely | 3 | |
| 5. Thanks customer with smile and personalised comment | 3 | |
| 6. Appearance is smart, clean and complete | 3 | |
| 7. Cleans work area regularly | 2 | |
| 8. Works safely and as part of a team | 5 | |

**Figure 36.4** *Observation checklist*

## ACTIVITY

The observation checklist shown above had two other sections: for service in the dining area, and for general service.

♦ Create two lists of criteria to judge staff on these other two areas of customer service.

♦♦ You also need to decide the possible scores for each criteria.

♦♦♦ If you had to grade staff on a five point scale from A to E, what sort of score would you need to achieve a grade A? What sort of score would suggest you need to warn the member of staff?

♦♦♦♦ Try out the checklist in your local fast food outlet by acting as a mystery shopper and without informing any staff.

## Observing staff at work

An example of one way of assessing customer care is to observe staff at work and record the quality of the service they give to the customer. The observation checklist shown above is part of a three-section sheet used for a fast food outlet.

## EXTENSION EXERCISE

• Look back at the features of customer service described in this chapter.
• Identify which features are likely to be used by your chosen business.
• Create ways of collecting information about the way your chosen business provides customer care and service. For example, you could create checklists and questionnaires, collect leaflets from the business, and arrange interviews with managers.

## What you need to do:

• To achieve Level ❶    you need to describe the customer service arrangements within your chosen business.

• To achieve Level ❷    you need to assess the quality of customer service arrangements within your chosen business.

• To achieve Level ❸    you need to create a thorough and detailed evaluation of the quality of customer service within your chosen business leading to recommendations for possible improvements.

CHAPTER 37
# Consumer protection

Protecting the consumer means making sure that the customer is receiving the actual goods and services he or she wants, and that they are in the right condition to work as expected. More formally, a series of laws set up the key principles that when a good is sold, it should be:

- 'As described', meaning the actual good should match its description
- 'Fit for the purpose', meaning the good should carry out the tasks it is supposed to do
- 'Of merchantable quality', meaning the good should work correctly.

*Figure 37.1*

## Current consumer laws

There are a number of other laws that also exist to protect the customer, on such things as the contents and labelling of food, consumer credit and claims about sale prices. Business is expected to know and keep within the law. In addition, in some cases business has set up its own help for the consumer through such things as **voluntary codes of practice**. A number of pressure groups also make it part of their role to protect the consumer from 'big business', with the Consumer Association probably the best known champion of the individual consumer. The consumer is also expected to look after his or her own interests by acting responsibly.

### Trade Descriptions Acts 1968 and 1972

These Acts makes it a criminal offence to give false or misleading descriptions on goods, services, accommodation and facilities. This also includes the sale prices, with the Acts stating that goods may only be described as reduced if they have been offered at a higher price for 28 consecutive days within the last six months.

### Sale of Goods Act 1979

This set up the principles of 'fit for the purpose, as described and of merchantable quality'. If these conditions are not met, customers are entitled to a refund or a replacement. This was strengthened by the Sale of Goods Act 1994 which replaced 'merchantable quality' with 'satisfactory quality'. This means that the quality of goods applies to appearance, finish, safety and durability as well as being free from minor defects. Consumers are given a reasonable time to examine goods to check for satisfactory quality.

*Figure 37.2* Products must be as described

## Food and Drink Acts 1955, 1976 and 1982

These Acts deal with hygiene, composition and labelling of food. In simple terms, food cannot be sold which is unfit to eat, and all food must be correctly labelled. This was reinforced by the Food Safety Act 1990, which requires all businesses handling food to take all 'reasonable precautions' when they manufacture, transport, store, prepare and sell food.

## Weights and Measures Act 1985

This Act makes it an offence for traders to give 'short' weight or measure. Inspectors visit shops to check the accuracy of scales, public houses to check pumps and optics, and petrol stations to check petrol pumps.

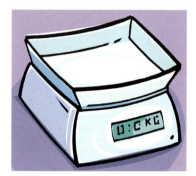

**Figure 37.3** *Scales must be accurate*

## Consumer Credit Act 1974

This requires all businesses offering credit to be licensed by the Office of Fair Trading. All borrowers must be given a written statement of the total cost of interest on any loan and credit agreement. This is shown as the annual percentage rate (APR). Consumers can also opt out of credit agreements after a 15-day 'cooling off' period.

## Consumer Protection Act 1987

This Act improved the law on the sale of dangerous goods. Certain goods, eg bleach, must be marked with warnings and safety advice. Other goods, including heaters and toys, are covered by safety regulations. The EU has added to this by issuing a directive that means damages can be claimed against suppliers of defective products which cause injury or death.

## Unsolicited Goods Act 1971

Finally, this Act means that consumers do not have to pay for goods which are sent to them but which they have not ordered.

# Consumer Rights

You can see from the descriptions of consumer law shown above that the range of rules is wide and they are also quite complicated. Some of a consumer's basic rights under these laws are therefore described below.

Customers can return a good that is:

- faulty
- does not work
- does not do what it is claimed it can do.

In all of these three cases, the customer can either have a replacement or a refund. A credit note should not be offered by the business in any of these cases. If a customer changes his or her

### For your portfolio

You need to understand the main principles behind current consumer laws covering:

- health and safety
- sale of products
- labelling of products
- misuse of information

The laws covering these are described in this chapter. As part of your investigation and report, you need to find out how your chosen business keeps within these laws as it carries out its business and provides customer service.

## KEY *TERMS*

Voluntary codes – agreements between members of a particular industry to police themselves rather than have laws passed to control them

British Standards Institute – an independent body which tests and certifies products

The Consumers' Association – an independent body which tests products looking for 'value for money' and reports the findings to consumers in their *Which?* magazine

Privatised industries – industries that were taken out of government control but are regulated by independent bodies such as OFGAS.

mind about the good when they take it home from the shops, the business does not have to offer either a refund or even a credit note. The business, however, may choose to do this if it wishes to extend its customer services and so help its reputation.

On a service that is not carried out properly or is not as described, customers can:

- have a refund
- have the service finished properly by the original business
- have the service finished properly by a new business with the charge being paid for by the original business.

## Voluntary Codes of Practice

Many businesses choose to offer a level of customer service over and above that required by law. In some cases, this leads to businesses within an industry setting up a voluntary code of practice. This code will lay down what is or is not acceptable. One code of practice is run by the Advertising Standards Authority (ASA). This organisation stops firms from running inappropriate advertisements; eg it has stopped companies using pictures and other images that are thought to be ethically or morally wrong.

The Association of British Travel Agents (ABTA) is a well known organisation with a major role to play in the travel business. It operates a code of practice that all members must keep to or they will be fined. All members must be insured through ABTA so that, if they go out of business, their customers either get their holiday or get their money back.

Some occupations and professions have a formal organisation that governs the behaviour of members. For example, the General Medical

*Figure 37.4*

## EXTENSION EXERCISE

New consumer laws and regulations are likely to appear in the next few years. Check that you have the most up-to-date information, both by searching the internet and by approaching the organisations described in this chapter.

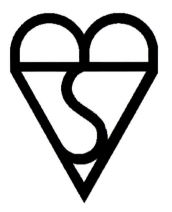

**Figure 37.5** *The British Standards Institution 'Kitemark'*

Council (GMC) can stop doctors practising medicine if they are found to be careless, dishonest or incompetent.

## Local Authority involvement

Local councils help to maintain standards and carry out checks laid down by laws through their Trading Standards Office. Officers will make regular and surprise visits to traders, checking scales are registering correct weights and that pumps are delivering the correct volume of petrol, for example. They will investigate complaints about dangerous goods being sold, such as toys with small parts that might break off, leaving sharp pieces that could hurt a young child. Sometimes they will investigate bad business practice, which when publicised puts pressure on to the traders to change.

Councils also have Environmental Health Officers who check for all forms of food hygiene. They will also investigate other health risks including sources of pollution and illegal waste disposal.

## Independent help

Various independent organisations have been set up to help consumers, either by setting high standards for products or through the giving of advice.

- The British Standards Institution (BSI) tests products to make sure they are reliable and of a high standard. Products that pass the tests can display the Institution's 'Kitemark'. This helps to reassure consumers that the product is both safe and of a high quality.
- The Consumers' Association is an independent body that investigates consumer issues and carries product testing to determine 'best buys'. It publishes its main magazine *Which?* to report on these investigations, and also publishes more focused magazines such as *Travel Which*.
- The Office of Fair Trading was set up in 1973 to provide information and advice to consumers. Much of this is achieved through leaflets available at Trading Standards Offices and Citizens' Advice Bureaux. The Director General of Fair Trading monitors consumer problems and whether consumer law is working well.
- Citizens' Advice Bureaux are 'staffed' by volunteers and give free help and advive on all sorts of matters including consumers rights and problems.
- OFTEL, OFGAS and OFWAT are examples of organisations set up to make sure that businesses in the privatised industries of telecommunications, gas supply and water supply do not exploit their consumers.

## Consumers self-protection

While consumers are protected by the law and other organisations, they are still expected to look out for their own interests. They are expected to be careful when buying goods and services. This means consumers should:

- read instructions and follow them
- read labels on food, drink and medicine
- read the small print.

## What you need to do:

• To achieve Level ❶    you need to describe the rights of customers under consumer law.

# BUSINESS

## Business Finance

# CHAPTER 38

# Business costs and revenue

Kent Clarke ran his own hairdressing business in Ashington, Northumberland, for nearly 25 years. For the first 15 of those years, he employed a fully trained assistant at his small salon, close to the town's main high street. In the last few years, Kent was the only stylist at the salon, and depended on a succession of trainees to do the less skilled tasks. He found it increasingly difficult to take holidays and, when he did, it meant closing the business. This affected his trade and he still had to pay all his overheads for that time.

**Figure 38.1** *Some of the costs for a hairdresser*

At the same time, competition in the hairdressing trade in Ashington had becomes quite intense. While costs continued to rise, Kent had to keep prices down. He found it more and more difficult to make a reasonable living from his salon-based business.

Kent did not want to return to working for someone else, and he felt that expansion was far too risky. Instead, he closed the salon and opted for the extra flexibility of operating as a mobile hairdresser. He realised that there would be new costs from being mobile, but he calculated that these would be outweighed by a considerable reduction in his overheads.

In the months leading up to the closure of the salon in September 1999, Kent asked his customers if they would continue to support him if he went mobile. Over 90% of his customers said they would, and some even suggested that other members of their families would probably use his services while he was at their homes. This market research, together with his cost calculations, gave Kent confidence that he could make a success of his new business operation. He was also able to reduce costs by not replacing his trainee assistant when she left after a few months.

## LEARNING ACTIVITY 1

1. Make a list of the likely types of costs Kent would have had when he operated the salon.
2. From this list of costs, decide which five costs would have been his largest when measured over a whole year. Give reasons for your choice.
3. Make a list of the likely types of costs Kent has in operating his mobile hairdressing business.
4. Create a new top five of Kent's largest costs for this new business. Explain the changes you have made.
5. To confirm some of your ideas, *either* talk to your hairdresser about the main types of costs in their business, *or* invite a hairdresser in to talk to your class.

# What are costs?

Any business, whether making and selling a good or providing a service, will require a large number of resources. These resources are likely to include workers, land and buildings, machinery and equipment, raw materials and parts or components. It is unlikely that these resources will be obtained 'free of charge' and most firms will have to pay either to purchase them or to hire them. Such payments for these resources are known as **costs of production** or more simply as **costs**.

**TRUE OR FALSE?**

Another name for a cost is price.

(see foot of page for answer)

# What are the typical costs of a business?

The types of costs that a business faces will depend on its size and on the nature of the good or service it is offering for sale. Some broad categories of costs, however, may be identified if we think of the typical groups of resources that a business will use.

- labour: salaries, wages, training, bonuses, fringe benefits
- land: rent or purchase price
- buildings: rent or purchase price, business rates, water rates, insurance
- power: heating, lighting
- equipment: hire or purchase price, maintenance/repairs, machinery/tools, furniture/furnishings, vehicles
- communications: telephone, post, stationery
- raw materials
- ingredients
- parts
- components
- depreciation
- interest on loans.

*Figure 38.2*

# What are the main types of revenue?

Revenue is income earned by a firm selling either the goods it makes or the services it offers:

- some firms in primary industry earn revenue by extracting raw materials; eg quarries might extract and sell stone, mines might extract and sell coal, while farms will grow and sell crops
- manufacturing firms make or assemble goods, and earn revenue mainly by selling them to other firms
- retail firms earn revenue mainly by selling goods or services to their customers from the general public
- other firms in the tertiary sector earn revenue by selling services either to the public or to other firms.

*Figure 38.3 Changing price will affect revenue*

## True or False answer

**False.** It is important to think of costs and price from the point of view of a business and not mix them up. Costs are the payments a business makes to buy or hire resources, to make and sell goods or provide services. When the good or service is sold, the business will set a *price*, which will bring in income or revenue to the firm before any costs are taken away.

From these examples, you can see that a firm's revenue is income received direct from its main production or trading activities. Sometimes, such revenue is called **turnover** or even **sales turnover** particularly when stocks are bought in and then sold on to customers.

A firm might change the revenue it earns in a number of ways:

1  It might change the price of the good or service. A lower price will bring in less revenue for each good or service sold, but the firm would hope that it would gain so many more customers that, overall, revenue would rise. Raising the price of a good would bring in extra revenue for each item sold but, if sales fell, some revenue would be lost. The firm, therefore, would have to consider any price change very carefully.
2  Other ways to earn more revenue might involve changes to the product, the use of promotion and advertising to boost sales or alternative ways to distribute the product to the consumer.

All methods would have to be considered carefully to see if the extra revenue would more than pay for any extra costs.

A firm might receive other income that is not directly linked to such activities; eg a retailer might rent out a flat above its shop, or a manufacturer might move to new premises and make a profit from selling its old factory. These sorts of income will not normally be included as part of revenue or turnover.

## Differences between start-up and running costs

### Start-up costs

Start-up costs are any costs that a firm needs to pay out before it is able to make and sell its goods or provide its services. Obvious examples of such costs include the purchase of premises, equipment, vehicles and furniture. Some of these items might be leased, and will probably involve the payment of a sum of money as a form of deposit in advance. Other start-up costs might include market research, payments for the installation of services such as electricity, water and telephones. A manufacturer will need to buy in a stock of raw materials, parts and components before it starting production; a retailer will need to stock the shelves with goods before it opens its doors to customers.

## Running costs

Running costs are the costs a business needs to pay out for its day-to-day operations as it makes the goods or provides its services. Some of these costs will be quite different to those paid to start up the business; eg wages will have to be paid once workers start to manufacture goods or serve customers. Electricity and perhaps gas will be needed once machinery starts to operate. Many running costs will, however, be start-up costs as well. If the building or machinery is leased, then rent will have to be paid out at regular intervals. Additional stock will have to be bought as production takes place or as customers make their purchases.

<table>
<tr><td>

**TRUE OR FALSE?**

*Another name for revenue is profit.*

*(see foot of page for answer)*

</td></tr>
</table>

## LEARNING ACTIVITY 2

**Key Skills:**
Communication C2.1b

*Either*  Think of a product or service that a firm has recently started to make or provide in your town or near to your school.

Or  Think of a product you would like to make and sell, or a service you would like to offer to your local community.

1. Research the possible costs and revenue of your chosen product or service.
2. Estimate the likely figures for these costs and revenue for a certain period of time.
3. Prepare a talk for the students in your teaching group that will explain these costs and revenue. Your talk must be illustrated with pictures of the product/service and with charts of the costs and revenue.
4. Deliver your talk, answer any questions and discuss your performance with the rest of the group.

**True or False answer**

**False.** Revenue is income to a firm before any costs are taken away. A profit is calculated by taking costs away from revenue.

203

| LEARNING ACTIVITY 3 | Key Skills: IT 2.2 and 2.3 |

Refer to the good or service which you researched in Learning Activity 2.

1. Create a three column grid with the headings 'Start-up Costs', 'Running Costs' and 'Both Start-up and Running Costs'.
2. Place each of the costs identified for your chosen business in the appropriate column. If you have access to a colour printer, use a different colour for each column.
3. Where possible, select some appropriate clip art to illustrate some of the costs.
4. Make a hard copy of the completed grid and make sure you save your work – you will need the file for other activities.

## What are fixed and variable costs?

It is sometimes useful for a firm to divide its costs into those that are either **fixed** or **variable**.

### Fixed costs

For a manufacturing firm making bar stools, its **fixed** costs are costs that will not change even when the level of its output changes. These fixed costs will stay the same whether the firm's output is 1,000 or 3,000 bar stools each week. If the firm produces no bar stools one week, it will still have to pay its fixed costs. A burger bar faces a similar situation. It will have some costs that are fixed and will not vary with the number of burgers sold or the number of customers served on any day. These fixed costs will be the same whether 100 burgers, 1,000 burgers, or no burgers are sold in a day. For both firms, typical examples of fixed costs might include rent, rates and insurance.

### Variable costs

**Variable** costs are the costs that change when the level of output changes. The firm making bar stools will find that some costs change directly with the number of stools it makes. A burger bar will be in the same situation, in that its variable costs change as it sells either more or less burgers to its customers. Strictly speaking, when no bar stools are being made or there are no customers to serve, each firm will have zero variable costs. Typical variable costs for the burger bar will be the food ingredients required to make the burgers. Similarly for the bar stool manufacturer, the metal, wood and plastic used to make the stools will be major variable costs.

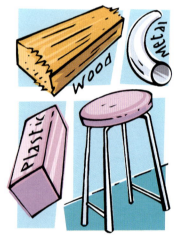
*Figure 38.4* Variable costs in making bar stools

## Fixed or variable costs

There are some types of costs that will be fixed for one firm and variable for another. For example, those firms that pay wages which are directly linked to the amount of goods made, will view the wages as variable costs. Other firms and organisations may pay wages or salaries which cannot be linked to the amount of goods produced or services provided, and these will be classed as fixed costs.

In some cases, a particular cost might have an element of both fixed and variable. For example, the power costs of a burger bar will include the fixed cost of heating and lighting the premises, which will have to be paid even if no customers buy burgers. Then, when customers do arrive, the burger bar will have variable power costs as the grills are used to cook the burgers.

**TRUE OR FALSE?**

*Fixed costs will never change.*

*(see foot of page for answer)*

## LEARNING ACTIVITY 4

*Key Skills:*
IT 2.2 and 2.3

Look back at the list of costs you created for Learning Activity 2 and the table you created for Learning Activity 3.

1. Create a three column table with the headings 'Fixed costs', 'Variable Costs' and 'Fixed or Variable'.
2. Place each of the costs you created for Learning Activity 2 under the correct headings. You might decide to do this part of the exercise by using the file you saved for Learning Activity 3.
3. Remember to save your new table with a new filename and print a hard copy.
4. Discuss with your colleagues in the class the differences between this table and the one you produced for Learning Activity 3.

## Total Costs

To find out the total costs of producing a certain number of goods or the total costs of providing a particular service, a firm would need to add together the fixed costs and the variable costs for that level of output. If it did this for different levels of output, the firm could compare its range of total costs with the range of total revenue earned if it sold those output levels. As a result the firm could start to estimate the amount of profit (or loss) it could make. It would also help the firm to consider the possible effects of any changes either to its fixed or variable costs.

**True or False answer**

**False.** Even fixed costs might change at some point. For example, the owner of the building you are using as a factory or a shop might put up the rent at the start of the next year; or the insurance company might have to raise the premiums it charges all firms because bad weather has increased claims for flooding. The point is, that these costs are not changing because of any changes in the level of output of goods or services.

Any increases in either fixed or variable costs will increase the total cost for a firm producing a certain level of output:

- Some of these costs might be outside the control of the business itself; eg a rise in raw material costs will result from a supplier putting up its prices.
- Some costs might be set outside the business but could be influenced inside the firm; eg electricity prices might be increased by the supplier, but a firm might try to economise on its use of such power.
- Other costs like wages are mainly under the control of the business itself, so any increase in wage rates will usually be the internal responsibility of the firm.

## Unit Costs

A final and very important measure of costs is to calculate the average or **unit** cost of making a single item or unit of production. The simple formula for unit costs is:

$$\frac{\text{Total costs}}{\text{Output produced}}$$

This calculation could be repeated for each level of output and then plotted on a graph to show the most efficient level of output. This would be where the unit costs are at a minimum. A typical unit cost curve is shown below.

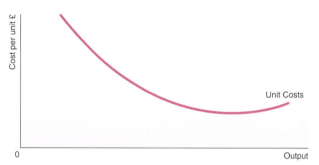

**Figure 38.5** *Typical unit cost curve*

## Creating graphs of costs

All of the calculations for total and unit costs may be shown in a table. Graphs may then be plotted to show the relationships for the production of bar stools in one month.

| Output Bar stools | Fixed Costs £ | Variable Costs £ | Total Costs £ | Unit Costs £ |
|---|---|---|---|---|
| 0 | 250,000 | 0 | 250,000 | — |
| 4,000 | 250,000 | 20,000 | 270,000 | 76.50 |
| 8,000 | 250,000 | 30,000 | 280,000 | 35.00 |
| 12,000 | 250,000 | 50,000 | 300,000 | 25.00 |
| 16,000 | 250,000 | 90,000 | 340,000 | 21.25 |
| 20,000 | 250,000 | 200,000 | 450,000 | 22.50 |

*Costs for bar stool production in one month*

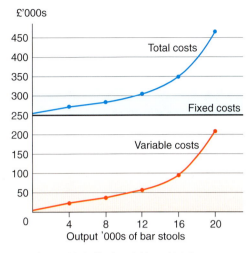

**Figure 38.6** *Fixed, variable and total costs of producing bar stools*

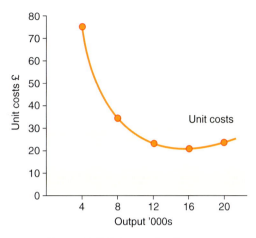

**Figure 38.7** *Unit costs of making bar stools*

## LEARNING ACTIVITY 5

*Key Skills:*
IT 2.2 and 2.3

1. Use the table shown on p 206 to create your own spreadsheet of the data, and then draw the graphs shown below the table using your spreadsheet data. Save and print the table and graphs.
2. Now change the fixed costs to £280,000 and reduce the variable costs for each level of output by £5,000. If you used formulas in the spreadsheet correctly, new totals should have been recalculated. Redraw the graphs, save and print.
3. Compare the original graphs with the new ones. How do they differ?
4. Why might the fixed costs have changed?
5. Why might the variable costs have changed?

## What have I learned?

1. Costs are payments for the purchase or hire of resources.
2. The costs of businesses may be divided up into start-up and running costs or into fixed and variable costs.
3. Unit costs measure the average cost of making a single item or unit.
4. Changes in costs will affect the profitability of business.
5. Revenue (a firm's income) may be earned either by making and selling goods or from selling services.
6. Revenue might change as the result of changes in price, and through changes in consumers' views on the goods or services being sold.
7. Changes in revenue will also affect a firm's profitability.

## KEY *TERMS*

- Costs – payments by firms for the purchase or hire of resources used to make and sell goods and services
- Running costs – costs that a business needs to pay out for its day-to-day operations to make goods or provide services
- Start-up costs – costs that a business needs to pay out before it starts to make and sell goods and services.
- Fixed costs – costs that do not change with the number of goods or services being made and sold
- Variable costs – costs that change with the number of goods or services being made and sold
- Unit costs – the average costs of making a single item or unit of output
- Revenue – income received by a business selling its goods or services

# EXAMINATION PREPARATION EXERCISE

Morell Ltd runs a small chain of burger bars in the north of England. It plans to set up a new burger bar outlet in Wallingford.

1. >> Make a list of the likely costs of setting up and running a new burger bar for Morell ltd.
2. > Make a three column table with the headings start-up, running, and start-up or running. Put the costs you listed in question 1 into the right column.
3. > Make a new three column table with the headings fixed, variable, fixed or variable. Put the costs you listed in question 1 into the right column.
4. >> How might Morell Ltd try to check the viability of its new outlet?
5. >>> Why might Morell's ingredient costs rise, and how might its new business be affected by this?
6. >>> How might Morell's try to increase the revenue it earns from its new burger bar outlet?

## CHAPTER 39
# Break even

Rowland and Hudson Ltd has been making and selling biscuits in the Borders area of Scotland for the past 50 years. It produces 20 different types of biscuits, including shortbread, digestives and gingerbread. The process for making each type of biscuit is very similar and the company uses two small production lines. Its two production lines each specialise in one type of biscuit usually for one or two days at a time.

**Figure 39.1**

The production lines are then cleaned and prepared for the next type. In this way the company is able to manufacture all 20 types each month. Stock is sold and sent out each day to wholesalers throughout southern Scotland and northern England.

Rowland and Hudson Ltd has set itself a number of objectives. One of its basic targets is to break even each month. The company has calculated that its fixed costs each month are £80,000. The basic ingredients for each type of biscuit are virtually the same, so variable costs are calculated to be £2.50 per kilogram of biscuits. Rowland and Hudson sells all types of biscuits to wholesalers at the same price of £5 per kilogram. It uses all these figures to create a break-even chart. This chart is used to interpret the effects of any changes to the company's costs. Rowland and Hudson can also use the chart to think through the possible results if it changes the price it charges for its biscuits. The company monitors production and sales very carefully to ensure that it will reach its monthly minimum break-even target.

## What is the break-even point?

This is the level of sales where the total costs of making and selling items of output equals the total revenue from selling them. Sales above this point will mean a firm is making a profit, but sales below the break-even point will result in a loss. This makes the break-even point an important target or objective for a firm.

Such a target is particularly important for small firms because it can be the difference between survival and closure. Medium to large firms may also set a break-even target when a new production line is started or a new product is introduced to the market. It may also be an important target for firms selling a service, as well as for those making and selling goods.

## How are break-even charts created?

These charts, and the graphs drawn from them, are created from five lots of data:

1. numbers of items sold
2. fixed costs
3. variable costs
4. total costs
5. total revenue.

All the figures have to be for a certain period of time; this could be for a day, a week, a month or even for a year. The actual break-even period will depend on the type and size of firm, and the good or service being sold. A firm is able to create a break-even chart using real figures from its business records or figures estimated from its plans.

A typical break-even table and graph for a textbook publisher are shown below. The costs and revenue are estimated for a new Business Studies textbook. The price of the textbook is set at £15, with variable costs estimated at £3 each. It is planned to print 12,000 books in the first year, with fixed costs for the year estimated at £100,000.

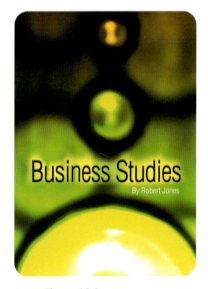

*Figure 39.2*

| Number of textbooks sold | 0 | 2000 | 4000 | 6000 | 8000 | 10000 | 12000 |
|---|---|---|---|---|---|---|---|
| Fixed costs (£'000s) | 100 | 100 | 100 | 100 | 100 | 100 | 100 |
| Variable costs (£'000s) | 0 | 6 | 12 | 18 | 24 | 30 | 36 |
| Total Costs (£'000s) | 100 | 106 | 112 | 118 | 124 | 130 | 136 |
| Total Revenue (£'000s) | 0 | 30 | 60 | 90 | 120 | 150 | 180 |

*Break-even table for a textbook publisher's new Business Studies textbook*

The break-even graph may then be drawn from this data. Costs and revenue are identified on the vertical axis, and sales on the horizontal one. Normally, three lines are plotted: those for fixed costs, total costs and total revenue. The break-even point is located where the total cost and total revenue lines cross or intersect. Dropping down from this point to the bottom axis, the publishing firm can see what level of sales of the new textbook are needed to break-even over the first year.

**LEARNING ACTIVITY 1** — Key Skills: Application of Number N2.2c and N2.2d

On graph paper, create your own break-even graph using the table shown above for the sale of the new textbook. Make sure you choose an appropriate scale, label everything correctly and give the graph an appropriate heading.

**LEARNING ACTIVITY 2** — Key Skills: IT 2.2 and 2.3

1. Use a spreadsheet program to create the break-even table, making sure you use formulas where appropriate. Save your work using a suitable filename.
2. Using the data in this spreadsheet file, create a break-even graph. Save and print your work.

## Results of the break-even graph

This graph shows the textbook publisher that it needs to sell just over 8,330 of this new textbook to break even over this year. Sales below this would mean the firm was making a loss. For example, sales of 6,000 would earn the publisher £90,000 of revenue, but its total costs would be £118,000; this would result in a loss over the year of £28,000.

On the other hand, if it achieved sales of all 12,000 books, revenue would be £180,000 while total costs would only be £136,000, thus earning a profit for the year of £44,000. These figures can be seen both by using the table and by analysing the graph.

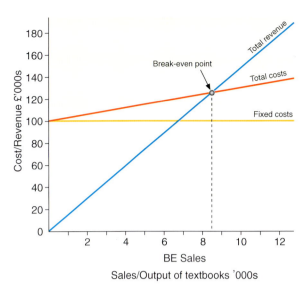

**Figure 39.3** *Break-even graph for the new business studies textbook*

The main drawback of calculating the break-even point using a graph is that the figures may not be exact. It is difficult to see from the graph whether just over 8,300 sales are needed to break even, or whether it is nearer 8,400. The graph method's big advantage is in showing the effects of changes both in costs and price on break even.

## Changes in costs and price

A change in fixed costs will cause a parallel shift in this line on the break-even graph. An increase in fixed costs will shift the line up the vertical axis, and a decrease will allow the line to move down. The total costs would then start wherever the new fixed costs line starts. Higher fixed costs will raise the break-even point, while lower fixed costs will reduce it. If the textbook publisher underestimated its fixed costs, it would have to sell more books than predicted to break even.

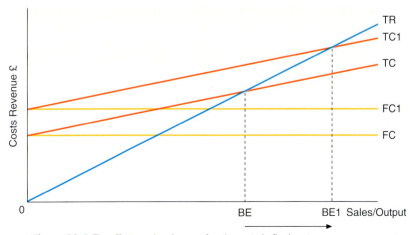

**Figure 39.4** *The effects on break even of an increase in fixed costs*

211

A change in variable costs will affect the slope of the total costs line, but the total costs line will always start from the fixed costs line. A rise in variable costs will raise the slope of the total costs line, while a fall in variable costs would flatten the total costs line. Rises in costs will mean that the publisher has to sell more textbooks to break even over the year.

An **increase** in the price of each textbook will increase the slope or gradient of the total revenue line, and will mean the publisher does not need to sell as many textbooks to break even. Any **fall** in price would flatten the total revenue line and mean the publisher would need to sell more textbooks to break even. Many firms find they are facing a number of such changes and will need to analyse them on a break-even graph.

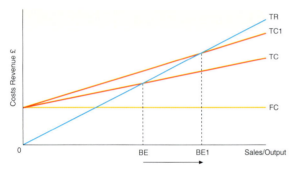

**Figure 39.5** *The effects on break even of a rise in variable costs*

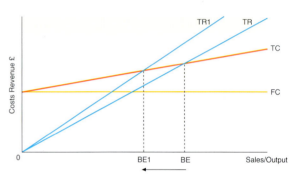

**Figure 39.6** *The effects on break even of a rise in price*

## LEARNING ACTIVITY 3

*Key Skills:*
Application of Number N2.2c, N2.2d, N2.1 and N2.3

The textbook publisher finds that its fixed costs rise to £110,000, while its variable costs rise to £3.50 per textbook. To help pay for these costs, the publisher decides to raise the price of the textbook to £16.
1. Use these new figures to create a new break-even table.
2. Using the new table, create a new break-even graph
3. Compare the new graph with the one you created for Activity 1. Explain in detail the changes between the two.
4. Using the new table and graph, identify the level of loss or profit at sales of (a) 6,000 textbooks (b) 12,000 textbooks.

1. Use the spreadsheet file you created for Activity 2 to input the changes to the publisher's costs and price. Save your work using a new filename.
2. Use this changed table to create a new break-even graph. Save and print your work.
3. Use the spreadsheet files to create the two break-even graphs on the same page.

## Calculating the break-even point

To overcome the problems of inaccurate calculation using graphs, a simple formula may be used. This is often called the **contribution method**, since part of it involves calculating the contribution the production and sale of each unit makes to a firm's fixed costs.

There are two parts to the formula:

1 Price per unit − variable cost per unit = contribution to fixed costs

2 $\dfrac{\text{Fixed costs}}{\text{Contribution}}$ = break-even level of sales

As with the graph, these figures must be for a certain period of time. This method may be illustrated using the first set of figures for the textbook publisher: price per textbook £15, variable costs per textbook £3, fixed costs for the year £100,000.

1 (Price per unit) − (variable cost per unit) = (contribution)
  £15 − £3 = £12

2 $\dfrac{\text{Fixed costs}}{\text{Contribution}}$ = break-even sales

  $\dfrac{£100,000}{£12}$ = 8,334 textbooks have to be sold over the year to break even

It is worth pausing at this point to consider the significance of calculation errors. In the case of break even, it might mean that a firm is aiming for the wrong sales targets, and unexpected losses might result instead of profits. If it does not identify this quickly enough, a firm may find itself in serious financial difficulties.

Calculate the break-even point for the textbook publisher when its fixed costs are £110,000, its variable costs are £3.50 per textbook and the price of each book has risen to £16.

## What have I learned?

1. Break even may be calculated using the contribution method or formula.
2. Data on sales, revenue, fixed costs, variable costs and total revenue may be used to create a break-even table and graph to show the break-even point.
3. The break-even point is for a particular period of time.
4. The break-even point will be **increased** by lower prices and by higher fixed and variable costs.
5. The break-even point will be **reduced** by higher prices and by lower fixed and variable costs.

## KEY TERMS

- Break-even point – the level of sales at which total revenue earned from those sales equals the total cost of making those goods or services
- Contribution – the sales revenue of an item (its price) minus the variable cost of making and selling that item

## EXAMINATION PREPARATION EXERCISE

This exercise is designed to check your knowledge and understanding of break-even. Go back to the beginning of this chapter and re-read the opening information about Rowland and Hudson Ltd.

1) > Create a monthly break-even table for Rowland and Hudson Ltd using the information in the data; calculate costs and sales revenue for sales figures of 0, 5,000, 10,000, 15,000, 20,000, 25,000, 30,000, 35,000 and 40,000kg.
2) > Create a labelled break-even chart from this table.
3) > Use the break-even chart to estimate the level of profit or loss if the actual level of sales in a month is (a) 27,000kg and (b) 37,000kg.
4) >> Calculate an accurate figure for the break-even point using the contribution method.
5) >>> Re-calculate the effects on the monthly break-even point if fixed costs rise to £85,000 per month, variable costs fall to £2.45 per kilogram of biscuits and Rowland and Hudson raises its price to £5.15 per kilogram of biscuits.
6) >>> Why might fixed costs have risen and variable costs fallen?
7) >>> To what extent do you think Rowland and Hudson was sensible in raising its price of biscuits by 15p per kilogram?

## CHAPTER 40
# Cashflow forecast

In Chapter 39 you were introduced to Rowland and Hudson Ltd, a manufacturer of biscuits in the Borders area of Scotland. Its main inflow of cash comes from the sale of its biscuits to a number of wholesalers in both southern Scotland and northern England. Most of these wholesalers expect at least one month's credit, while some can take up to more than two months to settle their bills.

Most of Rowland and Hudson's outflows of cash include amounts that have to be paid out regularly, either weekly or monthly. The largest item is the wage bill, followed by overheads such as power, rent and rates. Ingredients are the main variable

*Figure 40.1*

cost, with flour and sugar topping the list. Rowland and Hudson receives a small discount if it pays its ingredients suppliers within 14 days.

While Rowland and Hudson has a regular demand and is certainly profitable, it does have some problems with its cashflow. It is able to finance the regular monthly net outflow through a sizeable overdraft which it has negotiated with its bank. Nevertheless, Rowland and Hudson would like to reduce this overdraft and improve cashflow.

## Flows of money into a business

**Inflows** of cash will start when a business is being set up or when it is being expanded in some way. Owners will put some of their money into a business and they may be able to obtain grants from various organisations to help pay for the land, buildings and equipment. If there is a shortage of capital, loans might be arranged from banks

*Figure 40.2*

and other financial institutions, to help provide the necessary cash to pay for the start-up costs and some of the later running costs of the business.

Once the business is running, a firm's main income will be received from the sale of its goods or services, although the actual arrival of cash into the business might be delayed, or might vary from day to day or week to week. The firm might have other sources of income such as rent from parts of its premises that it no longer needs to use itself.

## Flows of cash out of a business

When a business is being set up, the main **outflow** of cash will be for all the start-up costs. If the business is already operating and it expands or introduces a new product, then again the main outflow of cash will be for these additional start-up costs.

Once the business is ready to operate, the main outflow of cash will be for the firm's running costs. It will also find that cash flows out to repay loans, to give owners a share of any profits and to pay any tax due through its business activities. All these outflows will be of quite different amounts and will take place at irregular times.

## Will the inflow of cash equal the outflow of cash?

It is extremely unlikely that on any particular day, week or month, the inflow of cash will equal or balance the outflow of cash. One week a firm may have a cash surplus but find the next week that it has a cash deficit. This is likely to be the case both for new and old firms, and for small, medium and large firms.

The difference between the inflows and outflows is called **net inflow** or **net outflow**, depending on which figure is bigger. A firm will have a problem if it has a net outflow, as this may mean it has a *shortage* of cash. This may prevent a firm paying its immediate debts. As a result, the firm might find it difficult to obtain new stocks of materials, or may even find it difficult to pay wages to its workers.

Overdrafts from banks can help the short-term situation, but the interest rates on these are quite high. A bank usually puts an upper limit on the size of the overdraft. If the net cash outflow becomes too large, the bank may refuse to honour cheques made out by the firm with the overdraft. In extreme cases, a firm might have to stop trading because of a cash shortage, even though it is relatively profitable. More businesses close because they have cashflow problems than through low profitability.

### TRUE OR FALSE?

*A profitable firm will always have enough cash to pay its bills.*

*(see foot of page for answer)*

**Figure 40.3** *Is there a net inflow or a net outflow?*

**True or False answer**

**False.** A firm might be able to make a large profit over the year but it may still find itself short of cash. It could even go bankrupt if it cannot find enough cash to pay its debts during a cash shortage.

# How will a cashflow forecast help?

A shortage of cash is not necessarily a problem as long as it has been forecast and planned for. Such planning will start with the creation of a **cashflow forecast**. This will estimate the likely flows of cash into and out of the business usually over several months. The forecast will help the firm to predict when it might suffer from cash shortages, and this knowledge will help it to control its business and financial operations. If the firm compares this forecast with the actual flow of cash, it will identify when it:

• needs to speed up the flow of cash into the business
• needs to slow down the flow of cash out of the business
• can afford to pay off some debts
• can afford to order new stocks or equipment
• needs to negotiate an increase in overdraft facilities at its bank.

# How is a cashflow forecast created?

Each firm and each set of accountants is likely to devise its own individual style of cashflow forecast to suit its own needs. Whatever the actual style, there are five key parts to any cash flow forecast and these are shown in the following simple table.

|  | Month | | |
| Amount in £ | 1 | 2 | 3 |
|---|---|---|---|
| A  Bank balance brought forward | 600 | (250) | (500) |
| B  Cash from sales | 1,100 | 1,505 | 2,320 |
| C  Total cash available (A+B) | 1,700 | 1,255 | 1,820 |
| D  Total cash out | 1,950 | 1,755 | 1,770 |
| E  Bank balance carried forward (C–D) | (250) | (500) | 50 |

*A simple cash flow forecast table for Ian Roberts, plumber*

From this cashflow forecast table we can see that the sole trader, Ian Roberts (operating as a plumber), starts month 1 with £600 in the bank. Over that first month, he estimates that he will earn and receive £1,100 of revenue from selling his plumbing services. This means that he has £1,700 cash available over this month to pay for his costs. Ian estimates that he will pay out £1,950 during the month, meaning that he will be overdrawn at the bank by £250 (shown by a brackets around the figure). This figure is then carried forward to the start of month 2. By the end of month 3, Ian Roberts estimates that he will have a surplus of cash in the bank of £50 and will no longer be paying interest on his overdraft.

   This may also be shown in a graph of the cash flow forecast showing the net inflow or outflow each month. This will be the bank balance carried forward at the end of the month and can show the overall trend over a period of time.

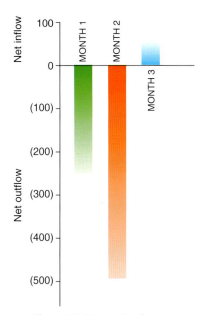

***Figure 40.4** A cashflow forecast for Ian Roberts, the plumber*

## A detailed cashflow forecast

The table and graph above show the main sections for the plumber Ian Roberts, but he will wish to see a more detailed breakdown. In particular, he will want to know the main categories of cash flowing out. This is shown in the table below.

| Amount in £ | Month 1 | Month 2 | Month 3 |
|---|---|---|---|
| Bank balance brought forward | 600 | (250) | (500) |
| Revenue from plumbing services | 1,000 | 1,405 | 2,220 |
| Rent from leasing out spare garage | 100 | 100 | 100 |
| Total cash in | 1,100 | 1,505 | 2,320 |
| Total cash available | 1,700 | 1,255 | 1,820 |
| Cash out | | | |
| Rates | 130 | 130 | 130 |
| Transport | 80 | 75 | 80 |
| Power | 20 | 20 | 20 |
| Stationery | 10 | 10 | 10 |
| Insurance | 160 | 0 | 0 |
| Wages | 1,200 | 1,200 | 1,200 |
| Materials | 230 | 200 | 210 |
| Other | 120 | 120 | 120 |
| Total Cash out | 1,950 | 1,755 | 1,770 |
| Bank balance carried forward | (250) | (500) | 50 |

A detailed cashflow forecast for Ian Roberts, plumber

This more detailed table allows Ian to identify the effects of possible changes in any of the individual figures. It also allows him to analyse his cash situation, and ought to help him to plan his business.

## LEARNING ACTIVITY 1

Key Skills:
Application of Number N2.1

Look at the three-monthly cashflow forecast, including the graph of net flows, for Ian Roberts the plumber. Describe the changes taking place over the three-month period. Use figures to support your descriptions.

*Key Skills:*
Application of Number N2.2c,
N2.2d and N2.3

1. Draw up a cashflow forecast table for Ian Roberts the plumber for months 4, 5 and 6, including an additional cash outflow for advertising costs.
2. Use the following figures to complete the cashflow forecast for months 4–6, remembering that month 4 will start with a bank balance brought forward of £50.
   - In month 4 and 5, income from Ian's plumbing services is constant at £2,000 per month but falls to £1,500 in month 6.
   - Income from renting out his spare garage is constant at £100 per month.
   - Power costs are £21 per month.
   - Transport costs are £80 per month for both months 4 and 5 but only £70 for month 6.
   - Rates are fixed at £130 per month.
   - Stationery is also constant at £10 month.
   - Other costs are estimated at £130 per month for months 4–6.
   - Ian attempts some advertising, costing £200 for each of the three months.
   - Ian plans to continue drawing out wages of £1,200 per month which he shares with his wife, who takes phones messages and deals with callers to his small workshop.
   - Materials are difficult to estimate, but as month 6 is traditionally a quiet month Ian estimates materials to be £210 in both month 4 and month 5 but only £150 in month 6.
   - Insurance continues to be an annual fee payable in month 1.
3. Describe the changes in the cashflow forecast over this second three-month period, remembering to use figures to illustrate your descriptions.
4. What problems might incorrect calculations cause with this forecast?
5. Ian regularly updates this cash flow forecast to create a record of his *actual* cashflow. At the end of month 6, while the business has had a reasonable amount of custom for the time of year, Ian finds that his actual balance at the end of month 6 is worse than expected. His overdraft at the bank is £640. This has been caused by late payments from some of his customers. How might Ian try to solve the cash problem?

## LEARNING ACTIVITY 3

1. Using a suitable spreadsheet program, create a spreadsheet file for all six months of the cashflow forecast for Ian Roberts the plumber.
2. Input the first three months' figures, making sure you use formulae to undertake all the calculations.
3. Check your figures against the three-month table shown above.
4. Now input the remaining data for months 4–6, using formulae where appropriate. Save your forecast with a suitable filename. Compare your totals with those you prepared for Learning Activity 2.
5. Alter some of the figures to see some of the effects on the cashflows. Explain the advantages of using a spreadsheet to calculate cashflow, and suggest any precautions you ought to take.

## What have I learned?

1. Flows of money or cash coming *into* a business include capital from owners, borrowed funds and revenue from sales.
2. Flows of money or cashflow *out* of a business include paying for start-up costs, all the running costs, and the payment of special items such as loan repayments, taxes and a share of profits to the owners.
3. A cashflow forecast should start with a cash or bank balance brought forward from the previous time period.
4. The cashflow should end with a cash or bank balance that is carried forward to the next time period.
5. The cashflow forecast will identify possible cash problems and will show when cash inflows need to be increased and cash outflows need to be reduced.
6. Making errors in calculating financial data in cashflow forecasts either by hand or by spreadsheet may cause serious consequences to the survival of a firm.
7. A firm may be profitable, but if it faces a serious cash shortage it may be forced to close down.

# KEY *TERMS*

- Cash inflow – cash flowing into the business from revenue, from other non-trading activities, from loans, from grants and from the owners
- Cash outflow – cash flowing out of the business to pay for start-up costs, running costs, expansion costs, repayment of loans, taxes and as a share of profits to the owners
- Net inflow – cash inflow is greater than cash outflow over a certain time period
- Net outflow – cash outflow is greater than cash inflow over a certain period
- Overdraft – permission is given by a bank for a firm to take out more money from its bank account than is actually in, with interest charged according to the size of the overdraft and the number of days overdrawn
- Cashflow forecast – a prediction or estimate of the future flows of cash into and out of a business which may be updated by and compared with the actual flow of cash

## EXAMINATION PREPARATION EXERCISE

This exercise is designed to check your knowledge and understanding of cash flow forecasting. Go back to the beginning of the chapter and re-read the opening information about Rowland and Hudson Ltd.

1. > Rowland and Hudson Ltd plans to open another small biscuit-making factory in northern England. As part of its plan it needs to identify the main categories of both cash inflow and outflow. These should include likely flows both when setting up the new factory and when running it. Set these flows out in a logical order in a column as the first step in creating a cashflow forecast for the new factory.
2. > How might a computer spreadsheet program help with the operation of the cashflow forecast?
3. >> Suggest possible problems for Rowland and Hudson from operating its cashflow forecast on a computer spreadsheet program.
4. >>> Describe the possible cashflow problems that Rowland and Hudson might have with its existing factory in Scotland.
5. >>> How might Rowland and Hudson attempt to overcome these cashflow problems, both in its Scottish operations and in its new English expansion?

CHAPTER 41
# Profit and loss

Greggs plc is the UK's leading retailer specialising in sandwiches, savouries and other bakery products. It particularly focuses on takeaway food and catering. It has over 1,100 retail outlets throughout the UK, trading under the brand names of Greggs and Baker's Oven. Greggs has achieved ten consecutive years of growth in profits. It has achieved this through careful planning, the development of new products and a programme of new shop openings – 35 during 2001 alone. As a public limited company, it must publish its reports each year. It also publishes interim six monthly results in June each year. Headline figures in June 2001 showed that its sales revenue for the six months up to 16 June was over £161 m. For the same period, it achieved a record pre-tax profit of £9.6 m, which was an increase of 22.4% compared to 2000.

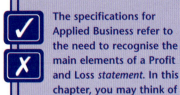

## What is profit?

Most firms will have the objective of making a profit. In simple terms, profit is the result of a firm's income being greater than its expenditure over a certain period of time. The opposite to this will be a loss – when expenditure exceeds income.

Even for the simplest form of business – a sole trader – this is too simple a way of explaining and measuring profit (or loss). A whole range of Profit and Loss accounts or statements are created and used by firms and their accountants to record all the elements that go into a measurement of profit. As firms change from being a sole trader to a partnership and then to limited companies, more and more complicated accounts are required, some of which are demanded by law.

Figure 41.1

## A Profit and Loss Account

This is a record of the firm's financial record in the past. In that sense it is like an historical document, but a firm may also choose to estimate its future profitability.

A Profit and Loss account will show the main sources of income and the main items of expenditure for a fixed amount of time, usually for a year. The more complicated forms of accounts will also show how any profit made is then distributed. The basic format you need to know for this course is shown below for a small electrical retailer operated as a sole trader, Gill's Electricals.

**GILL'S ELECTRICALS**

Figure 41.2

|  | £ |
|---|---|
| Sales Revenue | 450,000 |
| *less* Cost of Sales | 250,000 |
| Gross profit | 200,000 |
| *less* Expenses | 155,000 |
| Net Profit | 45,000 |

*Profit and Loss account for Gill's Electricals for the year ending 31 January 2001*

Sales revenue is the income received by Gill's Electricals when it sells its products to its customers. No costs have been deducted, and the firm will be able to calculate revenue by multiplying the price charged for each item sold, by the number sold at each price. In the case of Gill's Electricals, it has managed to sell its electrical products for £450,000 over the past financial year. The business will be expected to keep a record of this revenue and will be able to use this to estimate future levels. Estimates of future revenue will have to consider the possible impact of any proposed price changes, as well as the effects of other factors such as an advertising campaign or the setting-up of a rival electrical outlet.

*Figure 41.3*

Cost of sales may be simply thought of as the cost of buying in the electrical products sold at Gill's Electricals. Most of these will be finished products ranging in size from fuses and 3-pin plugs, to televisions and freezers. All such purchases made by Gill's Electricals will be included in its figure for cost of sales – amounting to £250,000 over the financial year. It will be important for the electrical retailer to make a record of all its expenditure on such items, to arrive at an accurate figure for its cost of sales. The firm may also use this as a guide to estimate its future cost of sales, taking into account any possible changes to the prices charged by suppliers.

## Calculating the gross and net profit

Once revenue and cost of sales figures have been measured, the firm may calculate its gross profit.

Gross Profit = Sales Revenue − Cost of Sales
£200,000  = £450,000   − £250,000

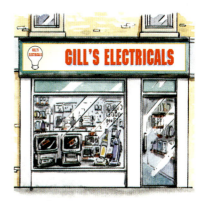

*Figure 41.4*

This is not the final profit figure, since a firm will also have many other expenses or overheads that it needs to deduct before it can accurately measure its final level of profits. Such expenses will include wages, rent and rates, water rates, power, insurance and equipment costs. A firm should be able to calculate a total figure for these expenses – usually for a year – and deduct this figure from gross profit to arrive at the **net profit** for the year. For Gill's Electricals, expenses came to £155,000 for the year, leaving a net profit of £45,000.

Net Profit  = Gross profit − Expenses
£45,000  = £200,000  − £155,000

Another way of expressing this is:

Net profit = Sales revenue − (cost of sales + expenses)
£45,000  = £450,000     − £355,000 (£200,000 + £155,000)

FOR YOUR
EXAMINATION

Not only must you understand the layout of a Profit and Loss Account, but you also need to know how to make basic calculations. These include how to calculate both gross and net profit, and how to complete a simple account, either like the short version here or the fuller version set out below.

A slightly fuller Profit and Loss account for Gill's Electricals up to 31 January 2001 would look like this:

| | £ | £ |
|---|---|---|
| Sales Revenue | | 450,000 |
| *less* Cost of Sales | | 250,000 |
| Gross Profit | | 200,000 |
| *less* Expenses: | | |
| Wages | 82,000 | |
| Rent and rates | 32,000 | |
| Advertising | 15,000 | |
| Power | 1,000 | |
| Other | 25,000 | |
| | | 155,000 |
| Net profit | | 45,000 |

*Fuller Profit and Loss account*

**TRUE OR FALSE?**

*Some firms use the term* <u>turnover</u> *as a substitute for revenue.*

*(see foot of page for answer)*

## LEARNING ACTIVITY 1

*Key Skills:*
Application of Number N2.1, N2.2c, N2.2d and N2.3

1. Create a fuller version of a Profit and Loss account for Gill's Electricals for the year ending 31 January 2002. Use the following figures to calculate and show totals for cost of sales, expenses, gross profit and net profit:
   - Revenue from sales of electrical items amounted to £480,000.
   - Gill's Electricals purchased £265,000 of electrical items over the year.
   - The wage bill came to £84,000 for the year with £33,000 being paid out for rent and rates.
   - Equipment purchases and maintenance amounted to £4,000.
   - Power bills for heating, lighting and cooking reached £1,000.
   - Advertising added up to £18,000.
   - Other costs accounted for a further £28,000 over the year.
2. Compare this account for 2002 with the one given earlier for 2001.
   - Write a report detailing the changes that have taken place.
   - Suggest why these changes might have occurred
   - Suggest ways that Gill's Electricals might try to improve its profitability for the financial year ending 31 January 2003.
3. The list of likely expenses for Gill's Electricals is rather limited. Produce a more detailed list of the likely categories of expenses that this firm might more usefully use in a Profit and Loss account.

True or False answer

**True.** Turnover is a short version of *sales turnover*, which is exactly the same as revenue or even sales revenue. They all mean exactly the same thing – income to the firm from sales of the good or service before any costs are deducted.

# Why is a Profit and Loss account created?

For most types of firms, it is a legal requirement to produce a Profit and Loss account in some form or other. All firms are expected to keep a record of their transactions for the two main tax authorities – the Inland Revenue, and Customs and Excise. A Profit and Loss account is one of the main documents used to check on the amount of taxes that have to be collected from firms. For public limited companies, the Profit and Loss account has to be published in an annual report that is then freely available for everyone to see.

One obvious reason for creating a Profit and Loss account is to use this record of financial transactions to check the performance of the firm. It might be checked against target figures for gross and net profit, or the figures for sales revenue, cost of sales and expenses might be reviewed to see if they are greater than expected. Comparisons with figures from previous years' accounts might be made to spot trends and analyse performance – just as you did in Learning Activity 1 above. Public limited companies could compare their accounts with those of other plcs, using the published annual reports.

## LEARNING ACTIVITY 2

*Key Skills:* Information Technology IT2.2 and IT2.3

1. Using a spreadsheet program, create the full version of the Profit and Loss account for Gill's Electricals for the year ended 31 January 2001. Make sure you use formulae to calculate the totals. Save this using a suitable file name, and print a hard copy.
2. Create a second file showing the figures for the year ended 31 January 2002 in separate columns to the right of the 2001 figures. Either change the figures for 2001 to italics or use bold for the 2002 figures. Again make sure you use formulae for calculating the totals. Save using a new filename and print a hard copy.
3. Explain the problems that would result from calculation errors. Illustrate this by producing a copy of the 2001 account alone with two errors in – one in expenses and one in sales revenue.

## Which factors might affect profitability?

There are a whole range of factors that might affect a firm's profits.

### Changes in costs

This will have an obvious effect, either because supplying firms have changed their prices or because the firm itself allows the costs to change. For example, a shortage of coffee worldwide would almost certainly push up the price of coffee sold in shops and restaurants; a firm would have to decide itself whether to award pay rises to its employees and therefore push up the wage cost element of making a good. Expansion plans involve a whole new set of costs that will have to be paid for, and it may take some time before enough income is generated to fully pay for them.

### Changes in revenue

This will have an obvious influence on profits, and will result from changes in sales. This might be the result of the firm's own actions such as greater promotion of its products or changes in prices. It might be the result of the actions of other competing firms who decide to change their prices, products and promotions.

### Changes introduced by external organisations

This will often affect profitability. These might include the actions of the government or of the European Union. New taxes or laws might affect both a firm's costs and sales.

## What happens to net profit?

There are three broad uses of net profit:

1 the Inland Revenue taxes a proportion of profit
2 profit after tax may then be used to reward the owners for risking their money in the business
3 in addition, some of the profit may be retained in the company either as a cash reserve or more usually for investment in new buildings and equipment.

## The importance of Profit and Loss statements to stakeholders

- **Managers** will want to compare the accounts with trading forecasts to see how well the company is performing. They will pay particular attention both to trends in sales and to changes in costs, as well as looking carefully at both gross and net profit.
- **Owners and shareholders**, who are not also managers, will be interested in the size of net profit earned, to identify their likely share of the profit.

- **Suppliers and lenders** will be keen to know that the company they are dealing with and lending money to is profitable and a safe risk.
- **Employees** will be keen to see that the company is successful and that their jobs are safe. Good profits might help them to gain a larger pay rise.
- **Customers** may not want a company to make too much profit out of their need for a product, but a profitable company may suggest that the products are of a good quality.

You should remember that only a public limited company's accounts are fully published and available for the public to look at. Stakeholders in other types of business might find it difficult to obtain an accurate picture of the firm's profitability.

## What have I learned?

1. A Profit and Loss account is a record of a firm's past financial performance, although estimates of future accounts may also be created.
2. Sales revenue less all the costs of production will give a firm its level of net profit (or loss).
3. The five main elements of a Profit and Loss account at this level are sales revenue, cost of sales, gross profit, expenses and net profit.
4. Records of both sales revenue and payments for costs of production need to be kept and used to create an annual Profit and Loss account.
5. Changes in costs, changes in price and changes in demand for the good or service will all affect the actual level of profit that a firm makes.
6. Calculation errors and incorrect procedures in computer spreadsheet programs will lead to serious mistakes in maintaining accurate records of profit and loss.

## KEY TERMS

- Sales revenue – income to the business from selling the good or service before any costs are deducted
- Cost of sales – the cost of purchasing stocks of raw materials, parts, components, ingredients and other inputs that go into the actual making of the product
- Expenses – all other costs or overheads (including wages) that are involved in making and selling the good or service
- Gross profit – the difference between a firm's sales revenue and its cost of sales
- Net profit – the difference between a firm's gross profit and its expenses

# EXAMINATION PREPARATION EXERCISE

This exercise is designed to check your knowledge and understanding of profit and loss accounts.

Go back to the start of this chapter and re-read the opening information on Greggs plc.

1. > Why will a company like Greggs plc produce a Profit and Loss account?

2. > Suggest typical items for Greggs' cost of sales and expenses.

3 >> Visit Greggs website at www.greggs.co.uk and find out its latest financial results, in particular its profit figures. Write a statement that describes the company's performance, giving a summary of the key figures and the suggested reasons for the changes.

CHAPTER 42

# Financial documents

**Figure 42.1**

Rowland and Hudson Ltd, manufacturer of biscuits, was introduced to you in Chapters 39 and 40. As you will recall, one of its main purchases of raw materials is for flour. Other types of ingredients are also required including sugar, flavourings and colourings. These items are usually bought from three main suppliers operating in southern Scotland. It is vital that Rowland and Hudson keeps an accurate record of its purchases and of the payments for these ingredients. Records of purchases of other items and especially services also need to be kept but such things as telephone bills, insurance premiums and business rates demands arrive virtually automatically from the providers of these services.

To help keep these financial records and to help it monitor stock levels of ingredients, Rowland and Hudson uses a number of financial documents in its purchasing activities, particularly when buying in stocks of ingredients. In the descriptions of purchasing documents that follow, an example of Rowland and Hudson buying flour from one if its three main suppliers, Angus Miller Ltd, is used to illustrate the *purchasing* and *selling* processes and the necessary documentation.

## Purchase order

The most common use of documents for a firm like Rowland and Hudson Ltd, will be to purchase the raw materials needed to make biscuits. The first important document it generates and uses is the **purchase order**. This is a form that requests another firm to supply Rowland and Hudson with a particular number and type of goods. It will be sent in the post or perhaps via a fax machine to the potential supplier. In some cases it might be the written confirmation of an order made by telephone, especially if Rowland and Hudson make regular purchases from the supplier. If the good is a piece of equipment that the company only buys occasionally, then Rowland and Hudson might request some written quotations before sending out a purchase order to the 'best' supplier.

You will notice that a purchase order has several sections that need to be completed. If any one section is incomplete, then delays may well occur in the goods actually reaching Rowland and Hudson. The name, address and telephone number of Rowland and Hudson will be in a prominent position so that the company receiving the order knows who has sent it.

Rowland and Hudson also include the name and address of the firm to whom it is sending the purchase order, to avoid mistakes and to help with its record-keeping. It is also then able to use envelopes with a clear address window which displays this name and address on the paper, and saves the address being written on the envelope.

An order number is used and the date of the order is located next to this, both helping with record-keeping. The main body of the order form has details of the goods to be purchased:

- The reference number is used to record any specific identification that the supplying company uses for the goods. This may be particularly important if there is a large catalogue of goods to choose from.
- The quantity and description then help to confirm the exact goods required, together with the unit price that has either been agreed for each unit or that Rowland and Hudson normally expects to pay.
- The amount is then calculated by multiplying the quantity by the unit price.
- Finally, a space is left for any special instructions, perhaps about the timing of deliveries, and the purchase order has to be signed by a person authorised to make the order.

A completed purchase order is shown here. Check that you understand each part before you move on to the next document. As the purchase order shows, Rowland and Hudson is ordering 10,000 kg of flour from Angus Miller Ltd. Rowland and Hudson uses three

*Figure 42.2*

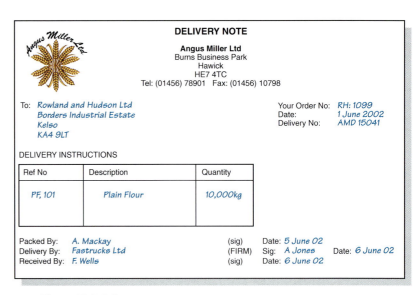

**DELIVERY NOTE**

**Angus Miller Ltd**
Burns Business Park
Hawick
HE7 4TC
Tel: (01456) 78901  Fax: (01456) 10798

To:  Rowland and Hudson Ltd
     Borders Industrial Estate
     Kelso
     KA4 9LT

Your Order No:  RH: 1099
Date:           1 June 2002
Delivery No:    AMD 15041

DELIVERY INSTRUCTIONS

| Ref No | Description | Quantity |
|--------|-------------|----------|
| PF, 101 | Plain Flour | 10,000kg |

Packed By:    A. Mackay      (sig)    Date: 5 June 02
Delivery By:  Fastrucks Ltd  (FIRM)   Sig: A Jones   Date: 6 June 02
Received By:  F. Wells       (sig)    Date: 6 June 02

**Figure 42.3** Delivery note

copies of the purchase order. One copy is sent to Angus Miller, one copy is kept by the purchasing department and one copy is sent to the accounts department in Rowland and Hudson.

## Delivery Note

Assuming that Angus Miller Ltd is willing and able to supply the flour to Rowland and Hudson, the next documents needed will be generated by Angus Miller Ltd itself. Firstly, once the order is put together, Angus Miller will create and send out with the order a **delivery note** that specifies the exact goods being supplied. A typical delivery note used by Angus Miller Ltd is shown here.

As you can see, Angus Miller's name and other details are shown at the top of the page, followed by the name of the company to which it is sending the goods. Other details show the order number of the firm, requesting the goods and the exact details of the goods being delivered. Most delivery notes will not include details of the price or the value of the order, but they may indicate if something has been ordered and cannot be included with the delivery, eg perhaps because it is out of stock. The actual signatures required will depend on the system being operated. If one copy each is to be retained by the company receiving the goods, by the company supplying the goods and by the company doing the actual delivery, then three signatures might be required. This is the system operated by Angus Miller Ltd, and each signature has space for a date.

The completed delivery note below shows 9,000 kg of plain flour being delivered to Rowland and Hudson by Fastrucks Ltd on behalf of Angus Miller Ltd. Notice how the delivery note states that the other 1,000 kg of plain flour ordered by Rowland and Hudson Ltd will follow on within 48 hours.

## Sales Invoice

Once the delivery leaves the Angus Miller warehouse its accounts department will be notified and a **sales invoice** prepared and sent

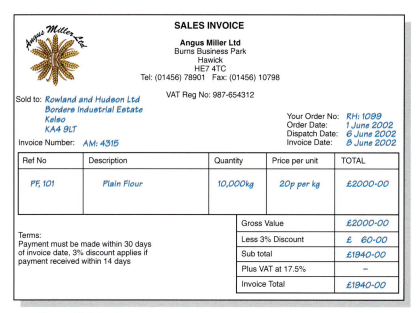

**SALES INVOICE**

**Angus Miller Ltd**
Burns Business Park
Hawick
HE7 4TC
Tel: (01456) 78901   Fax: (01456) 10798

VAT Reg No: 987-654312

Sold to: Rowland and Hudson Ltd
Borders Industrial Estate
Kelso
KA4 9LT

Invoice Number:   AM: 4315

Your Order No:   RH: 1099
Order Date:   1 June 2002
Dispatch Date:   6 June 2002
Invoice Date:   8 June 2002

| Ref No | Description | Quantity | Price per unit | TOTAL |
|--------|-------------|----------|----------------|-------|
| PF, 101 | Plain Flour | 10,000kg | 20p per kg | £2000-00 |

Terms:
Payment must be made within 30 days of invoice date, 3% discount applies if payment received within 14 days

| | |
|---|---|
| Gross Value | £2000-00 |
| Less 3% Discount | £  60-00 |
| Sub total | £1940-00 |
| Plus VAT at 17.5% | – |
| Invoice Total | £1940-00 |

**Figure 42.4** *Invoice*

to Rowland and Hudson. This is, in simple terms, the bill for the goods sent.

Angus Miller Ltd's name and key details will head the page, followed by the name and details of the firm that has purchased the goods. The exact description of the goods ordered and sent should match the purchase order and the delivery note, unless something could not be delivered. The price and value of the goods will partly depend on whether a fixed price had been agreed at the time of the order, and some firms may choose to charge for delivery. If VAT has to be charged on the goods being sent this will be shown in the section showing the sub-totals and amount due.

As in the example shown here, the firm preparing the invoice may also state the maximum amount of time it is prepared to wait for payment. In this case Angus Miller Ltd offers a 3% discount on the value of the sugar if payment is received within 14 days. As flour is classified as a food there is no requirement to charge VAT on it.

This invoice is sent to the accounts department at Rowland and Hudson soon after the goods are dispatched. Some firms may include the sales invoice with the delivery note when the goods are delivered, to reduce postage and to speed up the payment process.

You will notice that the invoice is for the full 10,000 kg of plain flour ordered by Rowland and Hudson, and shows the invoice total as net of 3% discount. If it is not paid within the 14 days Angus Miller would expect the full amount to be paid.

## Goods received note

Once Rowland and Hudson Ltd receives the goods, it will complete a **goods received note** for its own internal use. This will inform the department requesting the goods that they have arrived. The note here shows the typical information included about the goods received in this case as used by Rowland and Hudson.

**Figure 42.5** *Goods received note*

One copy of the note will go to the department ordering the goods and one copy will go to the accounts department. The key information on this note should match the information on the original purchase order. Both the purchasing department and the accounts department at Rowland and Hudson will use the note to check that all the details are correct. For the accounts department, it will be particularly important to check the details before it pays Angus Miller Ltd the amount shown on the sales invoice for the plain flour.

## Credit note

When the accounts department at Rowland and Hudson checks this sales invoice against the original purchase order and the goods received note, it will notice that the invoice is for the full order of 10,000 kg of plain flour, while the goods received note will record the receipt of only 9,000 kg. If the missing 1,000 kg does not arrive within the stated time delay, Rowland and Hudson may decide to obtain additional flour from another company.

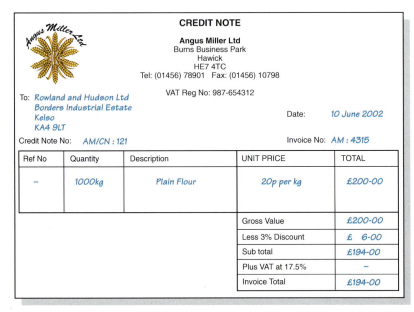

**Figure 42.6** *Credit note*

If it does this, the accounts department will contact Angus Miller Ltd to inform it of this and Angus Miller will issue a **credit note** for the undelivered 1,000 kg. This credit note will decrease the amount outstanding on the original sales invoice and saves Angus Miller producing a replacement sales invoice for the 9,000 kg of plain flour that were delivered on time. A completed credit note is shown here.

## Cheque and Remittance Advice Slip

Once the accounts department at Rowland and Hudson is happy that all the details of the transaction are correct, it will be prepared to pay for the goods received. This will involve writing a **cheque** and completing a **remittance advice slip**. Both of these are shown below.

The cheque is a standard one issued by a bank in books of 30 or 60. Larger organisations may have their names clearly printed on part of the cheque as well as the name and address of the bank. In this case, you will notice in the bottom corner underneath the space for the signature, that it states the cheque is written on behalf of Rowland and Hudson Ltd. The remittance advice slip is created by Rowland and Hudson to send with the payment explaining clearly what is being paid for. It will keep a copy for its own accounts records, so that it knows which goods and services have been paid, and it may be used as an additional check alongside the firm's cheque book record.

You will notice that the cheque includes the amount in both words and numbers, that it is made payable to Angus Miller Ltd who will have to pay it into its account because the cheque is crossed with

*Figure 42.7* Cheque

*Figure 42.8* Remittance advice slip

two parallel lines. The cheque has to be signed and dated to make it completely valid. The remittance advice slip matches the amount of the cheque and details what goods are being paid. Some firms supplying goods may provide their own copy of a remittance advice slip that the purchasing firm has to complete and send back with the payment.

## Receipt

A final document that might be generated in this buying process is a **receipt** for the payment of the goods. Some firms may not issue these if the participating firms are happy with all of the above procedures and feel that they have enough records to prove that goods have been exchanged for payment. If goods are bought using cash, however, then a receipt will be certainly required by the purchaser from the supplier. For example, Rowland and Hudson might buy additional stationery such as paper and pens from a local shop. Cash may be provided from petty cash and the person purchasing the goods will have to present a receipt to the accounts department showing the exact amount spent.

All of the documents explained so far have put Rowland and Hudson in the role as the purchasing firm. It should be remembered that Rowland and Hudson will also be selling biscuits and will create sales invoices of its own in response to purchase orders it receives. It is likely to issue receipts to small shops who buy boxes of biscuits from the company. A typical completed example is shown here.

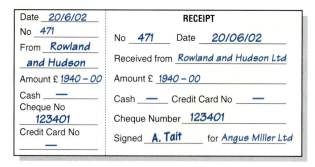

***Figure 42.9*** *Receipt*

## Business Statement of Account

Firms like Rowland and Hudson which are involved in regular transactions might produce a summary of sales and payments over a period of time. For example, Batey Ltd runs a small chain of tourist shops and is a regular purchaser of biscuits from Rowland and Hudson. To help small firms, Rowland and Hudson usually produces a three-monthly **business statement of account**. This will show the values of goods supplied to Batey Ltd and the payments received by Rowland and Hudson. This may be seen on the blank statement of account here.

The invoice numbers sent by Rowland and Hudson are recorded in date order, with the debit column showing the amount of each

## STATEMENT OF ACCOUNT

Account name: *Batey Ltd*

Account No: *451 – 0621*
Date: *18/6/2002*

Rowland and Hudson Ltd
Borders Industrial Estate
Kelso
KA4 9LT
Tel (01234) 56798
Fax: (01234) 98756
VAT Registration Number: 994-362457

| INVOICE NO | DATE | DEBIT | DATE | CREDIT | BALANCE |
|---|---|---|---|---|---|
| RH-00-10123 | | | 1/5/2002 | | 1020-45 |
| RH-00-10099 | 3/5/2002 | 232-55 | | | 1253-00 |
| RH-00-10144 | | | 8/5/2002 | 370-40 | 882-60 |
| RH-00-10103 | 16/5/2002 | 317-25 | | | 1199-85 |
| RH-00-10159 | | | 23/5/2002 | 541-67 | 658-18 |
| RH-00-10113 | 30/5/2002 | 234-14 | | | 892-32 |
| | | | 15/6/2002 | 424-19 | 468-13 |
| | | | | | |
| | | | | | |
| | | | | | |
| | | | | | |

Total balance outstanding

£ *468-13*

TERMS

**Payment must be made within 30 days of invoice date.**

*Figure 42.10* State of accounts

invoice. The right-hand section shows the amount of money received on a particular date by Rowland and Hudson from Batey Ltd in the credit column. The balance column shows the net amount owing to Rowland and Hudson at each date, with the final figure at the bottom showing the total balance outstanding at the end of the three-month period. This helps Rowland and Hudson to monitor its transactions with Batey Ltd, and this statement may be used as an additional reminder if bills have become too large or payment is being delayed for too long.

Rowland and Hudson may use these statements to monitor trends in sales and speed of payments over the whole year. They might also help it to identify possible cashflow problems at particular times of year. They will certainly help to identify 'slow payers' and those who might need some encouragement to settle accounts more rapidly. Notice how useful a spreadsheet program might be to Rowland and Hudson in creating these statements.

# The flow of documents

The description above of all the purchasing and selling documents also helps to shows you the typical order or flow of documents and who will actually generate or create them. This flow is shown below with Rowland and Hudson Ltd ordering goods from Angus Miller Ltd.

Rowland and Hudson Ltd sends out **Purchase Order** to Angus Miller Ltd

↓

Angus Miller Ltd sends a **Delivery Note** with the goods to Rowland and Hudson Ltd

↓

Angus Miller Ltd sends **Sales Invoice** to Rowland and Hudson Ltd

↓

Rowland and Hudson Ltd issue a **Goods Received Note** for use within the company

↓

Rowland and Hudson Ltd send a **Cheque** and **Remittance Advice Slip** to Angus Miller Ltd

↓

Angus Miller Ltd send **Receipt** for the payment to Rowland and Hudson Ltd

↓

Angus Miller Ltd sends out a monthly **Business Statement of Account** to Rowland and Hudson Ltd

## The importance of accurate completion of documents

The flow of documents is obviously very important, but so is the accurate completion of the documents. Inaccuracies might lead to wrong goods or wrong amounts being ordered, or wrong payments which might mean the difference between making a profit or suffering a loss, and possibly to soured relations between firms if mistakes lead to problems and even legal action. Internal problems within a firm might be the result of any inaccuracy if, for example, a goods received note shows less items than have been actually received, but are billed for on an invoice.

Some firms may use sets of blank pre-printed documents which are then filled in by hand, by typewriter or perhaps by use of a word processor or computer. The use of computers allows firms to set up a set of model documents which may be filled in on the screen. Each completed document may then be saved as a separate file and printed with the appropriate number of copies. The most sophisticated software systems allow data to be inputted which then complete a number of different types of documents. This obviously speeds up the process and so cuts costs. Document records ought to be more accurate under this system, but it does not stop the wrong data being inputted and, as with all documents and record systems, a checking process will be required.

## What have I learned?

1. Purchase orders, goods received notes, remittance advice notes and cheques are produced by the purchasing firm.
2. Delivery notes, sales invoices, credit notes, business statement of accounts and receipts are produced by the supplier.
3. Each document has a particular part to play in the buying and selling process and there is a normal sequence for the ordering, checking, recording and paying for goods and services.
4. It is important for firms both to complete forms and to carry out calculations accurately, as problems will result from mistakes.
5. Documents may be completed in handwriting, by typewriter, by word processor or computer program such as spreadsheets or database, or by a dedicated finance system.
6. All documents ought to be checked before they are sent out.

## KEY TERMS

- Purchase order – used by a firm wishing to buy goods and services and sent to a supplier with details of the goods or services required
- Delivery note – used by a supplier to accompany the goods being delivered, informing the purchaser of the actual items being sent
- Sales invoice – created by the supplier to inform the purchaser of the prices and total values of the good being sold, together with any conditions about payment of the bill
- Goods received notes – completed by the purchasing firm to notify the ordering and accounts departments that the goods have been received in the correct amounts and in good condition
- Credit notes – used by a supplier when the sales invoice sent includes a value for goods that were not supplied or were not in a condition to be accepted by the purchaser
- Business statement of account – generated by a supplier to show the value of goods being sold and the amounts of money received from an individual purchasing firm over a period of time
- Remittance advice slips – usually created by a purchasing firm and sent to the supplier with payment for an invoice, to show exactly what is being paid
- Cheques – the most common method of payment used by firms
- Receipts – provided by firms receiving payment for goods and services to show that a bill has been paid

# EXAMINATION PREPARATION EXERCISE

This exercise is designed to check your knowledge and understanding of the main documents used by a business to purchase goods and services. Go back to the beginning of this chapter and re-read the opening information on Rowland and Hudson Ltd. You might also re-read the information on the company at the start of Chapters 39 and 40.

Many of the tasks will involve you completing documents involved in the purchasing process. Blank masters of these documents are included in Chapter 50 at the end of this student book and may be photocopied for you to complete. The purchases will be by Rowland and Hudson Ltd from Angus Miller Ltd, so look through this chapter to identify any information required about company addresses etc.

1. > Complete a purchase order for Rowland and Hudson for 15,000 kg of plain flour at an expected price of 20p per kg, 5,000 kg of granulated sugar at an expected price of 55p per kg and 10 litres of ginger flavouring at £4 per litre. The previous order number was RH: 2034. Rowland and Hudson expect delivery within seven days of the order date, and delivery should be between 10 am and 2 pm Monday to Friday. Date the order on the date you start this exercise.

2. > Complete a sales invoice and a delivery note on behalf of Angus Miller Ltd for the above quantities and prices. The previous invoice number used by Angus Miller was AM: 4756. The previous delivery number was AMD: 5379. Date the two documents for four days after the date of the purchase order sent by Rowland and Hudson. The order is delivered by Fastrucks Ltd and uses the same names for signatures as shown above.

3. > Complete a goods received note on behalf of Rowland and Hudson, assuming that it receives all the goods ordered and they are in good condition. The goods arrive five days after the completion of the order form. The next good received note number is RH/RN-4234.

4. > Complete a cheque for the full amount of the sales invoice, less the 3% discount offered by Angus Miller Ltd if payment is made within 14 days of the date of the invoice. Date the cheque for eight days after the date of the invoice, and also complete a remittance advice slip for Rowland and Hudson for the same date.

5. > Explain when credit notes and a business statement of account would be used by Angus Miller Ltd in its trading with Rowland and Hudson Ltd.

6. >> The main body of this chapter explains all the documents used in the purchasing process. Use this description to create a poster illustrating the normal flow and sequence of documents from both the purchasing and supplying firms. You might wish to illustrate this poster with completed documents using the blank masters from Chapter 50. This task might be completed in pairs or small groups, if you wish to use your posters as part of a display.

7. >>> Explain the importance of completion and calculation errors when completing the documents both for Rowland and Hudson Ltd and for Angus Miller Ltd.

8. >>> Undertake some research to identify some of the computerised finance systems on the market. Write a brief report to both companies explaining the main features of the systems you discover, together with an explanation of any advantages and disadvantages.

# CHAPTER 43
# Balance sheets

When a firm wants to know what it is worth, it can use a Balance Sheet. This account shows a firm the value of what it owns, the value of what it owes and the value of the capital invested in the firm. The assets that Rowland and Hudson Ltd, the biscuit manufacturer, own include its factory and warehouse, most of the machinery in the buildings, the delivery vehicles, the furniture and furnishings in the offices, and stocks of materials and finished biscuits. It also has some liabilities in the form of two loans from banks and other debts owed to its suppliers. Contributions to the company's capital come from its shareholders and from profit retained in the company over a number of years. Company law requires Rowland and Hudson Ltd to prepare an annual Balance Sheet, but it is also a useful account to show how well the company is performing, and comparisons can be made with previous years' accounts.

*Figure 43.1*

## What is a Balance Sheet?

The Balance Sheet is an account that gives a statement of a firm's wealth on a particular date. It is sometimes said to be like a 'snapshot' because it records the company`s value at that moment in time, just as a photograph records people or events in an instant. By the next day, the value of the firm will have started to change. Normally, a Balance Sheet will be produced at the end of the firm`s financial year. It has three main parts:

- assets: everything that a company owns and which has a money value
- liabilities: everything that a company owes and which has a money value
- capital: the different forms and sources of money invested in the firm.

FOR YOUR
EXAMINATION

✓
✗

Balance Sheets will be set out in different ways according to the type and size of firm, but this chapter will keep to a standard layout. Whatever the layout, the Balance Sheet must always 'balance'.

*Figure 43.2*

## How is a Balance Sheet set out?

There are several ways to set out a Balance Sheet. This depends on the type of firm, its size and even which accountancy firm it uses. The balance sheet shown in Figure 43.3 is for a limited company and should be very similar to the ones used in your examination paper.

|  | £ | £ | £ |
|---|---|---|---|
|  | '000s | '000s | '000s |
| **Fixed Assets** |  |  |  |
| Land and buildings | 140 |  |  |
| Equipment and vehicles | 37 |  |  |
| Furniture and furnishings | 11 |  |  |
|  |  |  | 188 |
| **Current Assets** |  |  |  |
| Stocks | 15 |  |  |
| Debtors | 2 |  |  |
| Cash | 2 |  |  |
|  |  | 19 |  |
| *Less* |  |  |  |
| **Current Liabilities** |  |  |  |
| (amounts falling due within one year) |  |  |  |
| Creditors | 13 |  |  |
| Bank Overdraft | 1 |  |  |
|  |  | 14 |  |
| **Net Current Assets** |  |  | 5 |
| (Working Capital) |  |  |  |
| **Total assets less current liabilities** |  |  | 193 |
| *Less* |  |  |  |
| **Creditors** (amounts falling due in more than one year) |  |  | 25 |
| **Net Assets** |  |  | 168 |
| **Capital and Reserves** |  |  |  |
| Share Capital |  |  | 108 |
| Reserves |  |  | 10 |
| Profit and loss account |  |  | 50 |
|  |  |  | 168 |

**Figure 43.3** *Balance Sheet for Henry's Pizzas Ltd as at 31 March 2002*

## Why do 'Net Assets' equal the total for 'Capital and Reserves'?

The figure for the capital and reserves shows the total value of the funds used to obtain the company's net assets. Therefore, the two figures must be equal. In the Balance Sheet above you can see that they are equal at £168,000 each.

### LEARNING ACTIVITY 1

Use the balance sheet shown for Henry's Pizzas Ltd to answer the following questions.

> 1. What sort of fixed assets might Henry's Pizzas Ltd have?
> 2. What sort of stocks will Henry's have?
>> 3. Who might be Henry's debtors?
> 4. Who might be Henry's creditors?
>>> 5. Why might Henry's have such a large figure for its stocks?
> 6. Why will it be important for Henry's to have a large enough figure for its net current assets (working capital)?

## How is a Balance Sheet used?

As well as giving a snapshot of the value and wealth of the company, the Balance Sheet has many practical uses:

- it can help to measure the profitability of the company
- it can help to measure the firm's cash situation
- it can allow comparisons to be made with previous years and even with other similar companies.

Checking the performance of the company might help in key decision-making. For many firms, and especially for limited companies, it is a legal requirement to produce a Balance Sheet.

### The importance of balance sheets to stakeholders

- **Managers** will use the figures to help show trends when compared with forecast figures and with figures for previous years. The figures will show the value of the company, whether there are any problems in meeting debts, and will allow the managers to carry out further calculations to analyse performance.

## FOR YOUR EXAMINATION

The examination paper may present you with an incomplete Balance Sheet. You will be expected to select figures from a set of financial data, and to insert the correct figures in the correct place in the balance sheet. You may also have to calculate some of the totals shown in the Balance Sheet. The examination may ask you to deal with only a part of the Balance Sheet. If this is the case, it should be labelled as an 'extract from a Balance Sheet' and will usually stop at either the 'total assets less current liabilities' figure or the 'net assets' figure.

## TRUE OR FALSE?

*Fixed assets are the same as a firm's fixed costs.*

*(see foot of page for answer)*

### True or False answer

**False.** Fixed costs are the costs paid to purchase such items as machinery. The figures for fixed assets are the value of things such as machinery at this moment in time, and could be calculated by estimating how much they could be sold for.

- *Owners and shareholders* will want to see the net value or worth of the company. Any growth in value might help push up share prices.
- *Suppliers and lenders* will be keen to check on the company's ability to pay its debts, and will look particularly closely at current assets and liabilities.
- *Employees* will be keen to check on the company's cash situation so that they are sure their wages will continue to be paid.

Remember, only public limited companies make their accounts available for the public to look at, so stakeholders in other types of business may find it difficult to assess performance.

## What have I learned?

1. A Balance Sheet shows the value of a firm at a point in time.
2. It shows the value of the assets owned, the liabilities owed and the capital at work in the firm.
3. Balance Sheet figures can be compared to previous years and sometimes to other companies to help interested groups monitor progress and performance
4. The Balance Sheet must always balance, with the value of net assets equalling the value of the capital and reserves.

## KEY TERMS

Fixed Assets – assets that are used to help production take place, including buildings and land, vehicles and equipment, furniture and furnishings

Current Assets – assets that can be easily turned into cash, such as stocks of materials and finished goods

Debtors – people or business organisations who have obtained goods or services from this firm but have not yet paid for them

Current Liabilities – debts which the firm has to repay within one year

Creditors – people or business organisations who have supplied goods or services to the firm but have not yet been paid for them

Net Current Assets – this is sometimes called working capital because it is the amount of money a firm has available to meet its day to day needs; it is calculated simply as current assets less current liabilities

Net Assets – this is calculated by adding the value of fixed assets to current assets and deducting all liabilities

Share capital – this can be simply thought of as the value of the shares when they were first issued

Long Term Liabilities – debts which are due for repayment in at least one year`s time; these will mainly include medium- and long-term bank loans

Capital and reserves – the total amount of capital put into the business by the owners which is calculated by adding share capital, reserves and retained profit together

# EXAMINATION PREPARATION EXERCISE

The following Balance Sheet is Rowland and Hudson Ltd, biscuit manufacturer. The figures in the shortened account are for 2001. The account is a typical layout that might be used in the examination.

*Extract from a balance sheet for Rowland and Hudson Ltd as at 31 May 2001*

|  | £'000s | £'000s | £'000s |
|---|---|---|---|
| Fixed Assets |  |  |  |
| Land and buildings | 400 |  |  |
| Vehicles and machinery | 100 |  |  |
| Furniture and furnishings | 15 |  |  |
|  |  |  | 515 |
| Current Assets |  |  |  |
| Stock | 60 |  |  |
| Debtors | 80 |  |  |
| Cash | 10 |  |  |
|  |  | 150 |  |
| Current Liabilities |  |  |  |
| (amounts falling due within 1 year) |  |  |  |
| Creditors |  | 110 |  |
| Net Current Assets |  |  | 40 |
| Total assets less current liabilities |  |  | 555 |

> 1. Use the following figures to create an extract from a balance sheet for the same company as at 31 May 2002:
>    land and buildings – £410,000; vehicles and machinery – £105,000; furniture and furnishings – £16,000; stock – £67,000; debtors – £90,000; cash – £12,000; creditors (amounts falling due within 1 year) – £125,000.
>> 2. Use the Balance Sheets for each year to compare the performance of Rowland and Hudson Ltd.

CHAPTER 44

# Sources of business finance

When a firm is being set up and then operated, the owners will need money. They might be able to provide some of this money themselves, but most firms will have to look for additional sources of finance. Many of these sources will involve some form of borrowing. Some types of finance might be available for short periods of time only, while others might be available for many years; some types of finance will have very specific uses, while others may have a variety. Large firms find they may have several sources of finance open to them, while small firms usually

*Figure 44.1*

find only a limited number available. As firms grow, they will find that their financial needs change.

Limited companies have access to huge quantities of finance through the sale of shares. A private limited company might decide to 'float' itself on the stock market by inviting the public to buy shares. In March 2002 the financial sections of newspapers reported that Sir Richard Branson was planning to do this with his Virgin Mobile company, with the deal expected to value the group at £700 m. Companies that are already plcs can also raise additional finance from owners by selling additional sets of shares. Listen to the business sections on national television and radio news broadcasts, or read the business sections of newspapers to find out the latest examples of these share offers.

## Types of finance

These can be broken down into three broad categories:

1 owners' funds
2 borrowed funds
3 grants.

### Owners' funds

As the title suggests, this is money put or invested into the business by the owner. A sole trader or a group of partners might decide to use personal savings or perhaps redundancy money to set up a business. When a limited company is being set up, the owners are known as **shareholders**. They share in the ownership of the company and they share the responsibility of putting money into the business. Owners' funds or capital is permanently invested in the business. It is not a loan, so the owners will not earn any interest on this money. Instead, they will expect to share the profits made by the firm. When the business is a company, this share of the profits is usually called a **dividend**.

Instead of taking out all the profits earned, the owners might decide to retain some of the profits to reinvest in the business.

*Figure 44.2*

Retained profit is one of the most important sources of finance for most businesses. While the actual amount retained will be limited by the size of the profit made by the company, it has the advantages of being free of interest and does not have to be paid back.

Sometimes, the owners might decide that they no longer want to own the business and will want their capital back. For a sole trader, this will mean either selling the business to someone else or closing it down and selling off the assets such as the premises. A partner wanting to leave a partnership could also try to sell to someone else, but if no one is prepared to buy into the business it would probably close down after selling the assets.

For shareholders, the process is much easier: they just have to sell their shares in the business, and the capital will stay in the company.

Owners' capital can be increased. A sole trader might have further savings or might decide to find a partner. Partnerships might look for additional partners while companies can issue further sets of shares. The only problems from increasing the number of owners are that more people will share the profits and they might want to share the running of the business.

## Borrowed funds

This is sometimes called **debt finance**, as it will involve the firm in obtaining some form of credit or loan and therefore being in debt to someone. Any form of borrowed funds will probably involve an interest charge and, of course, the funds will have to be repaid. Depending on the type of credit, money can be borrowed for just a few days or for several years. Most of these sources of credit are explained further on in this chapter.

## Grants

Grants can be thought of as a 'gift' of money which does not have to be paid back. A wide range of grants is available to all sorts of firms. The amounts of money involved can vary from £50 per week for new, small firms starting up to many millions of pounds for multi-national companies. The grants might be targeted at firms providing certain goods or services, or at those in a particular region. Providers of grants vary from the EU to local councils, and from the UK government to charitable trusts.

## LEARNING ACTIVITY 1

Find out what grants are available to businesses in your locality. In groups, write to a number of organisations to find out this information. Use Yellow Pages as a starting point for the likely addresses.
Organisations might include:
local councils, local companies, Learning Skills Council, your local MP, your Euro MP, the Board of Trade, the EU.

## Why do firms need the finance?

Businesses need money for all sorts of things. Some money will be needed before the firm is ready to open. More finance will be needed just to keep the business running on a daily basis. Once the firm has been operating for a while, it may need further capital to help it progress into the future. So, we can identify four broad categories of financial need.

### Start-up

Most new firms are small and will have limited amounts of money available from the owners themselves. Large sums of money may have to be borrowed to pay for all the start-up costs. These will include both the purchase of fixed assets such as the premises and equipment and the purchase of current assets such as a first stock of materials. It may take several years for a new firm to become really successful and for any borrowed finance to be paid back.

### Cashflow

A firm needs a steady supply of funds to pay for the running costs of producing more goods and services. Delays in receiving payment for goods sold may lead to cash shortages when wages have to be paid and materials bought. Most firms will try to keep a pool of working capital available to cover any temporary cash shortage but may also need to negotiate an overdraft with a bank.

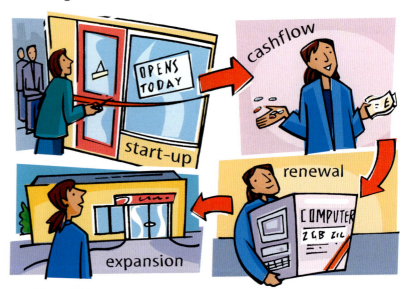

*Figure 44.3*

### Renewal

Most machinery and equipment (or **plant**) will have a certain expected life and at some stage will need to be replaced. So, finance will be needed to help renew and maintain these fixed assets. Some firms will find this a bigger requirement than others. It will depend on how much equipment there is, how expensive it is and how quickly it wears out.

## Expansion

If a firm is quite successful, the owners might want it to grow. In many ways, expansion will be similar to start-up but the firm may no longer be small. It may have a good reputation and own valuable assets such as land and property. Large amounts of money might be needed for any expansion and it might take several years for the expansion to be really successful. As a result, it may not be possible to pay back any borrowed funds for several years.

# Sources of borrowed funds

A firm's financial needs are clearly varied. Some finance will be required for just a few days, while other finance may be tied up in the firm for many years. There are, therefore, different sources of finance for these different time periods.

## Short-term finance

This refers to money that is borrowed for between one day and three years. It is mainly needed to help with cashflow, to buy assets such as vehicles and to buy in additional stocks of materials.

Types of short-term finance include:

- **Bank overdraft**: an agreement with a bank to overspend the business's account, up to a specified limit. The business will go into the 'red' and interest will be charged according to the amount overdrawn and the time involved. Many businesses arrange permanent overdraft facilities, with the overdraft changing as money flows into and out of the business.
- **Short-term loan**: a specific sum of money is borrowed for a fixed time period. Interest will be charged on the full amount borrowed. The loan will be for a particular purpose, eg for a new van or a small machine. Most of these loans will be repaid monthly.
- **Hire purchase**: this is a method of buying equipment by paying for it in instalments. The full price paid is likely to include a charge for interest. The firm buying the equipment will not own it until the final payment has been made.
- **Trade credit**: arrangements with a supplier to postpone payments for goods and services received until an agreed date. In most cases this will be 30 days of credit, but it depends on a firm's business reputation. There is no interest charge for this.
- **Factoring**: some firms deliberately delay payment of their bills for several months. This might leave a firm with a cash shortage while waiting for payment. The firm could approach a specialist factoring company who may offer an immediate payment of up to 80% of the amount owed. The remainder will be paid once the debt is settled. A fee will be charged for this service.

## Medium-term finance

This is money that is borrowed for between three and ten years. It may be used to buy assets such as machinery, to set up the business and to pay for small scale expansion.

- **Term loans**: these are similar to short-term loans, but the banks often offer a wider range of conditions. Interest rates might be either fixed or variable. Repayment might be made in instalments at the end of each year or might be made at the end of the loan period. The loans are likely to be for larger amounts.
- **Leasing**: the leasing company will buy the asset and then lease it to a business (the lessee). The leasing agreement will be for a fixed time period, after which it might be renewed or a new agreement reached for a more up-to-date piece of equipment. The lessee will pay a regular payment for the use of the asset. The leasing company may be responsible for repair costs but the lessee will not own the asset.
- **Instalment credit**: this is the same as hire purchase but will be arranged for longer time periods and probably for larger sums of money.

## Long-term finance

This is money that is borrowed for at least ten years. This will be used to start up larger businesses, to buy lifelong assets such as buildings and to pay for large scale expansion.

- **Term loans**: the same as for medium-term loans, but may be for as long as 20 years. Any lender would make sure that the borrower had sufficient security in case the loan could not be repaid.
- **Syndicated loans**: for very large loans, a group of banks or other financial institutions might jointly provide the money. This would spread out the risk of non-repayment.
- **Mortgage loans**: these are loans for the purchase of land and buildings. These may involve very large sums of money and so may be for between 20 and 35 years.
- **Sale and leaseback**: an asset, particularly land and buildings, may be sold to a company specialising in leasing. The seller then leases the property back from the buyer. This gives the selling firm a large sum of money, but it no longer owns the property and it will have to pay out a regular sum of money for its use.
- **Debentures**: large public limited companies can borrow through the City of London by issuing debentures (sometimes called stocks or bonds). These loans may be for as long as 25 years. The rates of interest may be fixed, or they may be lower than for other loans if the borrowing company can offer sound, specific assets as security.
- **Venture capital**: this is finance invested by organisations or individuals in small- or medium-sized businesses that are often considered too risky by most providers of finance. Some of the investment is likely to be in the form of a loan, but some of the investment may also be made in return for a share in the ownership of the business. The investment is more likely to support expansion of an existing business rather than a business start-up.

## LEARNING ACTIVITY 2

Most high street banks have business advisers. As a group, invite a representative from a local bank to talk to you about the financial products and services offered to local businesses.

## What have I learned?

1. Firms need finance to start up, to maintain, to expand and to run their businesses.
2. Finance may be provided by the owners themselves, through grants from various organisations or may be borrowed in a variety of ways.
3. Money may be borrowed for short, medium or long periods of time, according to the type and size of firm, the reason for borrowing the money, and the risk to the lender.

## KEY TERMS

- Owners' funds – money put into the business by the owner. This investment will be by the sole trader, partners or shareholders. The money will stay in the business as long as it continues to operate
- Grants – money given to a firm to help it to operate and expand. The sums given will vary according to the size of the firm receiving the grant, what it is to be used for and the organisation giving it
- Borrowed funds – money that is borrowed in some way and will have to be repaid, often with an interest charge
- Short-term finance – money that is borrowed for between one day and three years. It is mainly needed to help cashflow, to buy assets such as vehicles and to buy in additional stocks of materials
- Medium-term finance – money that is borrowed for between three and ten years. It may be used to buy assets such as machinery, to set up the business and to pay for small scale expansion
- Long-term finance – money that is borrowed for at least ten years. This will be used to start up larger businesses, to buy lifelong asset such as buildings and to pay for large scale expansion.

# EXAMINATION PREPARATION EXERCISE

Read each of the case studies given below. For each case study:

1. Decide which possible methods of finance might be used by the business in each case.
2. Describe the advantages and disadvantages of each method and decide which method or methods will be best.
3. Justify your choice.

## CASE STUDY A

An outside catering business is owned by a sole proprietor, John Hedley. He has three workers and wishes to expand the number of catering contracts. The owner will need an extra van priced at £8,000 and will need to hire two extra workers, increasing the weekly wage bill by £450. He will need to order extra ingredients which are usually obtained from suppliers that offer 14 days' credit. The owner finds that some customers take up to four weeks to pay for the catering services that John provides.

*Figure 44.4*

## CASE STUDY B

An optician that operates as a private limited company wishes to expand by opening a second branch. There are two shareholders with an equal share in the business. They have found a suitable building for the new branch which will cost £150,000 to purchase and fit out. Extra staffing costs for the second branch are estimated at £65,000 for the year with other overheads estimated at £30,000. An additional start up stock of frames and lenses will cost £9,000.

*Figure 44.5*

CHAPTER 45

# Budgets and financial planning

Almost everyone uses a budget. Most of you will be carrying out short-term planning by deciding how to use the money you are given each week. Slightly longer term-planning might see you budgeting for a holiday or buying Christmas presents. This can then be extended to plans for new furniture, a car, and, of course, a house.

In many ways, businesses are doing exactly the same type of planning and budgeting that individual people carry out: we are all trying to see into the future so that we can be prepared.

The problem for firms and people alike is being able to see into the future accurately.

*Figure 45.1*

# What is a budget?

A budget is a financial plan which is created and developed for the future. A short-term budget would be for up to one year, while a medium-term budget might be for as long as five years. This then leaves a long-term budget being planned for over five years.

Budgets in small firms might be developed and controlled by one person. In larger firms they might be put together by people from different areas of the firm, with each team setting objectives, obtaining information, and making decisions as the budget is prepared and used to control the business. In the largest businesses, there are likely to be several budgets, with separate departments having their own plans that then contribute to budgets for the whole firm.

# What are the purposes of budgeting?

- Budgets help businesses to predict what the organisation thinks will happen.
- Budgets help businesses to explore and weigh-up alternative courses of action. The research undertaken and the information gathered will help decisions to be taken.
- Budgets set targets which may then be communicated to people throughout the business. This will help everyone to work towards the targets.
- Budgets help to monitor performance within the firm by studying results and comparing them to the planned figures in the budget. If the firm can find out why the differences have taken place, it will help managers to control performance.
- Budgets are a vital part of the process of business planning. They give the firm sets of measurable data which help it to set objectives and to carry out planning for the whole business.

# Types of budgets

There are all sorts of budgets that a business might develop. These can include:

- cashflow forecasts (explained in Chapter 40)

- trading forecasts – estimates of sales, costs of production including overheads, leaving an indication of profit or loss
- capital budgets – plans for the purchase of fixed assets, which show the likely date of purchase and the expected cost of the assets
- research and development budgets – showing plans for the costs of creating and developing both new and replacement products
- advertising and promotional budgets – supporting individual products and the firm as a whole
- departmental expenditure plans – showing the planned expenditure of each department over a specified time period and giving the company a picture of total spending.

## Examples of budgets

### Capital budgets

Capital expenditure takes place when fixed assets are obtained for a business. This spending can be planned by using a capital budget. Many firms will identify the different categories of fixed assets that might be acquired. Typical categories of fixed assets will be: buildings, land, plant and machinery, furniture and furnishings, computer equipment, vehicles. These categories could be listed in a table with the possible expenditure planned out for each month of the year.

Some firms might find it more useful to divide the capital expenditure up into replacement, expansion and health and safety. In this way a business could see when it was actually achieving a growth in its capital assets and not just replacing worn-out or out-of-date capital. It would also help to show whether the items were essential or desirable. However the capital budget is designed, once it is planned out the figures can be put into the firm's cash flow forecast.

A capital budget for six months showing a mixture of these designs is shown below.

*Figure 45.2*

|  | Jan | Feb | Mar | Apr | May | June |
|---|---|---|---|---|---|---|
|  | £ | £ | £ | £ | £ | £ |
| **Replacement** |  |  |  |  |  |  |
| Land and buildings |  |  |  |  |  |  |
| Plant and equipment | 2,000 |  |  |  |  |  |
| Furniture and furnishings | 500 |  |  |  |  |  |
| Computer equipment |  |  |  |  | 450 |  |
| Vehicles |  |  |  |  |  | 400 |
| **Expansion** |  |  |  |  |  |  |
| Land and buildings |  |  | 15,000 |  |  |  |
| Plant and equipment |  | 5,000 |  |  |  | 7,500 |
| Furniture and furnishings |  |  |  |  |  |  |
| Computer equipment |  |  |  | 4,000 |  |  |
| Vehicles | 8,000 |  |  |  |  |  |
| **Health and Safety** |  | 2,000 |  |  | 3,000 |  |
| **Total** | 10,500 | 7,000 | 15,000 | 4,000 | 3,450 | 7,900 |

*Figure 45.3  A capital budget for six months showing a mixture of designs*

## Trading forecast

This is closely linked to the actual trading and Profit and Loss statement or account, since it will include the same main items. The items used in the forecast and actual account will depend on the type of firm and its products but are likely to include:

- sales – the value of the goods/services sold
- purchases – the value of materials, components and other stock bought
- wages – in a manufacturing firm these might be broken down into two categories:

1. direct labour costs of workers who make the product
2. indirect labour costs of workers not directly involved in making the product

- expenses – all the other items of expenditure and overheads including power costs, advertising, business rates, insurance, transport and interest charges
- net profit/loss –the figure showing the difference between the value of sales and the value of all the costs.

*Figure 45.4*

| | Jan | Feb | Mar | Apr | May | June |
|---|---|---|---|---|---|---|
| | £ | £ | £ | £ | £ | £ |
| Sales | 5500 | 6250 | 5765 | 5485 | 6755 | 5945 |
| Purchases | 1575 | 1985 | 1875 | 1685 | 1995 | 1875 |
| Wages | 1500 | 1550 | 1555 | 1550 | 1565 | 1550 |
| Expenses | 2175 | 2255 | 2345 | 2255 | 2185 | 2255 |
| Total costs | 5250 | 5795 | 5775 | 5490 | 5745 | 5680 |
| Net profit or loss | 250 | 455 | (10) | (5) | 1010 | 265 |

**Figure 45.5** *A typical example of a six-month trading forecast for Elaine Moore's flower shop*

**FOR YOUR EXAMINATION**

✓ You will not be expected to compile any budget or forecast from data. You ✗ may be presented with the budget and asked to make comments about it.

It should be remembered that the actual trading statement will show sales and purchases when they are made, and not when the money is actually received or paid out. This compares to a cashflow forecast which shows when each flow of cash is expected to take place.

## Comparing budgets

It is always difficult to be accurate when creating a budget. In any forecast, the figures may vary for all sorts of reasons, which is why it is important for a business to compare its forecast figures with its actual figures. This comparison will allow the business to update forecasts and to keep the business operating successfully.

These comparisons are sometimes called **variance analysis**. Any differences between the budgeted figures and the real figures are called **variances**. A favourable variance on a trading and Profit and Loss account will mean the net profit on the actual account is greater than the planned figure on the budget. An adverse variance would mean the actual net profit figure was lower than the forecast figure. Careful analysis of the variances can help a firm to understand why they have occurred and what might be done about them. The use of spreadsheet programs helps most businesses to do this analysis quickly and accurately.

## The importance of financial planning

The budgets explained and illustrated above will help the business as a whole and the separate departments within it to plan for the future. Estimates for both income and spending have to be made, usually for 12 months at a time. In addition to the budgets shown in this chapter, a business will pay particular attention to its cashflow forecast. Budgets may show figures for each week, month, quarter or even for the whole year.

As actual data is received by a firm, it will need to update the budgets and forecasts so that they are as realistic as possible. This will help the firm to monitor expansion plans being undertaken, will help to plan and deal with any unexpected costs, and hopefully may even lead to a reduction in costs. Poor planning can all too easily lead to a business failing.

## Business plans

When a firm is going to set up and when it is going to change or expand its operations, it usually needs a plan. In many cases, it will produce a formal, detailed business plan that sets targets, that includes a mass of data about the business, that allows progress to be checked and that helps the firm to obtain finance. The content of the plan will depend on the size and type of the firm, the good or service provided, and the reasons for producing a plan.

### Why will a firm produce a business plan?

There are five main reasons for making a plan:

1 To make sure any business activity is successful, a firm will need a plan so that nothing is forgotten. Whether a new, small firm is being set up for the first time or whether a multi-national company is about to build an additional factory, the owners and managers have to be sure that they have a plan that will work. Any mistakes could be both costly and risky.

2 To run and control the business successfully, the business plan can include a checklist of key guidelines. The managers can check that they are following the plan and can use it to see how to correct any problems. For example, a new sole trader might have a list of tasks to do each day; the distribution manager in a small company might have a set procedure to follow if a customer rings up to complain about a delivery problem. In other words, the plan is a working document and not just a glossy brochure.

3 To help the owners and managers review progress, the plan can include a set of aims, objectives or targets. These can be set out in specific detail with key dates set out for their planned achievement. For new firms these targets might be 'to break even by the end of the first nine months in business'. Established firms might be wanting their new production line 'to be fully operational

within six months of starting the installation'. Profit levels, sales figures or the number of outlets could all be targets included in business plans.

4  To help obtain loans and other forms of credit, particularly from banks and financial institutions, means that most business plans must be very detailed. This will be necessary both when the firm is being set up and when any additional finance is required. Any lender will expect to see that the plan has been well thought out, and that its risks when lending money are minimised.

5  To show potential investors that the firm is worth the risk of investing capital in it, a business plan can be used to attract additional partners or shareholders. A sole trader might use it to change the business into a partnership. Companies might use the plan as part of the documents needed to issue new sets of shares.

## What should be included in a business plan?

This partly depends on the type and size of firm and the reason for producing a plan. The contents shown below are the normal requirements when setting up a new, small firm. They are set out in a condensed format to show how a business plan might be laid out.

Name of business..........................
Address..........................
Telephone number..........................
Sole trader [ ] Partnership [ ] Franchise [ ] Limited Company [ ]
Target start up date..........................
Type of business..........................
Aims and Objectives..........................
Your ultimate goal..........................
What do you expect to achieve by the end of
Year 1..........................
Year 2..........................
Year 3..........................

### Your market
Describe the type, size and location of your market ..........................
Describe your customers ..........................

### Your product/service
Compare your product with two competitors using:
price...........................        quality..........................
availablity.....................        customers.....................
staff skills....................        reputation.....................
advertising...................        delivery..........................
location.......................        special offers................
after sales service......................
Why is your product/service special?......................
Why will it be better than your competitors?......................

### Pricing
Itemise your costs.............................................
Calculate your break even point.....................................

### Promotion and selling

How do your competitors promote and sell their products/services?................................

How are you going to promote and sell your products/service?..............................

Estimate the cost of this.............................

Why are your promotional and selling methods appropriate?..............................

### Staff

Personal details of owners...............................

Details of key staff to be hired...............................

Number/job descriptions/cost of staff to be hired............................

### Financial matters

What business assets do you have and what are they worth? (eg equipment, vehicles)...............................

What assets will you need to:

start up...............................

continue through your first year...............................

Give details of your premises eg lease, rent, rates, location, condition...............................

What credit do you expect from your suppliers?...............................

Who will keep your financial records?........................

Give an estimated:12 month cashflow forecast...........................

12 month estimated Profit and Loss account forecast......................

What finance do you require and what are your proposed sources?

Grants...............................

Own resources...............................

Loans...............................

Creditors...............................

## LEARNING ACTIVITY 1

Most banks produce a range of booklets giving advice on the completion of a business plan, and some provide a CD-rom to help in the preparation. Visit a bank or invite a representative to talk to your group about the type of data they would want to be included, and the business advice they offer firms.

## What have I learned?

1. To help it plan for the future, a business may prepare and use a number of budgets including a cashflow forecast, trading forecasts, capital budgets, research budgets and advertising budgets.
2. Budgets may be created for the whole firm and for the separate departments within a firm.
3. Budgets may be weekly, monthly, quarterly or yearly.
4. Budgets will help a business to predict what will happen, to weigh up alternative actions, to set targets, to monitor performance and to plan the whole business and its future.
5. When a business starts up or expands, it may produce a formal, detailed business plan which it will use as a set of guidelines and as a way of attracting additional capital.

*Elaine Moore's flower shop*

*Figure 45.6*

# EXAMINATION PREPARATION EXERCISE

Look back at the six-monthly trading forecast for Elaine Moore's flower shop. Create a further six-monthly forecast for July until December.

1. Use the following figures to fill in the appropriate parts of the forecast.
- Sales for July were £6,075, rising by £50 in August and a further £50 in September.
- Sales in October fell to £5,975, falling by £75 in November and a further £75 in December.
- Purchases in July were £1,850, rising by £50 each month during August, September and October.
- Purchases fell to £1,755 for both November and December.
- Wages were £1,550 for all six months.
- Expenses were £2,125 in July, increasing by £50 in August and a further £75 in September.
- Expenses fell to £2,150 in October, and rose again to £2,250 for both November and December.

2. Calculate the total costs and net profit or loss figures for the separate months of July to December.
3. Calculate the estimated net profit figure for the whole 12-month period.
4. Explain how creating a trading forecast will help Elaine Moore to plan her future business.

CHAPTER 46

# Methods of making and receiving payments

Most people have some sort of personal bank account. This means have a paying-in book, probably a cheque book, most people will have a debit card and, once over the age of 18, a credit card. On many accounts, regular payments can be made and received using either credit transfer or direct debit systems.

All businesses will have a business account which they will operate in a very similar way to the personal accounts described above. Businesses like Rowland and Hudson Ltd (the biscuit manufacturer) will receive payments in the form of cash, cheques, debit and credit card receipts, credit transfers, and direct debit payments. Some of these payments will go directly into its bank account, while others will be collected and paid in by an employee. Rowland and Hudson Ltd will be able to make payments from its bank account using exactly the same methods.

The main difference between a personal account and a business account is the cost charged by the bank for the services it offers. Most personal customers are able to use the services of a personal account, cost-free. They may even receive a small amount of interest on their account. Most businesses, however, will have to pay bank charges both for making payments from their account and for paying money into it.

*Figure 46.1*

## Cash

Cash or money is still central to many transactions between buyers and sellers. While fewer transactions are made in cash these days, there are still some purchases that will always be made using cash. Buying a newspaper, some stamps when posting a letter or a soft drink are small transactions and will take place using cash.

You might think that there will be no costs for a firm when handling cash, but this is not true. Counting and checking cash takes time and is therefore a cost to a firm. There is also a security risk with cash, so it will need to be kept in a safe or other secure locations. There is also a security risk when transferring cash to the bank. Banks may charge a business both for paying in cash to their accounts and for requesting change.

The quantity of cash handled by firms varies greatly. A firm like Rowland and Hudson Ltd finds that none of its customers pays in cash and, apart from buying odd items such as office pens and paper, it pays all of its suppliers by cheque. Kent Clarke (the hairdresser) receives 70% of his fees in the form of cash, with the remainder of his customers paying by cheque.

*Figure 46.2*

### LEARNING ACTIVITY 1

1. Make a list of your family's transactions in a typical week.
2. Identify and list those transactions which are only paid for in cash.
3. Explain why these transactions are paid for in cash.

# Cheques

A cheque is simply an instruction to a bank to pay a sum of money to someone else. For example, if a photographer called Michelle Hunt needed to pay her insurance company, Safecover plc, a fee for her annual insurance cover, she would usually write out a cheque and send it to the company. She would date the cheque, write in the name of the company she wished to receive the fee, write in the amount in both words and figures and, finally, she would sign it. Safecover plc would take this to its bank and pay it into its account. The bank would arrange for the money to be deducted or debited from Michelle's account and added or credited to the insurance company's account. If they banked at different banks, this could take between three and seven days.

Cheques are a safer and usually more convenient form of transferring money, compared to actual cash. However, they may also incur bank charges both for Michelle Hunt who wrote the cheque and for Safecover plc who paid it into its business account. The other problem for Safecover plc is there is no guarantee that the money will be transferred into its account if Michelle Hunt did not have enough money in her account to cover the amount of the cheque. If this was the case, Michelle's bank might refuse to honour the cheque and return it to Safecover plc marked 'refer to drawer'. This is often called a **bounced cheque**. Safecover plc would then need to contact Michelle Hunt to find out what the problem was and to obtain the money it was owed.

The **drawer** is the person who writes the cheque – in this case Michelle. The **drawee** is the bank of the person writing the cheque. The **payee** is the person or organisation receiving the cheque. If the drawer thinks there might be a problem with the payment after the cheque has been sent to the payee, the cheque may be 'stopped' if the drawer informs the bank. Most banks will charge a fee to a business for this service.

Most shops dealing with customers they do not know will only accept cheques if they are backed up by a cheque guarantee card. In most cases, the card will only ensure payment up to £50, so this limits the size of transactions paid for by cheques. This would not be such a problem where you are buying a service and the supplier has your details. For example, you could pay your telephone bill for £98 by sending a cheque to the company. The company would have all your details to chase up any problems with the cheque.

*Figure 46.3*

*Figure 46.4*

# Debit Card

Most retail businesses dealing directly with the public will accept debit cards. Customers with a debit card hand them to the salesperson and the card will be swiped through a machine that reads the magnetic strip on the back of the card. As long as the customer has enough funds in the bank account, the transaction will be approved. It can take up to three working days for the money to be taken out of the customer's account, and slightly longer for the business to be credited with the money.

This is a safer way of accepting payment for a business, compared

*Figure 46.5*

both to cash and to cheque payments. There will be a cost charged, however, by the banks to the business for using this system, and as with all payment systems this will be negotiated with the banks on an individual basis. The most well known debit cards are 'Switch' and 'Delta' cards. A firm may allow some of its employees to use debit cards drawn on the firm's bank account as a convenient way to buy small items for the business.

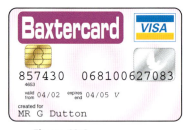

**Figure 46.6**

## Credit Cards

As the name suggests, this form of payment involves the possibility of credit being given to the buyer. The cards are issued to members of the public through financial institutions such as Visa, Mastercard and American Express. When a customer buys goods using the credit card in a shop, the card is swiped in a machine to check the details included on the magnetic strip. The machine is connected to a central computer by a special phone line and it is this computer that allows the transaction to go ahead.

The retailer swiping the card will have a record for the transactions which will either be automatically sent to the card issuer or will have to be posted to it. The retailer will receive the total payment for the various transactions at regular intervals, less 1–3% according to the deal struck with the card issuers. While this might seem to be a high cost, at least the payment is guaranteed which compares favourably with cheques.

The customer will receive a monthly account, showing a record of all the transactions and the minimum payment to be paid that month. The customer is being given credit by the card issuer and not the retailer. As with debit cards, a business might give some employees its own business credit cards when they have to pay out large sums of money immediately. For example, many coach drivers will have a company credit card to buy fuel, meals and accommodation when operating away from their base.

## Credit Transfer/Direct Debit

Many businesses have to make regular payments such as paying wages to employees. Some may have to collect sums of money from customers on an equally regular basis. Using any of the above systems will be less convenient than using a method that directly transfers money between bank accounts.

Most firms will use the bank giro credit system to pay wages into the personal accounts of employees. A list of employees and their personal bank account details will be prepared, together with the amount of money that has to be transferred to each account. This is given to a firm's bank who will transfer the money from the firm's account directly into the accounts on the list. It is a fast and convenient way of paying out large sums on a regular basis, but of course the bank will charge a fee for the service.

Many firms which need to collect regular sums of money from customers will ask them to pay by direct debit. A direct debit form giving details of his or her bank account and the amount of money to

### Direct Debit instruction
Please complete this form if you wish to pay by Direct Debit

1 Enter the full postal address of your bank/building society branch:
To the Manager

Bank/Building Society

Postcode

2 Names of bank/building society account holder(s):

3 Bank/building society account number

4 Sort code of bank/ building society branch
(Located top right-hand corner of your cheque book)

5 I/We instruct you to debit the above bank/building society account by the monthly amount due on our loan.

6 I/We instruct you to debit the credit card account below by the monthly amount due on our loan.

7 Credit Card Number

8 Signature(s)

Date

**Figure 46.7**

be paid out at certain dates is filled in by the customer. The company will then arrange for its bank to collect the sums on the specified dates direct from its customers' accounts.

This is a convenient system for the customer, and can be cancelled by them at any time. The firm collecting payment in this way does not have to send out reminders, and will normally receive the money by the set dates. A fee will have to be paid by the collecting firm to the bank. Most people with mortgages are expected to pay their monthly instalments by direct debit, for example, and it is a popular method with both buyer and seller.

## What have I learned?

1. There are five key methods for a business to make and receive payments.
2. Each method will have its own advantages and disadvantages in terms of costs, speed of transfer and security.

## LEARNING ACTIVITY 2

This is a research activity. You need to contact the business sections of at least two different banks to find out the following questions:

1  How much does the bank charge a business for each method of making and receiving payments?
2  Can firms negotiate lower fees for these services?
3  How long does it take for the bank to process each method?
4  What advice does the bank offer business about the advantages and disadvantages of each method?
5  Does the bank offer any special services to help businesses with payment methods?

## EXTENSION EXERCISE

Use your findings from Learning Activity 2 to prepare a table giving a basic description, the typical costs, the advantages and disadvantages of each of the five payment methods.

# BUSINESS

## Investigating Skills

# CHAPTER 47

# Making an oral presentation

Giving a good presentation is all about confidence and preparation. It is important that you are really confident in your knowledge of your subject matter. If you are, then you will find the whole business of making a presentation so much easier. Preparation is equally important – you must make sure that everything is ready for your presentation – and test it to make sure that it works – long before actually doing the presentation itself. You should also be clear about the purpose of your presentation. Not all presentations are about giving out information (in fact, there may be many more efficient ways to share information than through presentations). Perhaps you are trying to prove a point, or start a discussion, or even persuade your audience to do something?

**Figure 47.1** *Be confident and know your subject matter thoroughly*

## Preparation

Make sure that you know who your audience is going to be so that you can talk to them at the right level. Sometimes a presentation may be for someone your own age, sometimes for younger children, sometimes for older people. There may also be different levels of knowledge in your audience. Are they likely to be experts themselves in the area that you are talking about? Or can you safely assume that they know very little? In all of these cases (and combinations), knowing your audience is essential. A presentation which may be good in many respects but fails to hit the right level – is either too simple or too complex for the audience – is a presentation that has failed. Both content and language level need to be adjusted for your audience.

## Content

Prepare what you are going to say thoroughly. Decide on the main 'headings' for what you are going to say and write them on sticky notes. These can then be arranged in the order which you think is best for their delivery. By doing it in this way, you can move sections around until you are happy with the order. Under each note, you should then write bullet point lists of the points you wish to make. Your notes should be on cards that are easily read (use a plain font in a good size) and easy to handle. Postcard size is about right. You should never, however, read directly from your notes, but should be familiar enough with your material to be able to use them as prompts. When planning your presentation, you will find that writing your notes out helps you to become really familiar with what you want to say so can be used as a form of 'revision'.

## Language

Use straightforward English for your presentation. Do not try to 'sound good' with jargon that your audience may not understand. You must, however, use the correct business terms and concepts. Explain any technical or specialist terms that are necessary – this will depend on the audience that you are presenting to. This is particularly important when using words or initials that are specific to the subject – will your audience know what a 'P and L statement' is? And isn't it easier to just say 'Profit and Loss'?

## Images

Decide what images you will need for each heading and bullet point and familiarise yourself with them. If you know your subject well enough, the images may act as enough of a prompt and allow you to do your presentation without notes. Sometimes your images will be bullet points or sub headings. Never read the words that you put up on screen – your audience can do that for themselves – but use them as a way of prompting you so that you add to what they say. Other useful images include charts, graphs, photographs and diagrams. These should always be neat, clear, colourful and bright. Draw them carefully and make sure that all of your audience will be able to see them. If you are using projector technology, these can be easily created on a computer.

## Hand-outs

People in an audience often like to go away with a reminder of what they have listened to. They also might want to make notes during your presentation. You can let them have copies of your headings to refer to or, if using the technology, copies of computer slides. You might also like to provide them with extra material. If, for example, you refer to a newspaper article, you could provide them with a copy of it in full so that they can read it in their own time. You might also provide them with a list of suitable web site addresses for further information or discussion. You must make sure that you have enough hand-outs for everyone in your audience and that they are all ready before your presentation. Leave plenty of time, for example, for photocopying, as this can often go wrong and take longer than you think!

## Questions

Invite questions and comments. You can often demonstrate your confidence and understanding better by answering questions. Always answer questions as fully as possible. Never answer questions with a simple 'yes' or 'no' if you can use the answer to pass on more information or a better explanation. If you don't know the answer, say so – don't try to bluff your way out of it, it just makes you look amateur. It is better to be honest and say; 'I don't actually know that' than to bluff. You should always offer to find out the information for the questioner. 'I don't actually know that, but I'll try and find out and get back to you' or you can even ask your audience if they know. Some presenters 'plant' questions in the audience. If no-one else asks the obvious question that you have a brilliant answer to, you can get a friend to ask it.

## Using technology

Use the best technology that is available to you, for example computer graphics, scanners and digital cameras. If you are using computer presentation technology then there are some simple rules to follow to make your images effective. Always use a good font size (16 point as a minimum) and limit the information on each slide. Two or three bullet points at most should be used. There should never be too much information on the screen and it should always look clear and well laid out – pages should never be too 'busy'. If there is 'too much' happening on a page, then this takes away from the clarity of the point that you are wanting to make. Use the same – easily readable – font on each page, and the same colour scheme – this makes your presentation look a lot more professional. Link the pages with a common theme – a logo, for example, or a border or background. If the programme you use can do it, use it to 'build up' slides – so that each section of a chart, for example, is added as you talk about it.

## Check, check and double check

You must be absolutely certain that everything is in place and is working. Make sure that, for example, the room is booked; if you are using televisions or computer technology, that they are booked and ready; that your computer technology (discs and programs) is actually compatible with the hardware that you are using. Many a presentation has been ruined by a confident presenter saving slides to a CD and then finding that the hardware does not have the appropriate drive, or the appropriate programme. (You must check this thoroughly; even though it may look like the hardware has the correct program, it could be a different version and be incompatible with your version!)

## Self preparation

Make sure that you are relaxed and comfortable before your presentation. Wear comfortable clothes, go to the toilet, have a glass of water handy and always arrive in plenty of time.

## Giving the presentation

Don't start your presentation until you are sure that your audience is settled and paying attention. Try to start it with something that is immediately going to grab their attention. Don't fidget or shuffle about nervously. It is worth getting a friend to video you as part of your preparation. You will soon spot if you have any habits that are likely to be distracting to your audience such as fiddling with your hair or shifting your weight from side to side. Try to look at your audience (make eye contact) and not at your notes, equipment or images. This is a lot easier if you are completely confident in your subject material. Make sure that you are including all of your audience, however, not just one or two people. If you hold your head up, your audience will find it much easier to hear you and to relate to what you are saying. Speak clearly and slowly. Nervousness often shows itself in a rushed presentation.

Be yourself – you will then be much more relaxed – and smile at your audience. This shows that you are confident and will make you both feel and look better.

## Checklist

- Know your audience – adjust content and language level accordingly.
- Know your subject – you must be an expert in the area that you are talking about.
- Make sure that the structure of your presentation is clear and logical.
- Prepare thoroughly – make notes and use prompt cards and/or projected headings on screen to remind you of what you are going to say.
- Use images where they add to your presentation; these should always be neat, clear and colourful.
- Use technology to its best advantage, but don't rely on it totally.
- Check thoroughly to make sure that everything is in place and working properly.
- Check to make sure that any hand-outs or other materials have been photocopied in good time.
- Be on time, relaxed and well prepared.
- Be confident, smile – and be yourself!

**FACT FILE**

*Many television programmes which look 'live' are actually 'recorded live' to allow time for checking. The BBC's Question Time programme is actually recorded over an hour before it is transmitted. At the end of the 'live' recording, no-one is allowed to leave until the engineers have checked that all the film is OK. If it isn't, the programme has to be repeated and actually go out live. This has happened on only a few occasions but shows how important it is to check.*

# CHAPTER 48

# Perfecting a portfolio

The main part of the assessment for the Applied GCSE is through your coursework, called your portfolio work. You are examined on your knowledge and application of the finance unit of your course, but for the other two units, you must do your best to produce a portfolio. This is a collection of materials to show that you have carried out a detailed investigation into a number of businesses.

***Figure 48.1*** *Good organisation is the key to a good portfolio*

## Your marks

You are marked (assessed) on your ability to:

- **Demonstrate and apply knowledge and understanding of the subject content**
  This means that you must know and understand what you are talking about before starting your business investigations. For example, there is no point in investigating the recruitment issues at a business if you have no knowledge of how businesses would usually go about recruiting workers.

- **Use the appropriate terms, concepts, theories and methods**
  Again, this is not possible unless you have thoroughly learnt and understand the application of these concepts, methods etc. You must use technical (business) terms wherever possible. Anyone can say that this is a 'low price', only someone who knows business will be able to say if it is (for example) a promotional, a loss leader, or penetration price.

- **Plan and carry out investigations**
  You must make sure that you have a logical sequence to your business investigations and be able to manage your own time effectively to carry them out.

- **Gather, select, record and analyse information and evidence**
  You may be able to collect a great deal of information but not all of it will be particularly relevant, or even useful. You must show that you have selected the most effective information, and discarded that which is of no use.
  Include information selected from your own work, materials you have collected relating to the businesses and materials you have collected from the businesses. You should be able to keep good records of your sources of information.

- **Evaluate evidence, make judgements, present conclusions**
  You will also be judged on how effectively you evaluate information

– which is most useful, and why, which least useful, and why? How have you made those particular judgements and come to those particular conclusions. You should explain your thought processes when making any decision or drawing any conclusion.

# Section 1

For Section 1, Investigating Business, you need to produce a portfolio based on an investigation of two contrasting businesses. You are advised to choose two businesses which have as many contrasts as possible – for example, they could be in different industrial sectors, have different ownership, sell different products in different markets, be located in different places or be different sizes. The more contrasting they are, the easier it will be for you. Some examination boards recommend that one of your businesses is a sole trader or partnership and the other a private or public limited company. However, as long as there is sufficient contrast between the two businesses, you are free to choose whichever type you would like e.g. franchises, co-operatives, charities, even public sector organisations.

  You will need to be aware that many smaller businesses do not publish things such as aims, or intermediate targets, or organisational structures. However, such things will still exist for smaller businesses, and it is important that you research them. Your portfolio could be divided into sections as follows:

## Part 1

- A description of the main activities of each business;
- A description of the aims and objectives of each business;
- A description of the type of ownership of each business;
- A description of the liabilities of the owners of each business

## Part 2

- A description of the organisational structure of the business
- A description of how the business carries out the main functional areas
- A description of what the functional areas do, and how they do it

## Part 3

- A description of how each business communicates internally
- A description of how each business communicates externally
- The evidence for your presentation to show the different methods of communication (not all examination boards require this)

## Part 4

- A description of the location (and reasons for it) of each of your businesses
- A description of the competitors to each of your businesses

- A description of the environmental constraints on each of your businesses
- A description of the legal constraints on each of your businesses

## Possible portfolio outline

A possible structure for your portfolio is included below. Remember, this is only an outline and it will be up to you to check that you are covering everything – and in as much detail – as your own examination board requires. Your own outline and methodology may be an improvement on this one! This outline only applies to one of your chosen businesses; remember, you need to have studied two, contrasting, ones. In many cases, you will receive higher marks by being able to make a direct comparison between your two businesses. For example, what are the similarities and differences in location, or ownership, or activities, or aims and objectives – and why. In some cases, your examination board will only need you to refer to one business. You must check this for yourself! You should always try to justify any statements or conclusions that you reach and, wherever possible, show the evidence that you have used to enable you to reach those conclusions.

Your teacher may have work from previous groups to be able to show you what quality of work is needed to reach particular levels. Examination boards also provide examples, which may be accessed from their websites.

### Part 1

The business that I have chosen is called xxxx. These are the reasons why I chose it . . . . (This may be because you think it would be interesting; because you know someone who works there; because you work there yourself or have carried out your work experience there; because it is near to where you live . . . .)

The most important activity of the business is the production of xxxx. (You could describe what sort of industrial sector this puts it in; what sort of market, and how each has changed in recent years.)

The aims and objectives of the business are . . . (These should include the general aims of the business – perhaps it has a mission statement, or similar? You should explain the shorter term targets that the business has set itself and how it manages and monitors those targets. You should explain how the business uses its objectives to measure whether it is achieving its aims, and why it does this).

The business is owned . . . (describe how the business is owned, why you think this is so and what the main features of this type of ownership are, including the owners' liabilities. Explain why you think this particular type of ownership is suited to this business).

### Part 2

This is how the business is organised and how each of the necessary business functions is therefore carried out. (Is it a flat, tall or matrix structure? Or perhaps a combination? You could use charts or diagrams, and explain what this type of organisation means in terms of key features such as span of control and worker motivation.)

This is how the functions within my chosen business are actually carried out. (Explain who does the necessary work? Are there distinct functional areas, like departments, in the business or is there a different form of organisation. Why?).

This is how the functional areas support each other and the business. (You could give examples of how functional areas have to work together to carry out necessary business tasks; you should explain why this is vital to the efficient operation of the business. You should show how at least three different functional areas work together to support the business. You should explain how the operation of the functional areas helps the business to achieve its aims and objectives.)

This is how I think that the functions could be more efficiently or effectively carried out in order to achieve the aims of the business. This is how the three functional areas above could improve their effectiveness. (In particular, you could look at how new technology, especially information technology, could be used to help the business improve or develop for the future.)

## Part 3

These are the main ways in which the business communicates internally. (You could divide these into oral, written and electronic; formal and informal and comment on where each might be used and how effective each might be.)

These are the main ways in which the business communicates externally (i.e. with people and organisations that are not a part of the business. (You could comment on the types of people or organisations that the business might need to communicate with. These could include suppliers, customers, competitors, government, shareholders and other stakeholders. You could comment on which method might be used for each, and in which situations. You should also comment on the effectiveness of such communications.)

These are the ways in which I think that the various methods of communication (internal and external) could be improved by the use of information technology. (in particular, you could look at the ways in which IT could be used to improve communications with customers.

This is how I chose to carry out my presentation. (You should put in the evidence here, such as overheads, graphs and charts, slide projector print-outs, notes and witness statements. Look at the chapter on 'Making an Oral Presentation' on page 264 before tackling this.)

## Part 4

This is where my business is located, this is why it is located here. (Describe the area, you could use maps and other information to show why the business is there – it could be for historical reasons, it could be because there are customers nearby, or competitors, it could be because of suppliers, or ease of access, or special concessions from government . . . )

This is how my business markets its products. (Explain the various ways in which the marketing takes place. Remember, this should include all of the elements of the 'marketing mix', not just advertising and promotion. Explain how successful you think that these methods are in selling the product.)

This is how I think that the competition in this sector will affect my business. (Describe the number of other businesses involved in the same activity (or set of activities) and explain how their activities are likely to affect the ability of your chosen business to reach its stated aims and objectives.)

This is how the economic conditions in the country might affect my business. (Explain the current economic conditions. Are interest rates high or low? Is employment going up or down? Have there been any recent changes in taxation at a local, national or European level? Have any new regulations or rules been introduced that might affect your business? Is demand for the business's products increasing or decreasing? Explain why you think that this is the case.)

This is how the law concerning the environment affects my business. (Outline the main national and international laws which are important to the business and explain how the business ensures that it is not breaking them. )

I think that the most important external influence on my business is xxxx. (Explain why you think so; explain what effect it has had on the business in the past, or what effect it might have on the business in the future.)

# Section 2

For Section 2, you need to produce a portfolio based on your investigation of a medium to large sized business, which shows that you understand the importance of people in a business. You will need to demonstrate knowledge and understanding of how people's jobs in business are organised, their roles and the nature and importance of recruitment and training. You will also need to show that you know how disputes are settled and how the business copes with health and safety issues. You should also show that you understand who the other stakeholders are, and their importance. For some examination boards, you will also need to do a presentation.

Your portfolio could be divided into sections as follows:

## Part 1

- A description of the main stakeholders in your business;
- A description of the possible aims and objectives of each stakeholder group
- An explanation of how these aims might conflict with each other and how such conflicts might be solved.

## Part 2

- A description of the organisational structure of the business
- A description of the roles of workers in one of the main functional areas
- A discussion of a Contract of Employment, and suggestions for improvement.
- A comparison of the working roles, arrangements and rewards for workers.
- Suggestions as to how the business could benefit from more flexible working arrangements.

## Part 3

- A description of the main laws which protect people at work
- An outline of the health and safety issues that most affect the workers already described.
- A description of the groups which the workers may join.
- A description of how the business deals with disputes between it and its employees.
- An evaluation of how an employee group or organisation has helped with a recent change in working conditions.

## Part 4

- Your own CV;
- A letter of application;
- A description of the recruitment process at your chosen business;
- A description of the training you might receive if you were appointed and an analysis of its effectiveness.
- A description of continuous or further training in various areas.

## Part 5

- A description of the customer services at your business.
- An outline of how consumers are protected by law
- A description of how the business finds out about customer wants.
- Suggestions for improvements to customer services.

## Possible portfolio outline

A possible structure for your portfolio is included below. Remember, this is only an outline and it will be up to you to check that you are covering everything – and in as much detail – as your own examination board requires. Your own outline and methodology may be an improvement on this one!

## Part 1

The business that I have chosen is called xxxx. The main stakeholder groups in the business are ... (Describe the main groups e.g.

suppliers, customers, employees, owners/shareholders and explain both how they – or their actions – affect the business, and how the business affects them.)

This is what I think each stakeholder group probably wants . . . (Describe stakeholders' aims.) This is where they may come into conflict. (Describe at least three possible conflicts and suggest ways in which the conflict could be resolved.)

## Part 2

This is how the business is organised. (You can use notes, charts, diagrams or other visual aids.) This is why I think that this type of organisation is appropriate for this business.

I have chosen to look at the job roles of people in the xxxx functional area. (Explain why you have chosen this area; identify at least three different job roles then compare the working arrangements and rewards for your identified workers. Also look at the induction and training which each received.)

This is a typical Contract of Employment for one of the workers. (Suggest how effective this is at meeting the needs of employers and employees and suggest improvements to it.)

These are my suggestions for possible improvements. (You could suggest how the working arrangements could be made more flexible, or how workers could be better motivated, or make suggestions for improved induction or other training.)

## Part 3

These are the main laws that protect people at work. (Outline the legislation and point out which of these are most important to your chosen business, and why.)

The health and safety issues which most affect the workers I have described are . . . (identify possible hazards and other health and safety issues; explain what steps the business takes to minimise or eliminate these risks).

The possible groups which workers may join are . . . (these are likely to be trades unions but may also be professional associations or similar bodies.)

This is how the business deals with disputes . . . (Describe the disputes procedure at the business – there may be a published document to which you can refer – and explain how the business deals with disputes between employee and employer.)

I have identified xxxx as a change in working conditions that has taken place at the business in the recent past. This is how the employee group helped towards its implementation. (The 'recent past' in your business may be several years ago. You should ask your identified workers what changes – national or local – they think have been significant in their time there, and then investigate the role of the union or other organisation in the introduction and implementation of these changes.)

## Part 4

This is my own Curriculum Vitae.

This is the job which I have chosen at the business (and why). This is my completed application form for that job.

This is how the business recruits its workers. (Describe the process; include the preparation of a job description from a job analysis and the actual selection and interview process.)

This is the training that I would expect to receive if I was successful. (Describe the training, say how effective you think it would be and give suggestions for other or further training.)

This is how the business ensures that workers are always fully trained and motivated. (Describe the appraisal system at the business, how staff can have skills updated or be retrained, how health and safety training is carried out and any national training initiatives that affect your business. What suggestions could you make for improvements?)

## Part 5

This is my evidence of an oral presentation describing the customer service at my business. This is how I chose to carry out my presentation. (You should put in the evidence here, such as overheads, graphs and charts, slide projector print-outs, notes and witness statements. Look at the chapter on 'Making an Oral Presentation' on page 264 before tackling this.)

This is how the law protects the customers of my business. (Include a brief outline of consumer protection legislation and show which laws are most important to your business and its customers.)

This is how my business carries out market research to discover customer wants. (You should include desk and field research, their relative advantages and disadvantages, and say when each would be used, and would be most effective.)

These are my suggestions as to how customer service could be improved. (You should particularly look at how information technology could be used to provide better customer service. These suggestions could be contained in advice that you would give to the managers of the business.)

## Ten points to remember:

- Choose your businesses carefully.
- Check what your examination board requires.
- Learn first, then use your knowledge and understanding of business to describe, analyse and evaluate.
- Collect as much information as possible.
- Give yourself plenty of time to complete the portfolios.
- Cover as much detail as you possibly can.
- Keep accurate records of where you have obtained information.
- Use many different sources of information.
- Explain, analyse, evaluate – give reasons as to why you have made

particular judgements or decisions, or come to particular conclusions.
- Keep your portfolio tidy, and safe (you might consider keeping it electronically).

CHAPTER 49

# Tackling a test

Whichever examination board is assessing you for Applied Business Studies, all three set the examination paper for Unit 3 Business Finance in a real world or realistic context. This means that a case study is created that allows questions to be asked that needs you the candidates to apply your business knowledge and understanding. Each examination board will have its own style of papers and questions but they are all relatively similar and have to cover the same assessment objectives. The time allocation varies between 1 hour 30 minutes and two hours. One Board, Edexcel, currently plans to issue some of the case study material in the weeks leading up to the paper. The other two, AQA and OCR, do not plan to do this. Whichever you are doing, your teachers will tell you about the specific features set for your examination paper. As the papers from all three boards are very similar in style and structure it is worth considering some general advice first, set out as dos and don'ts.

*Figure 49.1*

## Some Dos and Don`ts

- Do not use a pencil, red or green pen to write your answers. Most examiners actually prefer black ink to be used, although blue ink is acceptable.
- Do not write in the margins and do not try to squash your answers in when you run out of lines. Use the extra blank pages at the back of the exam paper or ask for additional sheets from the exam invigilators. If you do use this stationery make sure you number each response correctly.
- Do try to write clearly as several candidates each year limit their potential marks because it is impossible to read some answers.
- Do read the question carefully and make sure you answer the question that is being asked – and not the one you would like to be asked. This is particularly important when the question appears to be similar to one that has been asked in the past.
- Do read the data carefully as there may clues to help your response: or the question may require you to select specific information from the data.

- Use the number of marks per question to guide you on the length of response needed and keep an eye on the time. If you do not answer all the questions you will automatically reduce your potential mark.
- Always read the instructions on the front cover. They include important reminders before you start to put pen to paper.
- Each question will have a 'command' word that will be telling you how to frame your answer. This is particularly important for questions using 'explain', 'why', 'describe', 'analyse' or 'justify'. Answers to these questions mean you have to make some points but then you need to develop or expand them. This does not simply mean that you rewrite the data provided. You have to say something extra about the point without getting repetitive. Using examples is one way to help you explain or develop an answer.
- Unless the question specifically asks you to give a list, always answer using sentences and paragraphs.
- Always try to use business terms rather than general words and phrases. For example, 'money' is often used by candidates when 'revenue', 'costs' or 'profit' would have been the correct specific term. Try not to mix up terms such as 'borrow' and 'lend', 'price' and 'cost' or 'revenue' and 'profit'.
- Some candidates take three or four lines of writing before they actually start to answer the question. Do not rewrite the question but try to find a quick way to introduce and start your specific answer. Remember, most introductions will not help you to score marks.

## Question styles

- Each Board has produced a specimen paper which includes the range of typical features. These features and question styles include:
- A front cover with space for you to put your name, centre, centre number and candidate number. It also has 'instructions to candidates' which you need to read before the examination starts.
- An opening piece of data that introduces the real world context for the questions. You are likely to be given background information about the type of business or businesses, the products sold and quite probably some of the people working for the business. Read this carefully as you may be able to use some of it in answers to some questions.
- Some questions will ask you to complete business documents such as a purchase order or an invoice from further data given to you. The business form will be produced on the examination paper and you complete it in ink by hand – neatly. In fact you answer all questions on the examination paper.
- Some questions on business documents may ask you to identify a specific number of errors. You will need to check each detail very carefully to find each one.
- Other questions may ask you how the documents might be improved and you may have to explain the purpose and importance of each document to a business. You might have to compete a flow

diagram showing the right order for a series of documents being sent between two firms. Finally, you may be asked to explain how computerized documents might improve the whole process as well as suggesting possible drawbacks of such a system.

- Some questions might be ask you to explain payment methods and you might be asked to suggest suitable methods for a particular purpose and be asked to give reasons for your choice. Remember to identify clearly how much has to be paid, to whom and in what way. You may also have to explain the problems if errors occur in documents and payment methods.

- On both Profit and Loss and Balance Sheets you may be asked to explain terms and to complete the accounts from the data given to you. This means you will have to do some calculations so make sure you have a calculator and that you use it. When you have completed the calculation take time to review your answer – is it a sensible figure for the type of calculation you have been asked to do? Other questions might ask you to recall reasons explaining why a business must keep accurate financial records.

- Some questions might ask you to complete a table. This could be the case for a cash flow forecast or for a table which you will use to draw a break-even graph. Take great care with the figures especially when there is a decimal point or when some figures are in tens some in hundreds and some in thousands or even millions. This is another occasion for a calculator.

- You might be asked to interpret a cash flow forecast or a break-even graph so you need to think very carefully what each shows. Use some of the figures shown to show that you are making use of the available data.

- The business in your case study might need some additional finance. If it does you are likely to be asked to suggest a suitable source or method of finance and to justify your choice. There may be two or three possible sources so try to think of the best by considering the amount of money needed, the use for the money and the type of business involved.

- Some questions may ask you to apply your knowledge in quite a specific way. For example you may be asked to decide from a list of costs which are fixed or variable or which are start-up or running. Take your time whatever the question; they will not be as simple as you might think. Read the description carefully.

Remember, examination practice is very important so that you get used to the style of questions and you learn to work at the right speed. To help you succeed you also need to revise all the content for this unit. Make sure you have a set of revision notes to help you prepare and get someone at home to test you on the key knowledge. Some students make revision posters that they pin up around their bedrooms.

Finally, remember to read the instructions, the data and each question very carefully: no one else can do this for you once you are in the examination room.

CHAPTER 50
# Blank financial documents

## PURCHASE ORDER

**Rowland and Hudson Ltd**
Borders Industrial Estate
Kelso
KA4 9LT
Tel: (01234) 56798   Fax: (01234) 98756

To:

Order No:
Date:
Delivery:   Above address

| QUANTITY | REF NO | DESCRIPTION | UNIT PRICE | AMOUNT |
|----------|--------|-------------|------------|--------|
|          |        |             |            |        |
|          |        |             | TOTAL      |        |

Special Instructions:

Order Authorised by:

*Purchase order*

## DELIVERY NOTE

**Angus Miller Ltd**
Burns Business Park
Hawick
HE7 4TC
Tel: (01456) 78901   Fax: (01456) 10798

To:

Your Order No:
Date:
Delivery No:

DELIVERY INSTRUCTIONS

| Ref No | Description | Quantity |
|--------|-------------|----------|
|        |             |          |
|        |             |          |

Packed By:                    (sig)    Date:
Delivery By:                  (FIRM)   Sig:        Date:
Received By:                  (sig)    Date:

*Delivery note*

## SALES INVOICE

**Angus Miller Ltd**
Burns Business Park
Hawick
HE7 4TC
Tel: (01456) 78901  Fax: (01456) 10798

VAT Reg No: 987-654312

Sold to:

Your Order No:
Order Date:
Dispatch Date:
Invoice Date:

Invoice Number:

| Ref No | Description | Quantity | Price per unit | TOTAL |
|---|---|---|---|---|
|  |  |  |  |  |

Terms:
Payment must be made within 30 days
of invoice date, 3% discount applies if
payment received within 14 days

| | |
|---|---|
| Gross Value | |
| Less 3% Discount | |
| Sub total | |
| Plus VAT at 17.5% | |
| Invoice Total | |

*Invoice*

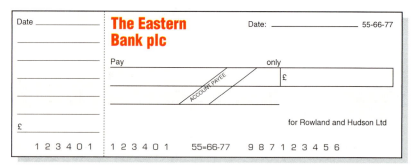

*Cheque*

**REMITTANCE ADVICE SLIP**

**Rowland and Hudson Ltd**
Borders Industrial Estate
Kelso
KA4 9LT
Tel: (01234) 56798  Fax: (01234) 98756

To:

Our Order No:
Your Invoice No:

For:
Payment enclosed:
Cheque No:
Date:

All queries should be addressed to the Accounts Department

*Remittance advice slip*

**GOODS RECEIVED NOTE**

**Rowland and Hudson Ltd**
Borders Industrial Estate
Kelso
KA4 9LT
Tel: (01234) 56798   Fax: (01234) 98756

GRN NO:
Date:
Delivery Note No:

Supplier:
Delivery by:

| Ref No | Quantity | Description | Ref No |
|--------|----------|-------------|--------|
|        |          |             |        |

Received by:
Action/Comments:

*Goods received note*

**CREDIT NOTE**

**Angus Miller Ltd**
Burns Business Park
Hawick
HE7 4TC
Tel: (01456) 78901   Fax: (01456) 10798

VAT Reg No: 987-654312

To:

Date:

Credit Note No:

Invoice No:

| Ref No | Quantity | Description | UNIT PRICE | TOTAL |
|--------|----------|-------------|------------|-------|
|        |          |             |            |       |

| | | Gross Value | |
|---|---|---|---|
| | | Less 3% Discount | |
| | | Sub total | |
| | | Plus VAT at 17.5% | |
| | | Invoice Total | |

*Credit note*

# INDEX

Note: page numbers in **bold** refer to Key Items.